All-Weather Warriors

MIKE SPICK

All-Weather Warriors

The Search for the Ultimate Fighter Aircraft

ARMS AND
ARMOUR

Arms and Armour Press
A Cassell Imprint
Villiers House, 41-47 Strand, London WC2N 5JE.

Distributed in the USA by Sterling Publishing Co. Inc.,
387 Park Avenue South, New York, NY 10016-8810.

Distributed in Australia by Capricorn Link (Australia) Pty.
Ltd, 2/13 Carrington Road, Castle Hill, NSW 2154.

British Library Cataloguing-in-Publication Data: a catalogue
record for this book is available from the British Library

ISBN 1-85409-202-2

Designed and edited by DAG Publications Ltd.
Designed by David Gibbons; edited by Jonathan Falconer;
printed and bound in Great Britain.

Jacket painting by Michael Rondot. Reproduced by courtesy
of the artist and Collectair Limited Editions.

Contents

Prologue

On the afternoon of 23 May 1942, a single German bomber took off from its base in Brittany. Weather conditions over England were ideal for it to penetrate undetected. Low clouds draped the hills, extending almost to ground level, blanketing the British fighter airfields. Above were further cloud layers extending to more than 20,000ft (6,095m). Even if the defending fighters were able to take off, interception would be like finding the proverbial needle in a haystack.

Droning across the English Channel, the bomber neared the Dorset coast. Its approach did not go unobserved; the unseen electronic beams of British radar pierced the clag and reflected from the bomber back to the Ground Control Interception (GCI) station. The British controller tracked it on his screen, establishing height, course and speed. As it became obvious that the intruder was going to penetrate inland, a request was made for an interceptor to be scrambled, even though the weather at ground level was marginal for flying.

The task fell to No 604 Squadron based at Middle Wallop, Hants, and, as it happened, to an exceptionally able crew. Sqn Ldr John Cunningham and his radar operator C. F. "Jimmy" Rawnsley, had already notched up an impressive tally of night victories in the Beaufighter. Now they were to hunt in daylight, in weather too bad for day fighters to operate with any chance of success.

Engines booming at full throttle, the big Beaufighter accelerated through the drizzle. On leaving the ground it was almost immediately swallowed up by the low cloud and Cunningham settled down to climb on instruments, setting course as he went for Swanage, on the Dorset coast. Outside the cockpit visibility was nil, just swirling white cloud, and at first only the blind flying instruments told the Beaufighter crew where they were going and what was happening.

Meanwhile GCI were still tracking the hostile plot, and after establishing contact with the hard-climbing Beaufighter, vectored it onto a pursuit course designed to bring it into the rear quadrant of the intruder, to a position where the onboard radar of the Beaufighter could make direct contact.

Higher up, conditions were a bit better. There were gaps between cloud layers, and while with no sight of the ground there were no visual cues to aid the pilot, limited visibility was available. Gradually the Beaufighter closed from astern until finally John Cunningham sighted the misty shape of the intruder about 3,000ft (914m) ahead and slightly to starboard. It was a Heinkel He 111.

At this stage of the war, it had long been apparent to the Luftwaffe that the British had developed an airborne radar which, coupled with a close ground control system, allowed them to intercept at night. In January of the previous year, just three

German aircraft had been lost to night fighters, but this figure had grown steadily until in May no less than 96 bombers went down. The invasion of Russia had then caused many Luftwaffe bomber units to be transferred to the Eastern Front, and night activity over Britain slackened, but the RAF fighter defences remained ready and waiting.

Aware of the dangers, the Heinkel crew had remained alert and spotted the British fighter instantly. Its pilot at once hauled it into a hard left turn – the classic break into an attack. Cunningham followed suit, but the unavoidable slight delay in responding, coupled with the higher speed and rather higher wing loading of his aircraft, meant that he was unable to turn with it. The two aircraft passed abeam of each other, about 300ft (91m) apart, the Heinkel gunners blazing away at their assailant. By the time the heavy Beaufighter had been reefed around the Heinkel was once more lost to sight.

Rawnsley, who had been unable to resist watching the contest from his position amidships, immediately stuck his head back in the visor of his radar scope but, dazzled by the muzzle flashes of the Heinkel's guns at close range, he was unable to see anything until his eyes readjusted. At first the German seemed to have escaped but GCI had retained contact, tracking him in a northerly direction. Vectored from the ground the Beaufighter took up the pursuit, and after a lengthy tail chase, once more gained visual contact. Again the German pilot hauled his aircraft into a hard turn, guns blazing, and vanished into the mists.

This time Rawnsley had thought to don sunglasses to protect his vision while watching the encounter and, on returning to the radar scope, he regained contact immediately. A further tail chase followed and after a few minutes the Heinkel was once again in sight ahead. Again it broke hard into the attack, but this time Cunningham was already turning with it. Round and round the two aircraft went, as though re-enacting a World War 1 dogfight. The German pilot, unable to shake off his tormentor, began to jink, then commenced a descending spiral hotly pursued by the Beaufighter.

Still the British fighter was unable to gain enough angle in the turn to bring its guns to bear. Airframe shuddering and engines screaming at full throttle, the altimeter unwound rapidly while indicated air speed built up to 340mph (547kmh), which was considerably faster than the maximum level speed of the Beaufighter. The ground grew nearer every second. That this state of affairs could not possibly last was quickly recognised by Cunningham, who broke off the combat and re-established level flight, rather to the surprise of Rawnsley who had imagined that the aircraft should be in a totally different attitude. Meanwhile the German bomber continued its downward plunge and was lost from sight.

Back on the radar scope, Rawnsley watched as the blip that was the He 111 vanished in the ground returns. GCI had also lost contact and nothing more was to be done. With the aid of a homing beacon, the Beaufighter returned to Middle Wallop and let down through the murk, touching down after a two-and-a-half-hour sortie.

The Heinkel, flown by Hauptmann Langar of Kampfgruppe 100, the Luftwaffe pathfinder unit, was not so lucky. Breaking cloud at low altitude, he found that he was over high ground near Cranbourne Chase. Hauling back desperately on the

7

stick, he tried to pull out of that screaming dive. He nearly made it, but not quite. His aircraft struck the ground near Alvediston in Wiltshire.

This interception is one of the great classics of all-weather air combat. It has all the ingredients necessary: one-versus-one; two exceptional pilots; suspense; with the advantage swinging from one to the other and back again; an exciting finish just when all seemed lost; and finally, evenly matched aircraft.

To some of course, the pitting of a fighter against a bomber may seem a mismatch. In many cases of course, it is, but in this instance there was little to choose between the two types, given that the task of one was to intercept while the role of the other was to escape. The Beaufighter was the faster of the two; had it not been, there could have been no contest. Its wing loading was rather greater than that of the He 111H, thus conceding an advantage in turning capability to the bomber, which was only partially compensated for by a significantly higher power loading. While the Beaufighter carried much heavier armament, it was never able to bring its guns to bear and did not fire a single shot during the entire engagement. The same cannot be said for the Heinkel, which fired both beam and dorsal guns, albeit without scoring. A lucky hit might have reversed the outcome.

The flying was of a very high order throughout. The most essential element in combat, whether attacking or evading, is to keep contact with the opponent. Once, Cunningham and Rawnsley failed to do this, but GCI was able to rectify the situation. Visual contact was lost on a second occasion, but direct radar contact was retained. An outstanding feature was the ability of both pilots to perform hard manoeuvres without either losing control or becoming disoriented while operating in what amounted to a visual vacuum, with limited visibility in all directions and no horizon. This demonstrated an ability to fly partly visually and partly on instruments which was well beyond the average. While it might be thought that as Hauptmann Langar finally crashed his aircraft, this should not apply in his case, it should be remembered that he was unfortunate enough to break cloud over high ground. While it cannot be proven, it is reasonable to think that he assumed that he would have had rather more clearance than was in fact the case. Cunningham, the local man, would have been far more aware of the likely proximity of hills than his German opponent.

Finally, the victory went to the best team and the best technology. The combination of GCI, a radar-equipped fighter, and teamwork between the pilot, the radar operator, and the ground controller, proved unbeatable on the day.

Another, equally important factor, was that the Beaufighter was able to take off in extremely adverse conditions, fly its mission, then find its way back to base and land safely with a minimum of fuss and excitement. This was not of course the first occasion that it had been done, but it still demonstrated an extremely important capability in providing round-the-clock air defence for 365 days of the year.

The expression "all-weather fighter" has been current now for many decades. Even today there is no fighter that can fly, let alone fight, in all weather conditions. To take an extreme case, let us consider an arctic blizzard. Visibility is nil, a complete whiteout. The fighter may easily get lost simply taxying out to the runway, or even stuck in a snowdrift. Add a 100kt crosswind and you get some idea of the problem. Nor are extreme conditions the prerogative of the polar regions. Sandstorms can easily reduce visibility to feet, at the same time choking the engines, while extremes of rain and wind in monsoon conditions can also render flying impossible. With a deal of luck it is sometimes possible for a fighter to take off in virtually nil visibility. The clever bit is in recovering it safely. Having therefore established that the expression "all-weather fighter" is an exaggeration, we must settle for the more accurate "adverse weather fighter".

This is not the only expression that needs redefining. The term "fighter" has been considerably misused in recent years. It now seems to refer to almost anything with an offensive capability, notwithstanding that the popular press dubbed the Tornado GR1 a bomber during the Gulf War of 1991. For the purpose of this work, a fighter is an aircraft used to deny the air to enemy aircraft, whatever their function, by opposing them in aerial combat.

The early days of military aviation saw aeroplanes, and to a lesser extent airships, used for a variety of functions: artillery spotting, reconnaissance, and the dropping of objects, not always bombs, designed to cause the enemy maximum distress and inconvenience. At first these could only be carried out in daylight and clear weather, simply because the crews could not see enough at night to carry out their missions effectively. The early fighters, or scouts as they were widely known, operated by day in conditions of at least moderate visibility, because no opponents were likely to be encountered at other times.

It has been a truism for many years that war does not cease at sunset. Operational necessity soon demanded that certain missions be carried out at night, or in bad weather, providing that the target could be found. Night raids were often much safer than those by daylight, due to the reduced effectiveness or even absence of opposition. The early Zeppelin raids were a case in point. British night air defences were virtually non-existent. Even on moonlit nights, inland targets were notoriously difficult to find but London, with the moon shining on the river Thames, was relatively easy. At the same time, the Zeppelins were themselves rather large targets and the cover of darkness reduced their vulnerability.

Bad weather daylight flying was another matter altogether, to be resorted to only when troops on the ground were hard-pressed. Aircraft were sent to support them, even if conditions made this a very hazardous undertaking. This normally involved very low level flying, so as not to lose sight of the ground, but at least the front lines were very hard to miss.

In both night and bad weather, aircraft carrying out these tasks had to be opposed, and ways were found of enabling fighters to fly and fight at night and in adverse weather. This did not of course cover the combination of night and bad weather. Either was bad enough while both together was out of the question for many years.

During World War 1, many aircraft were designed specifically for night interception. Most were failures. As had been the case in day fighting, few early theories worked. The burden was carried in the main by orthodox day fighters with one

9

or two small modifications, and such external help (ie, searchlights) as could be given. This was the origin of the all-weather fighter, which can therefore be defined as an aircraft which can operate and engage in combat in conditions under which the primary sensor, the human eye, is inadequate for the task.

Between the wars the ability of an aircraft to operate at night was paid a great deal of lip service, particularly in the field of strategic bombing, but in practice remarkably little was actually done, and virtually no effort was made to produce a true night fighter. This was due in part to the technological limitations of the time, but also because the maxim "the bomber will always get through" had gained considerable currency.

Two factors tipped the scales. The first of these was two-way radio telephony. This enabled fighters not only to talk to the ground controller, but also to each other. The second was radar. This allowed a ground detection and reporting system to point the fighter to the vicinity of the enemy, and secondly provided an electronic eye with which the fighter crew could penetrate the darkness and detect not only the presence of an enemy, but where it was and what it was doing. It was at this stage that a fighter able to operate at night and in adverse weather conditions emerged. This was still not a true all-weather fighter, for the rather perverse reason that it was ineffective in clear skies in daylight. A heavy and bulky load of electronic equipment was carried which needed a second crewman to operate it. In many cases it was festooned with draggy aerials. By contrast with the standard day fighter of this era – which extended from 1940 at least into the late 1950s – it was a large and relatively unmanoeuvrable aircraft that lacked performance. If caught in clear skies by its day-only counterpart, it was a dead duck.

The final change was wrought by three major technical advances. With the development of the afterburning jet engine, sufficient power finally became available to enable the bigger birds to match their smaller daylight-only counterparts in performance. Agility was improved by advances in aerodynamics and flight control systems. The third advance was in weaponry. The advent of homing missiles made it possible to kill oponents from far beyond visual range, which gave aircraft possessing this capability an enormous theoretical advantage in combat.

There were of course many operational problems to be overcome, not the least of which was that of identification. But at last the all-weather bird was able to operate effectively round-the-clock in almost all conditions, ceding superiority to no-one in any field from medium range night interception to close combat.

The most recent advances have been made in the field of low observable technology, or "stealth". Any fighter is vulnerable if it is visible, whether to eyesight, to radar, or in the infra-red spectrum. Moves to confer a measure of invisibility date back to World War 1, but a worthwhile degree of success has only been obtained in recent years. The final question to be answered is where this will lead.

The quest for the ultimate fighter is ongoing. While this may seem to be a matter for advancing technology only, this is far from the case. Despite many past predictions, the fighter pilot is far from redundant. The story of the development of the all-weather fighter is equally the story of the pilots who led the way, and who "did it for real".

1. The Night Sky was a Big Place

In the early days of military aviation little enough was known about flying by day, let alone at night or in cloud. True, a few intrepid aviators had climbed into the night sky, and yet others had blundered into cloud, mainly by accident and rarely by design. Those who lived to tell the tale showed that it could be done, but also how dangerous it was.

Taking off in the dark was not too difficult, provided that the engine kept running, there was enough field in front of the nose, and the pilot held a straight course. Getting lost was the next hazard. There are many recorded instances of inexperienced airmen getting lost on their first solo within a matter of minutes, often to find that the airfield was right beneath them all the time. And this was in broad daylight! Night navigation at first was all but impossible except in moonlight, with the aircraft at a modest altitude, following clearly defined landmarks such as canals or railway lines, as did Claude Graham-White when taking part in the London to Manchester Air Race in April 1910 (he still only came second!).

Landing was the worst of all. Finding the right field was bad enough, but while a horizon might be visible at altitude, even on the clearest night it was almost invariably lost in ground haze as the aircraft descended, leaving the pilot with no visual cues, and nothing by which to accurately judge his height above the ground. Landings in such conditions were often noisy and expensive. Only later were the first rudimentary landing aids and blind flying instruments developed. Even these availed little against the worst enemy of all, fog, which stole insidiously over airfields while the airmen were still aloft, making recovery from a night sortie an undertaking fraught with peril.

Most dangerous of all was disorientation. After the human eyeball, the most commonly used aviation sensor was widely held to be the seat of the pants, though actually located in the inner ear! Used as a backup to visual cues, this was a valuable flying aid, to the extent that equestrians were often favoured by flying selection committees. But on its own it was treacherous, liable to give all sorts of false impressions. It is as though the gyros in one's head topple, making one feel that one is flying straight and level when actually in an overbanked, semi-inverted position, or climbing when one is diving. It has killed many a pilot in the past, and even now can still endanger anyone insufficiently skilled in the art of instrument flying.

An early example, and fairly unusual because he lived to tell the tale, was provided by Lieutenant Randall of the Royal Flying Corps (RFC). Piloting a Maurice Farman Longhorn, he became disoriented in cloud. On emerging into clear air, he saw a huge hill looming directly ahead. At first unable to recognise it, he finally realised that he was in a vertical dive and the hill was in fact Salisbury Plain! Hauling back on the stick had no effect; the Longhorn continued its stately plunge downwards. In desperation, Randall pushed through, and the Longhorn recovered into an inverted position, miraculously without shedding its wings, which were hardly stressed for negative "g" manoeuvres. Rolling – if that is not too positive a word for a Longhorn – into an upright position, Randall recovered safely to Upavon.

The frailties of aircraft of the pre-1914 period, their low speeds coupled with the unreliability of their engines, meant that air operations could only be attempted in fair weather, and precautionary landings were often made when conditions grew gusty. The RFC was no exception, but even as early as 1913, attempts were made to achieve a measure of night capability. The effects of this would be threefold. It would allow reconnaissance aircraft to take off before dawn so as to arrive in their designated area at first light. It would allow them to continue a late patrol until dusk, returning to base in darkness. Finally it would allow a measure of communications capability at night.

The way was led by No 3 Squadron and on 16 April 1913, a Lieutenant R. Cholmondeley flew a Maurice Farman biplane from Larkhill to Upavon and back, a round trip of just under 14 miles (22km), by moonlight. In this modest, but successful start, he discovered that while there was a reasonable horizon at several hundred feet, it vanished as he came in to land. Neither was the ground illuminated enough for him to judge his height properly on final approach, although after a rather too exciting few minutes he arrived safely on terra firma.

Further night flights were made from Larkhill over the next few weeks, with airfield illumination provided by turning on the hangar lighting with the doors wide open. Then in June, petrol flares were used for the first time. The first pilot to use flares as a landing aid was a Lieutenant G. Carmichael, who had his machine fitted for the attempt with what was probably the first night flying aid, a light to illuminate his compass and rev counter. After this, flares became standard for night operations.

But even as these experiments were made, what was probably the first ever war sortie involving night flying was carried out, albeit mainly fortuitously. In the Balkans, the Ottoman Empire was at war with Bulgaria, whose army was advancing towards Constantinople. As usual, communications were poor, the situation was confused, and the Turkish High Command desperately needed to find out what was going on.

In the late afternoon of 7 April 1913, a DFW Mars biplane took off from the Turkish airfield of St Stefano to reconnoitre the Bulgarian army positions. The pilot was Mario Scherff, a European, while the observer was none other than Mustapha Kemal, later Kemal Ataturk, the future founder of the new Turkey, but then just a Staff Captain. At Kemal's insistence, they flew over almost every Bulgarian-occupied village along the way, being shot at as they went. This took some considerable time, and nightfall, made worse by a gathering storm, overtook them.

The return flight was made in inky darkness with, as Scherff later commented, not even a glimmer of light. Unable to see even the few instruments he had, and buffetted by the storm, he became completely lost. Luck was with them. Descending to a lower altitude and heading in the general direction of the Sea of

Marmara, which was sufficiently large as to be unmissable, they eventually spotted a lighthouse, which gave them a fix on their position.

At last they arrived back over the airfield, which was marked by two petrol fires. The only other cues were the lights of a nearby village in a valley below the field. Invisible in the darkness were telephone wires and a war memorial. Unable to judge his altitude, Scherff lined up his aircraft, switched off the ignition, and at the same moment the wheels touched the ground. Collision with not very solid obstructions followed, but the flyers escaped injury. They had been luckier than they knew.

World War 1 began on 4 August 1914 and the new fangled aeroplanes at once started to prove their value on reconnaissance and artillery spotting missions, with a little ineffective bomb dropping thrown in. At first most flew unarmed, but it was soon realised that it was necessary to deny the enemy these missions, and the first air combats took place. These were haphazard affairs, as no-one really knew how to go about fighting in the air. Many theories abounded, a significant proportion of them involving multi-seat aircraft bristling with gunners, flying along exchanging broadsides in the manner of ships of the line in the days of sail.

But even as a Napoleonic era three-decker was unable to catch a fast frigate, so flying battleships were unable to catch small and fast reconnaissance aircraft, while the problems of hitting a target able to move rapidly in three dimensions from an unstable and vibrating aircraft proved equally intractable. After much trial and error, the dedicated fighter emerged as a fast and agile single seater, with fixed, forward firing machine guns. But the early development of air fighting as such is another story.

Even before the outbreak of war, it had become obvious that air attacks against the British Isles were possible. The threat was posed by the German airship fleet, which was obviously capable of carrying bombs over the sort of distances necessary, and which had actually trained for bombing missions before the war, achieving quite respectable standards of accuracy. They were also routinely flown at night. Operated by both the Imperial German Army and Navy, these were generally called Zeppelins, although they were in fact of two types. The aluminium framed Luftschiff Zeppelin machines were operated by both services, designated L by the Imperial Navy and LZ by the German army, while the plywood framed Schutte-Lanz types, designated SL, were used by the army only.

Few defensive measures were taken; a few searchlights, even fewer quickly modified high angle guns, and four totally inadequate aeroplanes, were the sum total of Britain's early defences against this new threat. The RFC, which should have taken responsibility, pleaded that it had insufficient aircraft, which was quite true, and a handful of Royal Naval Air Service (RNAS) aircraft assumed the task as a temporary measure.

In practice, with no advance warning system, interception by the aircraft of the era was a fairly hopeless proposition. Taking off when a Zeppelin was sighted, they took something like 45 minutes to reach its operating altitude of 10,000ft (3,050m), by which time it would be long gone. Standing patrols demanded far more aircraft than were available, and even then interception would have been very much a matter of chance, with the odds stacked heavily against the fighter.

Of course, a Zeppelin was a simply enormous target. Even the early ones were nearly 500ft (152m) long and 60ft (18. 29m) in diameter. Provided that an armed aircraft could get within range, it was almost impossible to miss although judging the range against such a huge target was a problem, particularly at night. In theory, they were almost equally easy to hit from the ground, while the fact that they were filled with highly flammable hydrogen gas made them exceptionally vulnerable to fire. The theory of the vulnerability of airships was reinforced early in the war by the destruction of three army machines while on tactical bombing missions over the Western Front, but in each case they had approached at low altitude. Surprisingly, not one of them burned. This was yet another theory of air warfare which did not quite work out in practice.

The first air attacks on England were not carried out by Zeppelins, but by fixed wing aeroplanes in daylight, but these were ineffectual. They did however indicate to the Germans that British air defences were virtually non-existent. Then on the night of 19-20 January 1915, the airship raiders struck. As raids go, it was an unimpressive start. Two headed for the mouth of the Humber, but due to unexpected winds and poor navigation, eventually arrived over Norfolk, dropping bombs on Great Yarmouth and Kings Lynn, while a third, heading for the lower reaches of the Thames, turned back early with engine failure.

Further raids followed, and the defences proved ineffectual. Even when searchlights illuminated the monsters, the guns seemed unable to inflict serious damage on them, while RNAS aircraft searched in vain. The night sky was a big place.

It was not until 17 May of that year that the first interception was made. On that night, LZ38, commanded by Hauptmann Erich Linnarz, was illuminated by searchlights over Essex. Nearby, and fortuitously at the same level, was Sub-Lieutenant R. H. "Red" Mulock, flying a modified Avro 504. Closing undetected, Mulock opened fire at an estimated 2,000ft (600m), but after a short burst his Lewis gun jammed. LZ38, made rudely aware of Mulock's presence, escaped into the darkness apparently unscathed.

This first interception was followed a few hours later by another, when LZ39 was spotted recrossing the Belgian coast by no less than three RNAS fighters. Of these, Sub-Lieutenant Reginald Warneford, flying a Morane-Saulnier L, was unable to reach the dirigible's altitude, but the other two managed to attack. Squadron Commander Spenser Grey in a Nieuport 11, tucked in close beneath the giant airship and emptied the magazine of his Lewis gun into its belly, while Flight Commander S. Bigsworth in an Avro 504 dropped four 20lb (9kg) Hales bombs on it from above. Five gas cells were ruptured, a propeller torn off, one crewman was killed and five others injured. This was not enough to prevent LZ39 from reaching base safely.

This action made it obvious that Zeppelins were not as vulnerable as had been thought. Hydrogen would not burn unless oxygen was present, and rifle calibre bullets simply went in one side and out of the other, causing leaks that were insignificant when one considers the volume of gas carried – typically nearly 27,000 cubic metres in 18 separate cells. To picture such a large volume, imagine a building 16ft

(4. 90m) high, covering the area of an average football field. Then imagine how long it would take all this gas to leak out through a couple of dozen small holes. And later Zeppelins were considerably larger.

In any case, providing they were accessible, small holes could be patched in flight to minimise gas loss. The failure of the Hales bombs to achieve decisive results was harder to explain, but it seems possible that they simply bounced off the envelope before exploding. Had they penetrated, they must surely have ignited the hydrogen.

The earliest anti-Zeppelin measure had been to bomb them in their sheds, and this had met with considerable success. On the night of 6-7 June Reginald Warneford, who we last met failing to get to grips with LZ39, took off with three others to bomb the airship base at Berchem Ste Agathe. He had never before flown at night, but was equipped with the latest blind flying instrument, a length of red wool tied to a cabane strut, the angle of which in the slipstream would warn him of a sideslip. Inexperience told, and almost immediately he lost contact with the others.

Searching the sky for them, he sighted engine exhaust flames in the distance and set off in their direction, only to find that he was pursuing LZ37 which was returning to base at 7,000ft (2,133m). As he closed, he was sighted, and the Germans opened up with machine guns, keeping him at a distance. The Zeppelin commander, Oberleutnant von der Haegen, accelerated and climbed, but Warneford hung grimly on. Nearing base, the Zeppelin at last started to descend. This was his chance. Climbing above it for the first time, he lined up and released his bombs one by one.

The result was spectacular. LZ37 was ripped apart in a giant fireball and Warneford's frail Morane was flung almost upside down by the blast. On recovering control, no mean feat at night in the notoriously sensitive Morane, he found that his adventures were not yet over. A broken petrol pipe caused his engine to fail, forcing him to land in an unlit field behind enemy lines to effect a temporary repair. This done, he took off, still in darkness, and flew home to receive the Victoria Cross for his exploit, only the second airman to be so honoured. It was in fact a double victory, for Wilson and Mills, two of the pilots with whom Warneford had lost contact, bombed the target successfully, destroying LZ38 on the ground.

The year 1915 saw the London's defences stiffened. Searchlights and guns were improved and their numbers increased; specifically anti-Zeppelin weapons were developed, and a great deal of effort was put into producing an effective night fighter. As from the middle of the year, the RFC had sufficient aircraft available to start taking over the air defence of Britain from the RNAS.

The standard . 303in machine gun had proved ineffective against dirigibles, and would remain so until incendiary and explosive bullets became available in the early spring of 1916. Bombing was the obvious alternative and there were many variations on this theme. Carcass bombs were a variety of mortar bomb, simple iron cases filled with explosive. Hales grenades were ordinary "pineapple" fragmentation grenades with a steel rod which enabled them to be fired from a rifle. Flechettes were sometimes carried – plain or incendiary, and a delightful contraption called the anti-Zeppelin bomb which consisted of a petrol container with a fuse to ignite it;

spring-loaded hooks were designed to catch in the fabric of a Zeppelin and ignite it. A variation on this theme was the Ranken dart, which combined an explosive head with four spring-loaded vanes on the tail. But any form of munition which had to be dropped on the German monsters was foredoomed.

Warneford had managed to catch LZ37 descending near its base. Over Britain there was little chance of finding a Zeppelin so low. As anti-aircraft fire grew heavier and more effective, so the German airships were driven to ever greater attack altitudes. Neither had their design stood still; before long they were able to ascend to over 20,000ft (6,096m). In cold figures, the British fighters were faster than the Zeppelins, but not if they had to climb to intercept, while if the raider discovered their presence it could evade by soaring upwards at a rate which they were unable to match. At lower altitudes fighters were theoretically able to outclimb their opponents, but the Zeppelins stayed higher up, where this did not apply.

Bombing Zeppelins was therefore never a viable proposition. Apart from any other consideration, an evading Zeppelin would have made a difficult target, even given its vast size, while it was not long before dorsal machine guns were mounted, ready to give an attacker a hot reception.

What was really needed was a more orthodox weapon, throwing a heavier and more damaging projectile than a rifle bullet. The Hales grenade has been mentioned, but this was short ranged, none too accurate due to its trajectory, and there was no guarantee that it would be in the right place when it finally decided to go off. The Le Prier rocket, used on the Western Front against observation balloons, seemed to offer possibilities, but this also was short-ranged and inaccurate. Attacking a huge target like a Zeppelin at night might sound easy, but the slightest misjudgement of speed and range could all too easily end in a mid-air collision, which was not the object of the exercise.

A hard-hitting medium range weapon which would allow the fighter to stand off from its opponent seemed to be needed. The trouble was that the flimsy airframes of the day were unable to take the shock of the recoil, and an aircraft which fell to pieces when its gun was fired was of little value. Two feasible alternatives were the Vickers Crayford rocket gun, and the Davis recoilless gun, which came in various sizes and fired shells weighing up to 2lb (1kg). As even on moonlit nights the fighters were dependent on searchlights to show them where the raiders were, it seemed like a good idea to give the fighter its own searchlight.

In retrospect this appears totally potty. The aircraft of the period had what is most kindly described as very modest performance, which fell off rapidly when any extra weight or drag was imposed. Warneford, carrying six light bombs, had not even been armed with a machine gun, despite accounts to the contrary. Sticking extra crew members, with large guns (the Davis gun was actually more than 7ft (2.13m) long) and a searchlight into existing machines, was out of the question.

Undaunted, various designers attempted to produce a Zeppelin killer. Among them was Noel Pemberton Billing, one of the more colourful characters of the time. In his book *Air War: How to Wage It* he laid down what he regarded as essential requirements. These were a searchlight with a range of one mile, and armament effective at the same range; a maximum speed of at least 80mph (129kmh);

minimum flying speed of 35mph (56kmh); 12 hours endurance, which made two pilots essential; and a rate of climb of 10,000ft (3,050m) in 20 minutes.

Pemberton Billing's first attempt resulted in the huge PB.29E quadruplane, powered by two 90hp Austro-Daimler six-cylinder engines driving pusher propellers. Both these and the fuselage, which carried a crew of three, were mounted on the second wing. First flown during the winter of 1915-16, it crashed before its full potential could be explored. Unfortunately no data has survived.

It was followed by the even larger PB. 31E Night Hawk, which first flew in February 1917. Also a quadruplane, the PB. 31E was powered by two 100hp Anzani radials and carried a trainable searchlight in the nose. Armament was a 1½lb Davis gun in a traversing mount level with the top wing, and two . 303in machine guns. Planned endurance was 18 hours, and the idea was that it could lie in wait for Zeppelins by flying very slowly into the wind. As the prevailing winds over England tend to be south-westerly, while the Germans were coming from the north east, this does not seem a good idea. Slow and unhandy, the prototype was scrapped in July 1917.

More workmanlike in appearance was the Parnall Scout, unofficially known as the Zeppelin Chaser. A conventional single-seat biplane powered by a 260hp Sunbeam Maori engine, it had an estimated top speed of 113mph (182kmh). Intended to carry the Crayford rocket gun mounted at an angle to starboard and inclined upwards at a 45deg angle, it was only ever fitted with a .303in machine gun. Seriously overweight from the outset, and considered to have unacceptably low safety factors, it is believed to have flown no more than twice.

One of the earliest anti-Zeppelin fighters, and one of the more promising, was the Port Victoria PV. 2 floatplane. A single-seat sesquiplane, it was powered by a 100hp Monosoupape rotary engine and first flew in June 1916. Proposed armament was the 2pdr Davis gun, but this was never fitted. Early promise was such that it was decided to develop it into the PV. 2BIS, and while this flew early in 1917, the type failed to enter service.

Also designed around the Davis gun was the Robey-Peters RRF. 25, an unorthodox biplane powered by a 250hp Rolls-Royce Eagle in-line engine. The pilot sat in the rear of the fuselage just ahead of the fin, while two gunners occupied nacelles slung under the top wing, the starboard of which housed a 2pdr Davis gun with 10 shells; the port wing was fitted with a .303in machine gun, although it was later decided to use Davis guns on both sides. The first flight took place in September 1916, but the prototype crashed on its third flight and burnt out. The slightly different Mk II flew in January 1917, but this crashed on take-off and further work on the type was abandoned.

Several other proposed Zeppelin chasers used the single-engined pusher configuration which, though it gave the gunner an uninterrupted field of fire ahead, was less aerodynamically efficient than the tractor layout due to the drag caused by the "birdcage" of booms and bracing wires needed to support the tail, which reduced performance. Typical of these, which included the Admiralty Air Department AD Scout and the Vickers FB. 25, was the Royal Aircraft Factory NE. 1. Derived from the FE. 9, which was in turn developed from the FE. 2, the NE. 1 (Night Experimental) was powered by a single 200hp Hispano–Suiza eight-cylinder engine, and carried a crew of two. Initially the pilot sat in front, with a . 303in Lewis gun and a searchlight, power for which was provided by a wind-driven generator beneath the nacelle, while behind him the observer was armed with a Vickers rocket gun with forward and aft-firing mountings. These positions, and the weaponry, were later reversed. First flight was in September 1917 and the type took part in official trials at Martlesham Heath in November. But at this stage of the war the performance of the NE. 1 was judged inadequate and, of six prototypes built, only one was issued to an RFC Home Defence squadron.

With not one successful purpose-built Zeppelin destroyer entering service, the most commonly used type with RFC Home Defence squadrons was the BE. 2c, which also saw extensive service in France, mainly as a reconnaissance aircraft and artillery spotter, or a makeshift bomber. A two-seat tractor biplane, with the observer awkwardly placed in the front cockpit, the BE. 2 lacked both agility and performance and in the presence of enemy fighters, by day it was a turkey. It was however an exceptionally stable aeroplane which made it suitable for night flying by pilots of limited experience. In Home Defence squadrons it was flown as a single-seater, with instruments marked with luminous paint, and a cockpit lamp. Armament was a fixed Lewis gun firing at an upward angle over the top wing, and/or anti-Zeppelin bombs.

Throughout the rest of 1915, Zeppelins roamed the night skies of England, hampered far more by the weather than the defences. The makeshift night fighters roamed far and wide, but failed to make contact, occasionally losing one of their number in a landing or other accident. Not until 15 October did a fighter even get close.

On that night, six Zeppelins set course, among them LZ15, commanded by Kapitän-Leutnant Joachim Breithaupt, on his first mission over England. After aiming some bombs at a troublesome anti-aircraft gun near Broxbourne in Hertfordshire (which he near-missed), he flew south to bomb central London. Meanwhile, five night fighters had risen to intercept, among them young Lieutenant John Slessor from Sutton's Farm near Hornchurch, who had orders to patrol at 10,000ft (3,050m).

Meanwhile LZ15 dropped some of its bombs, then throttling its engines back to idle, it drifted above the stricken city while its commander listened for the aircraft that he suspected were on their way to attack him. Even without the searchlights, LZ15 was clearly illuminated on the underside by the lights of the city, and was visible for some considerable distance. Sure enough, he heard the sound of an aircraft engine at full throttle as it tried to claw its way to his altitude. He may even have sighted Slessor's BE. 2c held in a searchlight beam as it climbed. Slessor, still 1,000ft (305m) below, saw sparks stream from the exhausts of LZ15's engines as they were opened up, then the huge ship swung away and climbed at a steep angle, leaving his BE. 2c floundering, before disappearing into cloud.

Slessor's troubles were not yet over. Following the course of the Thames, he sighted the L-shaped flares that marked the landing ground. After patrolling a while longer, he let down, only to find that a layer of fog had rolled in. This would have been bad enough, but the local searchlight decided to help by illuminating the field, blinding Slessor in the process, who finished in a turnip field with a bent aeroplane.

Slessor's experience clearly showed that without at least initial parity in altitude, the BE. 2c stood little chance of catching a Zeppelin. It has often been asked since why higher performance aircraft could not have been used. The answer is simple. Of the five aircraft that ascended that night, three crash-landed. Worse was to come. On one disastrous night in January 1916, of 15 aircraft that took off, 11 crashed and three pilots were killed. Given the experience levels current at that time, with anything other than the docile BE. 2, attrition would quickly have become unacceptable.

Not until 31 March 1916 did the defenders score a victory, and then it was a combination of AA guns and fighters which did the damage. Seven airships set out to bomb London of which five, including LZ15, once again commanded by Breithaupt, crossed the English coast. Near Dartford, LZ15 came under fire from AA guns. Then it was hit amidships; the steering gear was damaged and four gas cells torn open. Turning back, Breithaupt jettisoned his bombs in a vain effort to maintain altitude. As his huge ship lost height, British fighters arrived. The first of these, flown by Lieutenant Ridley, gave it a short burst with its machine gun before losing contact. Shortly after, a BE. 2c flown by Lieutenant Alfred Brandon of No 39 Squadron, attacked. Coming under fire from the German gunners, he flew ahead of it, then turned in when about 500ft (152m) higher. Unable to get his incendiary bomb into its tube (release from which would have which ignited the fuse) in time, he dropped two boxes of Ranken darts which caused further damage. He then lost contact in the darkness. Shortly after midnight, by now down to less than 1,000ft (305m), LZ15 buckled in the middle and subsided into the Thames Estuary.

Months passed and the destruction of LZ15 appeared increasingly to have been a fluke. The raiders continued to come and go almost at will and the defences seemed impotent. The problem of locating them and directing fighters towards them had still not been solved. Not until the night of 2-3 September did the tide finally turn.

There were no less than 14 German airships over England that night. Also airborne was Lieutenant William Leefe Robinson of No 39 Squadron. Patrolling between Sutton's Farm in Essex and Joyce Green in Kent, he sighted a Zeppelin caught in searchlights over Woolwich, and started his BE. 2c in pursuit, before losing it in cloud. This was probably L98.

Resuming his patrol he then sighted a red glow to the north and turned towards it. Closing in a slight dive for maximum speed he sighted a Zeppelin which proved to be SL11, commanded by Hauptmann Wilhelm Schramm. Arriving about 800ft (244m) below it, Leefe Robinson raked it from bow to stern without effect, even though he was using a mixture of Brock and Pomeroy explosive ammunition. Turning, he replaced the empty ammunition drum with a full one and raked SL11 along one side, still with no apparent effect. Putting a third drum on his Lewis gun, he closed to 500ft (152m) below, and coming in from astern concentrated his fire on one spot. Soon he saw a red glow: the rear of SL11 erupted in flame with a tremendous roaring noise, and the giant Schutte Lanz started to settle. Frantically Leefe Robinson wrenched his aircraft around and away from the falling, blazing mass, which crashed near the Plough Inn at Cuffley in Hertfordshire. Low on fuel and oil, he made his way back to Sutton's Farm, and the immediate award of the Victoria Cross. For the British night fighters, it was the start of an era.

Further successes followed quickly. Shortly after midnight on 24 September Lieutenant Brandon, who had attacked LZ15 in March, encountered LZ33 near Chelmsford. After chasing it for several minutes he closed and fired a drum of . 303in ammunition along its length. As with Leefe Robinson's initial passes, no fire was caused. Shortly after changing drums his Lewis gun jammed and he then decided to climb above it for a further attack. In doing so he lost sight of it against a cloud bank. Brandon was unaware at the time that LZ33 had sustained heavy damage from AA fire previously, and after his attack it was unable to maintain height, finally coming down on marshland near West Mersea. Kapitän-Leutnant Alois Bocker and his crew were taken prisoner.

This was a fine start for the defenders, but more was to come. LZ32 was homeward bound when yet another pilot from No 39 Squadron, Lieutenant Fred Sowrey, intercepted. Attacking from below, he fired three drums of ammunition along its length. The first two of these appeared to have little effect, but the third ignited the Zeppelin from end to end. A blazing mass, LZ32 reached the ground near Billericay in Essex. After months of no results, two down in one night seemed almost miraculous. Still more was to come. Eight nights later, Kapitän-Leutnant Heinrich Mathy, the doyen of Zeppelin commanders, was caught at 12,000ft (4,267m) over Potters Bar by Lieutenant W. J. Tempest of No 39 Squadron and his Zeppelin LZ31 went down in flames.

From this point on, the defenders had the measure of the Zeppelin menace. Never again did the raiders strike at London, but confined themselves to safer areas. Further victories came the way of the night fighters, and after the disastrous (for the Imperial German Navy Airship Service) raid of 19 October 1917, when five out of 11 Zeppelins were shot down, the monsters of the night sky only rarely appeared.

Like many other seemingly hopeless battles, the pendulum had suddenly swung from one extreme to the other. What had made the difference? A combination of factors was involved.

First, the gun and searchlight defences had increased immeasurably. These indicated the whereabouts of the Zeppelins to the defending fighters with increasing frequency. Secondly, the reporting system, and also the monitoring of German radio transmissions had improved, allowing the British to locate the raiders with increasing accuracy. Thirdly, the number of fighters aloft patrolling likely lines of approach had also increased, which meant that the chances of a fighter being within reasonable interception distance at any given moment, were far greater. Fourthly, as Home Defence squadron pilots gained experience, high performance aircraft were increasingly used at night, making interception following a sighting far more certain. These could also carry heavier armament. Finally, as we have seen, raking a Zeppelin from end to end with machine gun fire did not always cause its destruction. Better results could often be obtained by shooting at the engine nacelles, with their vulnerable fuel tanks. But this called for more accurate aiming than was normally possible at night, when the gunsights were often not visible. A Sergeant Hutton of No 39 Squadron first overcame this by boring tiny holes in both fore and back sights, which were illuminated from within. These final points made little difference to the anti-Zeppelin campaign, but came in very useful later, as we shall see.

With the waning of the Zeppelin raids came a new threat. In the late afternoon of 25 May 1917, a formation of Gotha bombers raided Folkestone. It was the shape of things to come. Other raids followed, and on 13 June they appeared over London, causing extensive damage. Flying at between 14 and 15,000ft (4,267–4,571m) they were above the effective height of AA fire, while defending fighters took too long to reach altitude, arrived in one and twos, and were generally ineffective.

The first night raid by bombers came on 3–4 September the following night they reached London. On both ocasions the raiders escaped unscathed. Finding a relatively fast and much smaller Gotha in the vast night sky was far more difficult than finding a huge Zeppelin. On 28–29 September the stakes were raised yet again, when Gothas were accompanied by two giant Riesenflugzeuge, in the form of the Staaken R. IV, which carried a far greater bomb load than its smaller counterpart, and with six machine guns, was more heavily defended.

At a stroke, slow night fighters such as the BE. 2c became obsolete. Catching Zeppelins had been difficult enough for them, but against the smaller and faster bombers their performance margins were totally inadequate. Yet this problem was soon to be solved.

On the night of 3 September, Captain Gilbert Murlis-Green, the acting CO of No 44 Squadron, received permission to try to intercept the raiders with Sopwith Camels. The Camel was a very tricky aircraft to fly even in daylight and had killed many experienced pilots. Flying it at night was regarded as next to impossible, but Murlis-Green, with two other hand-picked pilots, took off and patrolled. Almost inevitably they found nothing, but all landed safely. This proved conclusively that high performance fighters could be used by experienced pilots at night, which at that time was not as obvious as might be thought.

Raid followed raid, and while AA accounted for a couple of Gothas, the night fighters had no luck until 18 December when Murlis-Green blundered (there is no other word for it) almost into one. Quickly pulling in behind it, he opened fire, and was immediately dazzled by the flash of the two Vickers machine guns which were mounted directly ahead of him. On recovering his night-adapted vision, he attacked once more, trying to aim, then looking away before he fired. Each time his night vision was ruined, and after several attacks he finally lost sight of his quarry. However, he had damaged its engines and it force landed in the sea off Folkestone.

Steps were put in hand to adapt the standard Camel for night fighting. Flash eliminators were fitted to the gun muzzles and the engine exhaust flames were masked. Finally the Neame illuminated gunsight ring was fitted, designed to match the wingspan of a Gotha at 300ft (91m) range.

By this time, other high performance fighters were in use with Home Defence squadrons. These included the SE. 5A and the two-seat Bristol F2B.

Camels modified specially for night fighting were also introduced. These had twin Lewis guns on a Foster mounting above the wing in place of the twin Vickers, thus removing the muzzle flash from the pilot's line of sight. The fabric to the wing centre section was removed to improve vision forwards and upwards. The cockpit was moved aft and the petrol tank placed in front of it. An experimental ground to air radio telephony station was set up at Biggin Hill, although the shortcomings of this were such that it proved of little use.

This notwithstanding, few further interceptions were made in the first months of 1918. But on the night of 19-20 May the night fighters scored their greatest success. On clear nights in summer the sky never gets completely dark and this was to the advantage of the defenders. No less than 38 Gothas and three Staakens were launched towards London. One Gotha was attacked by the SE. 5a of Fred Sowrey, now a major, from whom it escaped, only to fall to the guns of a Bristol F2B flown by Lieutenants E. Turner and H. Barwise. Another Gotha fell to the F2B of Lieutenant A. Arkwell and Air Mechanic Stagg, while the Camel of Captain Quintin Brand accounted for a third in an encounter at such close range that his moustache was singed by flames from the bomber. Three more fell to AA fire, while a seventh came down in Essex with engine failure. Such a loss rate was unsustainable and further raids on England became few and far between.

The night fighters had convincingly defeated the Zeppelins, but the bomber was another matter. All that can be said is that they had made bombing raids fairly hazardous during clear light nights, but to claim that they had defeated the bomber would be far too ambitious. In any event, such a claim would be disproved 22 years later. One thing that was clear was that neither Zeppelin nor bomber had defeated the weather, which accounted for a significant proportion of casualties among the raiding forces. Neither were the defenders exempt.

On the Western Front priorities were different. The gaining of air superiority over the front lines was of the greatest importance in order to allow friendly aircraft to carry out reconnaissance, artillery spotting and bombing missions unhindered, while preventing the enemy from doing the same. Consequently, most sorties took place in daylight, albeit sometimes in extremely bad weather. This took its toll in terms of individuals, and occasionally entire formations were lost. For example, on 21 July 1916, five FE. 2ds of No 20 Squadron RFC flew into a hillside in fog, killing all 10 crewmen.

The German homeland was bombed extensively at night during the latter half of 1918, notably by an Independent Force of the RAF formed specifically for the task, but the Luftstreitkräfte never looked like providing an effective fighter defence. British bombers raided a variety of mainly industrial targets over a wide arc stretching from Cologne to Stuttgart, thus dissipating the defences. Of course, had Berlin been attacked, the reaction might have been stronger. As it was, the Luftstreitkräfte relied mainly on attacking Independent Force airfields and encounters in the air at night were rare, although on one occasion an FE. 2d of No 100 Squadron, the first dedicated night raiding unit in the RFC, stumbled across a Gotha and shot it down. But as the FE. 2 was returning from a bombing mission at the time, it hardly counts.

Over the Western Front itself, sporadic night raiding took place, often with little effect. Although distances were relatively short, good landmarks were in short supply which made targets difficult to find. Then following the disastrous night of 19-20 May, the Gotha and Staaken force was switched to rear area targets in France, in support of the ground war.

Up to this point, airfield attack had been favoured in many quarters as a means of reducing enemy air power. Interception was often attempted but, as in other theatres, with little success. With this escalation of the night air war, two RAF squadrons were formed to counter the Gotha threat. No 151 Squadron, flying Night Camels and commanded by the redoubtable Gilbert Murlis Green, arrived in France in June 1918.

Circumstances on the continent were rather different. When defending England, fighters could patrol up and down a line marked by flares on airfields, which were left alight for the pilots to land by. Any attempt to do this in France was to provide a target marker for a raider, and a different system was evolved. A pattern of light beacons was set up, each flashing a different letter in Morse, the letter being changed at intervals to prevent the Germans from using it. These beacons allowed the pilots to navigate around the night sky after a fashion, although it was far from easy. For landing, each aircraft was fitted with a signal lamp. On returning to his airfield, the pilot flashed his individual callsign. If the coast was clear, this was answered from the ground and a lighting trolley, mobile so that it could be pointed into the wind, was switched on, casting a beam of light across the field by which the pilot landed.

No 151 Squadron flew many defensive sorties during the final months of the war. They also carried out intruder sorties in support of night attack squadrons, notching up 26 victories before the Armistice. The second night fighter squadron, No 152, only arrived in October 1918 and did not see action before hostilities ended.

By the time of the Armistice in November 1918, night flying had made great strides. Night fighting, however, was still in its infancy, while bad weather flying had been barely attempted. As later chapters will show, the night bomber was still a force to be reckoned with.

2. The Limbo Years

In one way, the situation in the years following the end of World War 1 was similar to that of the early 1990s. With the defeat of Imperial Germany the major threat to world peace had evaporated, leaving a vacuum in which those responsible for forward defence planning floundered. With no visible threat to guard against, it became very difficult for the services to obtain funding for new schemes which only might – but equally might not – prove useful at some future date. The industrial nations of Europe were impoverished, even those on the winning side, and they were far more concerned with rebuilding their shattered economies than in maintaining a strong defensive stance.

The massive British air fleet was reduced from 185 squadrons in 1918 to a mere 28 in 1921, of which 21 were based overseas. Over the next few years it was to be touch and go whether the RAF would remain in being as an independent service, as both the Army and Royal Navy wanted to recover their elements now incorporated in the new air arm. France, on whose territory most of the war had been fought, was much slower to denude itself of air power and retained 126 squadrons at that time, mainly at home.

Over the next few years, many lessons of World War 1 were forgotten. In Britain, the so-called "10-Year Rule" was adopted, which in essence stated that a valid threat in Europe would take 10 years to emerge thus giving plenty of warning for a rearmament programme to be initiated. This gave little incentive for further progress. Most of the aircraft in use in the early 1920s had been developed during the war and were forced to soldier on, often for many years. For example, the Bristol F2B of 1917 vintage remained in service until 1932.

From April 1920 to September 1922, the sole fighter defence of England comprised just one squadron, No 25, which was equipped with Sopwith Snipes. Based at Hawkinge in Kent, No 25 Squadron was therefore theoretically responsible for both day and night defence, although such a small force indicates that the possibility of it actually being needed was not taken too seriously.

A development of the Camel, the Snipe not only had better performance than the latter, but also its handling was rather less fearsome, making it more suitable for night operations. What was more it carried oxygen, a parachute, and a heated flying suit. The armament consisted of twin . 303in Vickers machine guns on the engine cowling with flash eliminators on the muzzles. Flash was still a problem at night, and eventually an improved propellant, giving less flame, was introduced, although this was only a partial answer.

During the closing years of the war, day fighter pilots had often used tracer ammunition as an aid to aiming. Hitting a fast moving target at even quite small angles off was beyond the capability of all but the most gifted marksmen. Tracer could show a pilot where his shots were going, and help him to adjust his aim. At night, tracer simply added to the problem of dazzle, and it was not until afterwards that a less bright form was developed for night use. Unfortunately there were still problems. Tracer could lie quite convincingly. If it burned out before reaching the target, which it often did, it gave the impression of bullets vanishing into an enemy aircraft whereas in fact they were falling short. Yet another theory bit the dust.

Meanwhile another good theory was making the rounds. In 1921 General Giulio Douhet, an Italian, wrote a book entitled *The Command of the Air*. In it he assumed that worthwhile strategic targets were normally concentrated in areas of about 500m diameter and that each could be totally destroyed by 10 aeroplanes each carrying two tonnes of bombs. A fleet of bombers sufficient to obliterate 50 such targets per day was to bring any war to a swift end. Enemy fighters were to be destroyed on the ground, although heavily armed gunships would escort the bombers until this was done, then afterwards revert to the bombing role.

The Command of the Air seems to have had little effect on the thinking of serving officers, mainly because it required an accuracy of bombing far beyond the capabilities of the time – and, indeed, for the foreseeable future. This notwithstanding, the RAF, the Armée de l'Air and the Regia Aeronautica (which was still the Italian Air Corps at that time) all started to build strategic bomber fleets. The thinking behind this was that interception was problematic even in daylight, while standing patrols required an unaffordable number of aircraft. The alternative was deterrence. As Lord Trenchard, the founding father of the RAF, stated in 1922:

"It is on the destruction of enemy industries, and above all, on the lowering of morale of enemy nationals, that ultimate victory rests...."

Building a strategic bomber fleet was a slow process. It was also politically unacceptable to entirely forego all fighter defences. Hamstrung by both financial constraints and the 10-Year Rule, progress was slow. In Britain, roughly three bombers entered service for each fighter. Development and production of the latter lagged in consequence.

However, there were certain advances. In May 1925 the Hawker Woodcock entered service with No 3 Squadron. Interestingly, this was the first aircraft ordered specifically as a night fighter, although apart from docile handling, a wide track undercarriage which was proof against all but the most hamfisted landings, and an improved blind flying instrument panel, it otherwise had little to commend it. Performance was slightly inferior to that of the Snipe, which it superseded, although its Bristol Jupiter radial engine was far more reliable. Acknowledging that muzzle brakes were not the answer to flash, the two machine guns were mounted externally well down on the fuselage.

Perhaps the most important innovation of the 1920s was the widespread use of radio telephony for fighters, allowing speech communication between aircraft and ground controllers. While this made more impact on the day fighter squadrons, whose leaders could now direct both individual aircraft and widely scattered flights on exercises, it was obviously useful at night. In theory it allowed a controller on the ground to direct a fighter towards a hostile. In practice, the controller had only the vaguest idea of the whereabouts of the raider, and probably none at all of the fighter. This was one of the most difficult problems to solve, as will be seen later.

Neither was radio telephony a panacea for communication. It was unreliable and quality was poor: speech was often distorted to a degree where it became completely unintelligible, while even at the best of times it helped if the hearer had some idea of what the message was about. It was to overcome this defect that code-words were adopted, such as "Bandit" for a hostile, or "Bogey" for an undentified aircraft. Squadron callsigns were also adopted, initially named after flowers until "Pansy" Squadron strongly objected.

Wartime experience had firmly established two lessons. The first was that night flying was dangerous. The inherent problems of flying at night, coupled with adverse weather, had caused far more casualties to both sides than enemy action. The second was navigation. Finding ground targets within about 100 miles (160km) of base on a clear night, by pilots familiar with the topography of the region was difficult enough, but Zeppelins droning about over a blacked out England had often reported bombing targets which were over 100 miles from where they had actually been. London of course was such a huge area, and so well marked by the Thames and its estuary, that it was difficult to miss. But precision attacks on specific small targets in the London area, such as munitions factories, were virtually impossible. The only realistic target was therefore the morale of the civilian population, as Trenchard had pointed out.

Given this, it was hard to take the threat of night bombing seriously, and the art of night fighting fell into almost total disuse. Lip service was still paid to it, but little practice was carried out. Accidents were most definitely not wanted in the peacetime service, and not flying at night was as good a way of avoiding them as any.

It therefore became a vicious circle. Little night flying was undertaken because it was dangerous, while little attempt was made to make it safer because hardly any night flying was carried out. How seriously the whole subject was taken can be appreciated by the fact that the Woodcocks of Nos 3 and 17 Squadrons, the only dedicated night fighter units in the entire RAF during the 1920s, carried bright day fighter colours during their entire service. They were finally replaced by Gloster Gamecocks in 1928, and the Gamecock was also the standard day fighter.

The seeming aversion of the military fighter community to night and bad weather flying was shared to a degree by their bomber counterparts, but in RAF service at least, dark green night bomber camouflage became standard from 1927 onwards, with red-and-blue-only national insignia. Despite this, most of their planning and exercises involved day operations. Little night flying was undertaken although the Vickers Virginia, which entered serice in 1924, was the first RAF bomber to be fitted with an autopilot.

In only one country was the problem of finding one's way from place to place at night tackled in a systematic way. Inevitably this was the USA, where good communications over vast distances had always been at a premium, and where innovation often took precedence over hidebound tradition. The traditions of the Pony Express were carried over into the US Air Mail service, including the need to keep going at night.

There was a price to be paid for progress. Aircraft going astray, pilots becoming disoriented, and forced landings due to engine failure were common events, making the mail service not exactly reliable. The first aids to navigation were huge bonfires at frequent intervals, marking the way across country, but as can be imagined, the logistics problems involved were enormous. The bonfires were eventually replaced by powerful revolving electric beacons which acted as street lighting for the airways. However, these were purely visual measures and depended on the pilot being able to see the ground. In conditions of poor visibility they could not be seen from the air; something better was needed for bad weather.

That something turned out to be radio aids. The illuminated beacons were supplemented with, or replaced by, radio beacons. Then in the early 1930s a scheme was developed whereby directional radio beams were transmitted, typically having Morse code dots on one side of the beam and dashes on the other, the two merging into a single tone in the centre, so that a suitably equipped aircraft could follow the continuous tone and know when it was straying to left or to right. While not foolproof, it was a significant advance.

The most significant factor about this new navigational aid was that as it made night flying more commonplace, it pointed up the need for improved facilities: hard runways, proper airfield lighting, radio landing aids etc. And with the emergence of a more affluent society, a new possibility arose. Radio direction finding was in its infancy, but cross-bearings taken on two or more of the new civilian radio stations that were then springing up, could provide, by a process of triangulation, fairly accurate navigational fixes.

For the moment, although these systems had little military application (ie, no enemy would be so obliging as to provide radio navigation beams for a raiding force to use) night flying became a much more practical proposition, for the bomber at any rate, although the problem of target identification remained.

With the rise to power in Germany of Hitler and his National Socialist party in the 1930s, the 10-Year Rule was finally abandoned and an expansion scheme was instituted for the RAF. To the British, the main threat was soon perceived as massed formations of unescorted German bombers coming in over the East Coast and Thames Estuary during daylight. Consequently the accent was on building up the day fighter force. As always, the night fighter was the poor relation.

The perennial problem of fighter interception, whether by day or by night, is arriving in the right place at the right time. The crux of the matter was in receiving a warning early enough for the fighters to take off, form up, gain altitude, then intercept. This was difficult enough even by day. In air defence exercises in the summer of 1934, raiders were simulated by elderly Vickers Virginia bombers, with a cruising speed of barely 75mph (121kmh). Successful fighter interceptions were minimal. If we look at the following scenario it will become apparent why.

Assume that a bomber raid is planned and the aircraft will be flying at 12,000ft (3,657m). The bombers are sighted, their course plotted, and the order to scramble defending fighters is given. The fighters then take off, form up and climb to this altitude in the general direction of the raiders. Roughly 30 minutes have elapsed. In a cloudless sky, the bomber formation can probably be seen at a range of

10 miles (16km). The area of visual search for the fighters at any given point on their course is thus just over 314 square miles (804sq km). In the elapsed time the bombers have moved another 37 miles (60km). Allowing for changes of course since the original report, they are therefore somewhere within an area of no less than 4,301 square miles (11,310sq km), giving less than a one-in-five chance of a sighting at any given moment. This is made far worse by the presence of clouds, which are a feature of most sunny days over England. Given cloudy conditions, it was quite possible for two formations to sail right past each other within five miles (8km) or even less without seeing each other, while heavy cloud could turn the difficult into the hopeless.

A further factor which made life more difficult for the biplane fighters of the early 1930s was the rate of technical advance that took place. A combination of improved aerodynamics and structures, giving rise to all-metal monocoque construction monoplanes with retractable undercarriages and enclosed cockpits, with more powerful engines, made several bombers of this period faster than the fighters which were supposed to intercept them.

Of course, this paints a blacker picture than was actually the case, although not by much. The answer was early detection, then a comprehensive tracking system, so that ground controllers had an idea of where the raiders were at all times. But how?

The Observer Corps, later to become Royal Observer Corps, was founded in 1925, and gradually a network of observation posts was set up over southern England. These were responsible for tracking enemy aircraft and reporting on altitude, speed, course, numbers and type. On the other side of the coin, they could only "observe" inland and so could give no early warning of aircraft approaching from over the sea; they were often baulked by cloudy conditions, and were blind at night. In non-visual conditions sound locators could be used, but these were inaccurate, gave no indications of numbers, altitudes and types, and only the vaguest idea of locations, courses and speeds. As bombers grew faster, so the sound lagged the aircraft by an ever-increasing amount, thus compounding the margin of error. Finally, by the time the report had been made and processed, a time lag of several minutes had elapsed. Even under ideal conditions, by the time that ROC reports had been processed and transmitted to the fighter controllers, the information was already five minutes out of date.

The task of the fighter controllers was to bring the fighters into visual contact with the bombers. The simplest way was to bring them in behind on the same heading, but the ensuing tailchase was time-consuming. It was preferable to project the known or estimated course of the raid ahead by the required amount, then send the fighters towards it by the most direct route. This was called vectoring. However, problems arose when trying to calculate the best course.

Attempts were made to find a mathematical formula to suit all cases, but finally it was realised that by taking the projected position of the bombers and the known position of the fighters as the base of an isosceles triangle, calculated by eye, then giving the fighters a course down one of the long sides, the superior speed of the fighters would invariably put them into an interception position, provided that the raiders made no radical change of heading.

The major problem was of course early warning. However good the tracking system might be inland – and as we have seen, at first it wasn't very – the time lag between initial detection and getting fighters airborne, to the right altitude, and in the right area, was too great. Bombers raiding targets on the coast, or only a short distance inland, would be long gone before the fighters could arrive. The only answer to this was to fly standing patrols, but the number of fighters needed to make this effective was prohibitive.

Although the shortcomings of sound location were well known, for many years there was nothing better to replace it with and although attempts were made to improve the system, they met with little success. The main use of sound location was to direct searchlights to illuminate the raiders. Other means were tried. One of the most promising was infra-red (IR), to detect the heat from aircraft engines, but this had many shortcomings. By 1937 IR could detect an aircraft at about 1,500ft (457m) but the problem of placing the fighter within this distance remained. IR was also far too easily distracted by alternative heat sources such as fires on the ground, or blast furnaces, which could be detected at much greater distances, while it gave no indication of range. Nor could it see through cloud. But as it happened, the eventual means of night and bad weather detection was already to hand.

The principles of radio-location, or radar, as it later came to be called, had been known for years. The first experiments had been carried out in the early years of the century by a young German scientist, Christian Hulsemeyer. His apparatus projected a radio signal outwards, and these bounced off any solid object within the field of view. These echoes, on returning to the receiving apparatus, caused a bell to ring. Although widely patented, this device was not developed. Its range was short – just a few hundred yards, and it had no directional capability. All that could be said of it was that when the bell rang, it showed that something was out there somewhere.

The means of displaying the whereabouts of what was out there had existed even longer, in the form of the cathode ray tube which was first built by Professor Ferdinand Braun in 1897, also in Germany. Moreover, the basic form of radio valve, the diode, had been invented by Professor Ambrose Fleming in England in 1904.

The fact that these two developments existed so early did not mean, as some commentators have suggested, that a workable radar could have been in use in World War 1. There was far more research and development work still to come before the detection of aircraft by radar became a practical proposition. As we have seen, even a relatively simple thing like speech transmission from ground to air and vice versa took many years to develop before it became fully workable.

The lack of effective early warning was highlighted by the rise of the threat to Britain represented by Hitler's Third Reich, and in 1934 a committee was formed to investigate ways and means. One of the proposals examined was a "death ray". In order for such a device to work, the location of the target had to be known with great precision. Initial work had therefore to proceed on two fronts: transmission of very high power, and precision detection. While it was quickly proved that it was impossible to generate sufficient power to harm even a gnat at the ranges required, the location of aircraft with radio beams was found to be feasible. The "death ray" idea was dropped, and work proceeded with radio detection, which promised an answer to the perennial early warning problem. Progress was rapid and by 1936 work had started on a chain of radiolocation stations around the south and east coasts of England. At first very temperamental, the early sets were soon achieving detection ranges of up to 100 miles (161km) as well as giving tolerably accurate height indications.

Meanwhile Germany was not standing still, and in many ways was ahead of Britain in the field of electronics generally. The difference though was one of outlook and usage. While Britain was concentrating on defensive systems, the Third Reich was geared to the offensive, not the least of which was the development of blind bombing systems. In the field of radar the Gema company had developed Freya, an early warning set with a range of about 75 miles (120km) which in some ways was superior to the British system, although it gave no height indications; and also a gun ranging radar for warships, both of which were in service by 1938. Meanwhile Telefunken had developed Wurzburg, a short-ranged (about 25 miles/40km) radar with sufficient accuracy to allow Flak gunners to engage unseen targets. It was this last, rather than the prowess of his vaunted Luftwaffe, which shortly after the outbreak of war caused Reichsmarshall Hermann Goering to boast that if enemy aircraft ever succeeded in bombing the Ruhr, the nation could call him Maier; a statement he lived to regret.

The British early warning stations, called Chain Home, had an eventual maximum range of 120 miles (193km). Unlike Freya which could rotate through 360 degrees, they were fixed, and could only look out to sea through an arc of 120 degrees, and to avoid possible confusion, were electronically screened to prevent contacts behind them from being picked up. On one notorious occasion in the first few days of the war, the screening at one station failed, allowing formations inland to be presented as coming in over the North Sea, giving rise to the fratricidal encounter known as the Battle of Barking Creek. It was fortunate that this mishap occurred before the air war started in earnest.

While the Germans set up a handful of Freyas along their coast, they made little effort to produce a comprehensive reporting and tracking system, unlike the more defensively minded British. The Chain Home system, which could not only determine aircraft altitude to within certain limits, but also give an approximation of numerical strength, provided early warning, while inland tracking was the function of the Observer Corps. The raw information from both sources was fed into a central system where the confusion factor, caused by raids being plotted by more than one reporting site, was filtered out, and the situation data was then passed to the operational fighter controllers for action.

The next step was to make it work, which was done during an intense series of exercises; the first ever fighter to make an interception with the assistance of ground radar was a Gloster Gauntlet of No 32 Squadron, which intercepted a civil airliner over the Thames Estuary in November 1937. With constant practice, the British detection and reporting system became finely honed.

In many ways, the Chain Home radar detection system was the forerunner of all that came later, in that it demonstrated that aircraft could be detected and tracked at long range by day and by night, regardless of weather, and that approximate heights, courses, speeds and numbers could be determined. It was not however at all suitable for actual night interception.

All that was needed in daylight was for the fighter squadron to be brought within visual distance of the enemy formation; perhaps five miles (8km) or so, and preferably with a height advantage. In conditions of poor visibility, even this modest requirement often proved difficult.

The requirements for night interception were much more stringent. Visual distance even on a clear starlit night was rarely more than 1,000ft (305m), and often much less. The night fighter had to be brought rapidly into proximity, then positioned astern, so that it could close to firing range slowly to minimise the risk of colliding with its unseen target. Precision altitude finding was essential. Chain Home was simply not accurate enough for this, let alone the Observer Corps network inland. The final factor was that bombers do not fly in formation at night, but singly. A couple of dozen raid plots caused a fair amount of confusion by day, but this was manageable. A couple of hundred bombers flying individually at night would swamp the system, making effective control nearly impossible.

A dual solution was needed. The first was an overlapping network of ground radars inland, which for all practical purposes gave 360 degrees of coverage, combined with accurate target location and height finding. Real time information was also essential, and the only way of achieving this was to locate the fighter controller at the radar station with the display in front of him. The second was a radar set which would fit into an aircraft. Bringing a fighter to within visual distance of a bomber using ground control alone was extremely difficult, but if the requirement was to bring it within say one or two miles, the problems were eased enormously. But this would only be a practical proposition if the fighter carried some means of detection which would allow it to make contact with the target at far beyond normal night visual range.

Of the two requirements, the second was by far the most technically exacting. The Chain Home stations were enormous, with aerials hundreds of feet wide and almost as high as St Paul's Cathedral, while the power supply could only come from the National Grid. Of course, the German radars were much smaller, and something like these was needed for the inland ground stations. But the problems of producing a workable radar to fit into even the largest fighter was a mammoth task.

Experiments commenced early in 1937. By this time, the BBC had inaugurated a television service, which meant that a lot of equipment, such as cathode ray tubes (CRTs) and thermionic valves, was readily available. This helped considerably. On 16 August of that year, the first airborne radar set was flown in an RAF Anson Mk I. A simple dipole array was used for transmission, while the receiver aerials were mounted on the wingtips. If the radar echo from the contact was stronger on one aerial than the other, it meant that the target was off to that side, while other aerials, mounted above and below the wings and working on the same principle, gave an indication of whether it was above or below. The echoes were displayed on two CRT scopes, one showing azimuth, the other elevation. Quite good results were achieved against shipping targets, but aircraft proved far more elusive. The main problem was lack of transmitted power.

Work continued, further progress was made, and the design hardened. The first few pre-production articles were hand-built, but more or less standardised under the designation of AI (for Air Interception) Mk I. One of these was mounted in a Fairey Battle light bomber for evaluation, and first flew on 21 May 1939. Results were deemed satisfactory, although it should be remembered that up to this time the set had been operated solely by scientists who had worked on it since its inception, who knew all its foibles, and had grown adept at getting the best out of it. In squadron service this was to prove another matter.

Controversy had arisen in the early stages as to who was to monitor the set. One school of thought felt that it should be the pilot, while others wanted a specialist radar operator. To a degree this argument was to continue for the next 35 years, and the single versus two-seat fighter debate continued until after the end of the Vietnam War in 1973, but in those days it was really no contest.

The pro-pilot school argued as follows. The pilot had to fly the aeroplane in such a way as to make the interception, and this was best done if he had all the data immediately available. Reliance on instructions given by a second crew member who was not a pilot, was a method prone to error, misunderstandings, and communication problems. Furthermore it would reduce the pilot, in theory at any rate, to the status of a chauffeur/gunner. Of course, much the same arguments could have been applied to bomber pilots, but nobody queried their need for navigators, wireless operators and bomb aimers.

The counter-arguments were that at night or in bad weather, the pilot had quite enough to do flying on instruments, without having to make sense of a load of squiggles in a pair of scopes. To aggravate the situation even more, the relatively bright light from the displays would impair his night-adapted vision when it became time, as it inevitably would, to take his head out of the office and search visually. Finally a pretty large aeroplane was needed to carry the heavy and bulky radar set, with its array of aerials and black boxes and a power supply, which gave plenty of room to accommodate a radar operator. The dispute was settled by the AOC-in-C of Fighter Command himself, Air Chief Marshal Dowding, who settled on a large aeroplane with twin engines, and a specialist crew member to operate the AI set. With hindsight, we can see that he was absolutely right.

The next step was to select a suitable aircraft. There was not a lot of choice at this time. The RAF's standard day and night fighter was the Gloster Gladiator, which first entered service in February 1937. A biplane, it was little more suitable for night operations than its predecessors. The first RAF fighter to have an enclosed cockpit, it was fitted with a reflector gunsight, and carried four . 303in Browning machine guns, placed where muzzle flash would not dazzle the pilot at night. Two were carried in sponsons under the lower wing, while the other two were located in troughs low on the front fuselage, their breeches extending into the cockpit where a wooden mallet was carried to clear the cocking handles in the event of a jam. When fired, the bullets passed inside the engine cowling and past the cylinder heads, perilously close to the plug leads.

The following month saw the service entry of the Bristol Blenheim light bomber, which caused a mild sensation because it was appreciably faster than the

Gladiator. This, coupled with low wing loading and quite respectable endurance, made it an obvious choice for conversion to the long range escort role, which had hitherto been neglected, and late in the following year a programme was begun to convert 200 Blenheim Mk I light bombers to Mk IF long range fighter configuration. A number of "long nose" Blenheim Mk IVs were also modified in this way in 1939.

The modification involved fitting a pack of four . 303in Browning machine guns, each with 500 rounds, to the underside of the fuselage and providing the pilot with a fighter-type reflector gunsight. The mid–upper gun turret, armed with one (IF) or two (IVF) Vickers K .303in calibre machine guns, was retained.

The Blenheim fighter squadrons which were formed from December 1938 onwards operated officially by day and by night, but their lack of performance compared to the Hurricanes and Spitfires then entering service was such that they gradually came to be regarded more as night fighters. When it came to selecting an aircraft to carry the new AI radar the Blenheim, already in service, was the obvious first choice.

Meanwhile the hand–built AI Mk I had been revised to make it suitable for mass production as AI Mk II, and further "tweaks" produced the Mk III. From July 1939 onwards, AI radar began to be fitted to 21 Blenheim Mk IFs, all of which were in service by the end of September of that year. From November 1939, the radar-equipped aircraft were issued in ones and twos to the Blenheim night fighter squadrons for operational evaluation, and to allow the crews of these to gain experience on type. The first six months of 1940 saw more than 60 further Blenheims fitted with AI Mk III.

As is often the case with an expedient, the Blenheim Mk IF was hardly ideal for its role. One of the primary requirements of any fighter, day or night, is a significant speed advantage over its opponent. Let us take for example the case of a night fighter being directed towards a hostile contact which is 20 miles (32km) ahead, cruising at 200mph (322kmh). The official maximum speed of the Blenheim was 260mph (418kmh), giving it the seemingly adequate margin of 60mph (96kmh). Assuming that the machine in question could actually achieve this speed at the required altitude, which was unlikely, it would take around 20 minutes in time and 67 miles (107km) in distance to overhaul its quarry. This was far too long. A pursuit starting over mid Kent might easily end over Northern France, and this was with a contact only 20 miles distant to start with. An unladen German bomber going home in a hurry, especially the fast Junkers Ju 88, was virtually impossible to catch.

In the rare event of an interception being made, the armament of the Blenheim was demonstrably inadequate, and often the bombers, although damaged, escaped. Events in the Battle of Britain were to show that even the eight . 303in Brownings of the Spitfire and Hurricane lacked both weight of fire and penetrative ability, and were soon to be replaced by 20mm cannon.

The Blenheim was a fairly docile machine, and in this respect was suitable for night flying, while its low wing loading made it fairly manoeuvrable. The cockpit however, had one bad fault. The glazed nose was made up of a multitude of flat perspex panes, which at night tended to reflect the instrument lighting. Sighting an

33

enemy aircraft on a dark night was difficult enough, even at close range, without handicaps of this sort.

What was really needed was a purpose-designed night fighter, big enough to carry the AI equipment and its operator, with bags of power, enough performance to close quickly on a contact, and the firepower to ensure a quick kill. The solution was at hand.

Towards the end of 1938, the Bristol Aeroplane Company commenced work on a high performance long range fighter. To speed progress, it was decided to use components, specifically the wings, rear fuselage, and tail assembly, from their rather undistinguished Beaufort torpedo bomber, married to a new front end, and with the far more powerful Hercules radial engines instead of the original Taurus. Sufficient punch was given by four drum-fed 20mm Hispano cannon. This became the Beaufighter Mk IF.

A production order for 300 was placed in July 1939, just two weeks before the first flight of the prototype. Official RAF trials began in April 1940, and the type started to reach the operational squadrons in September. A little later, production aircraft mounted six . 303in Browning machine guns in the wings which, added to the four cannon, made the Beaufighter one of the most heavily armed fighters of the war.

Although still not a purpose-designed night fighter, the Beaufighter Mk IF was destined to reverse the course of the night air war. But this was not until the spring of 1941, by which time it had become available in numbers. Until then "cats-eye" fighters and the inferior AI Blenheims were forced to hold the ring.

3. About Radar

From 1940 onwards, the story of night and all-weather combat is inevitably closely tied to radar and its development. While a certain understanding of the subject is necessary in order to follow events, technical explanations within the main text slow the narrative and lead to all manner of digressions. To avoid this, there follows a simplistic overview of radar from 1940 to the present day which, while not pretending to be definitive, addresses the basic questions of what, why, how, and when.

The simplest analogy for radar is to imagine a smooth pond. Drop a pebble in the centre. The energy of the falling pebble is transmitted to the surrounding water, creating a ripple which spreads out from the point of impact. This simulates a radio emission spreading out from the transmitter. The ripple is a tiny wave, and similarly the radio emission is an electro-magnetic wave. The only real difference is that while the ripple we see on the surface of the pond is two-dimensional, the radio emission acts in three dimensions.

A single ripple is hardly enough to obtain any worthwhile results, so we now drop a series of identically sized pebbles into the pond at precise intervals. These cause a series of identically sized ripples or waves, spreading out from the centre. The spacing between the ripples is determined by two factors: the speed at which they travel through the water, which is constant, and the time lag between each pebble hitting the water. If the pebbles are dropped at exactly equal intervals, the spacing between the tops of the ripples will be constant. The distance between them is called the wavelength.

Gradually, as the energy in the water is dissipated, the ripples die down as they get farther and farther away from the point where the pebbles were dropped, until they are no longer perceptible. This distance is their effective range.

Now imagine a toy boat floating off to one side of the point of impact, but one that is too heavy to be rocked about by a small ripple. Part of the ripple reaches it and breaks against it. Some of the energy from this small part of the ripple is reflected back towards its source, even though this effect may be too small to be seen.

If, very close to where the pebbles are dropping, there is a tiny piece of straw floating, this may be moved ever so slightly by the returning fraction of the original wave. The direction of this movement will indicate that there is a solid body somewhere out there in the opposite direction. The piece of straw thus represents a very sensitive receiver. This is the basic principle of radar detection, and of sonar for detecting submarines.

As the ripple travels across the water at a constant rate, the time difference between the original ripple starting and the arrival of the reflected ripple, multiplied by the speed of the ripple, will provide a total distance measurement for the round trip. The boat is therefore just half this distance away.

To continue this aquatic analogy, what if the boat is too far away for the reflected ripple to be detectable? The answer in this case is to cause bigger ripples by dropping the pebbles from a greater height, thus increasing their energy. This will increase detection range at the cost of using greater power.

So far the boat has been broadside-on to the ripples, giving the greatest possible reflecting surface, but if it then turns bow-on, the reflecting surface is much smaller and detection range for the same power will shorten. In the same way, the amount of radar energy reflected by an aircraft varies in relation to its aspect to the transmitter.

It is relatively easy to detect where the boat is at any given moment. But what if it is moving? How does one tell which direction it is going, and how fast? The answer is to produce a series of ripples which will each reflect back from the boat in succession, giving a number of fixed points and times from which both movement and speed can be calculated. The greater number of fixed points, or contacts that can be made, the more accurate the tracking will be. Therefore the greater the number of ripples which can be produced, the better. This of course demands a faster rate of pebble dropping, and means that the distance between the tops of the ripples, the wavelength, will be reduced. The rate at which the pebbles are dropped is the frequency.

From this simple analogy we can see that detection depends to a large degree on the amount of transmitted energy – ie, pebbles dropped from a greater height, or simply larger pebbles; while tracking ability is aided by a higher frequency – ie, a faster rate of pebble dropping.

Wavelength and frequency are expressions which continually crop up when discussing radar, and the two are linked inasmuch as an increase in frequency leads to a decrease in wavelength and vice versa. Wavelengths are measured in metres, centimetres, and millimetres, and finally, microns. Frequencies are measured in cycles per second, called Hertz after an early radio pioneer. The early radars started by using Megahertz (1MHz = one million cycles per second), and eventually progressed into Gigahertz (1GHz = one thousand million cycles per second). If like me you have a job visualising such large numbers, think of them as a lot, and ever such a lot!

Two more factors need discussion before we leave our "pebbles in a pool" analogy. Assume that the pool is an irregular shape, and that one of its banks projects to a point where it is slightly nearer the receiver than is the boat. Reflected ripples from the bank will be larger than those from the boat. The larger reflected ripples will swamp the smaller ones, making them undetectable.

A partial answer to this is to make the original ripples more or less directional by putting a curved screen, something like half a bucket, around the point where the pebbles are being dropped. This confines the ripples in a small space, and their energy is only released over a limited area instead of around the full circumference of the circle. While it is true that this reduces the area being searched, it can often eliminate unwanted reflections, which in radar terms are echoes from the ground, called ground returns.

This naturally brings us to the case where the boat and the bank are in close proximity, where large reflected ripples from the bank arrive at the piece of straw slightly earlier than the smaller ones from the boat, masking them and making the boat undetectable. This has its counterpart in low flying aircraft, which are masked by ground returns. For many years there was no real answer to this problem. Its eventual solution was the exploitation of the Doppler principle, which we shall see later.

Next we have the problem of range ambiguity. For various reasons we have seen that very high frequencies have certain advantages, not the least of which is greater transmitted power. This however has one serious disadvantage, although it only became evident much later, when greater AI range was sought while frequencies were increased. If several ripples are on the water at the same time, how does one tell which ripple the echo comes from? Like the problem of low flying aircraft, this too was only solved by clever gadgetry, which will be dealt with later.

In its most basic terms, radar consists of an emitter which sends out electromagnetic waves which bounce off anything that gets in their way; a receiver which picks up those echoes which just happen to bounce back in the right direction; and a means of displaying the echoes in a manner which will allow the observer to deduce where they are, what they are doing, and sometimes what they are.

Radar has certain inherent shortcomings. These stem from the wavelengths used, which although now much shorter than they used to be, are still very long compared to the visible light spectrum which is, like radio emissions, an electro-magnetic wave. But whereas the wavelength of visible light gives absolute clarity to our eyes, radar does not. If we could see the target through the eyes of a radar, we should see a fuzzy picture, constantly growing and diminishing and changing shape.

Because of this, angular discrimination is not very good, and radar has difficulty in discriminating between closely spaced targets, which tend to merge with each other. For example, two or three aircraft flying in tight formation might appear on a radar screen as one large blip, and only when the range closes sufficiently to increase the angle between them can multiple targets be discerned. On the other hand, range discrimination is very accurate, and remains constant at any distance.

Having established a means of detection, the next step was to provide a suitable form of display, showing not only that something was out there, but how far and in what direction. The cathode ray tube (CRT) was for many years the chosen form of display. This needs little description as, in the form of the television screen, it exists in virtually every home in the developed world. What we see on our TV screens is a series of dots built up line by line in quick succession to form electronic images, which our brains interpret as being people, places and events. We do not actually see people, but it seems as though we do. For the TV viewer, there is no skill involved, but radar is a totally different matter and in its early days, with raw analogue information presented, this was even more so.

The power of radio waves decays very rapidly. The strength of an echo is inversely proportional to the target's range to the fourth power – ie, $1/R^4$, which is pretty tiny, and is conditioned still further by the size of the reflectivity of the target, known today as the radar cross-section (RCS).

The radar receiver had to be very sensitive in order to detect extremely weak returns from a target. Because in an aircraft it obviously had to be in close proximity to the transmitter, there was a very real danger of it being damaged by the extremely strong radiated power. This was overcome by using short pulses, with intervals between them long enough to allow the echo to return to the receiver. Radio waves travel at a known speed, almost exactly 186,000 miles per second (299,793km/sec); by measuring the time taken for the echo to return, range could be calculated with a high degree of accuracy. For this, a very short timescale was needed. Ranging times are generally expressed in microseconds – one microsecond being one-millionth of a second. To give some idea of the problem, a range of one statute mile (1. 6km) gives a time lapse of about 11 microseconds between pulse and echo.

The difference between the transmitted power and the echo is therefore extreme; the latter can be measured in fractions of a millionth of the original output. For example, an AI radar might put out 150kW, but receive echoes of only a couple of microwatts. The situation can be likened to throwing the Hilton Hotel at an immoveable object and having a single brick bounce back. Enormous power is needed at the transmitter in order to throw the Hilton Hotel an appreciable distance, coupled with extreme sensitivity at the receiver in order to detect the single brick. Of course, it is always possible that the brick will not bounce back hard enough to reach the receiver. There will of course be other bricks bouncing around the place, but these will be heading off in other directions rather than returning to the receiver, and are therefore of no value.

Radar echoes from distant targets are therefore miniscule, and at extreme ranges they can be too small to be detected. Two other factors enter here. The first is glint. The radar impulse bounces off the target and is scattered in all directions. At certain angles and under some conditions, more is reflected back towards the receiver than at other times. This varies the strength of the echo considerably, often many times per second.

The second factor is the amount of background noise, or clutter. Noise comes in two varieties: electrical noise in the receiver, coming from an almost infinite variety of sources, and unwanted echoes from the surface, known as the ground return. The echo needs to be strong enough to show up against the background noise; a weak echo will be lost. For this reason, detection is always a probability, never a certainty, although the probability of detection of a specific target at a particular range can be predicted with a high degree of accuracy.

Radar requires high average transmitted power for long range, and precise angular discrimination for accuracy. The British CH ground stations used HF, and at first a wavelength of about 50m, later halved to 25m, while transmitted power approached 200kW. This combination provided long range, but accuracy, especially in height-finding, suffered. For AI use, a much shorter wavelength was required, while much less power was available.

The first British AI radars worked on the much shorter wavelength of 1. 5m. This was too long for a dish antenna to be used, and as stated in the previous chapter, a dipole antenna, harpoon shaped in the case of AI Mk IV, was situated on the nose of the aircraft, with receiver aerials placed out on the wings. A reflector behind the antenna directed some of the radiated energy forward, but much was wasted in other directions; even astern. Inevitably the pulses were reflected back from the surface, with the result that the ground returns swamped echoes from anything else around that was at a greater distance from the fighter than the altitude at which it was flying.

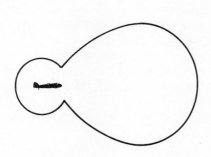
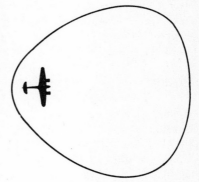

As can be seen, the coverage of AI Mk IV not only reached out ahead, with a maximum range limited by the altitude of the fighter but gave a certain amount of cov-erage astern. Unless this was recognised in time by the operator, it could lead to some very embarrassing moments.

Effective range was therefore limited by altitude, with the result that nothing could be detected at low level, and little below 5,000ft (1,524m) when flying over land. A calm sea was much less reflective, giving better results at lower altitudes.

The emission of radiation rearwards had one particularly unfortunate effect. Inexperienced operators sometimes assumed that a contact was ahead when it was actually behind them, with the result that the more the fighter accelerated, the more the range seemed to open. The answer was simple. If one turned towards the contact and the blip moved towards the centreline of the fighter, it was ahead. If however it appeared to move away from the centreline, it must be astern.

Yet another problem was ambiguity, when the radar could indicate that a contact was above and to starboard when it was actually below to port. This problem, known as squint, first became obvious during practice intercepts in daylight, when the pilot could actually see the target aeroplane, and wondered why his radar operator was trying to steer him in the opposite direction. The cause was a simple directional misalignment, and easily cured once it was known to exist. Modern radars are very carefully calibrated to eliminate this failing, but in the early years of the war it caused much grief to night fighter crewmen of both sides.

Whereas altitude determined the effective, as opposed to the theoretical, maximum range of the early AI radars, they also had a minimum range, at less than which detection was not possible. This, which has been an enduring problem with all pulsed radars, was conditioned by the duration of each pulse. As we saw earlier, the need for high transmitted power conflicts with the need for extreme sensitivity at the receiver, and the latter must be shut off during transmissions lest it be damaged. The result is that echoes from a very close contact would return while the pulse was still being transmitted, while the receiver was still closed down. The timespan involved determined the minimum range, which for early AI radars was typically several hundred feet. On a very dark night, or in heavy cloud, it was therefore possible to close to within minimum radar range without being able to make visual contact. Modern radars have very short pulse durations, with a high ratio of "listening" to "sending" time, but the problem persists.

The quest for improved radar performance has always hinged around three factors: shorter wavelengths, greater average transmitted power, and greater data processing capability. Prior to 1940, none were attainable.

The first breakthrough came early in 1940 with the development of the cavity magnetron, a device which produced high power at short wavelengths. Quite early in its development the cavity magnetron was producing 50kW on a wavelength of slightly more than 9cm. This enabled centimetric radar, as it was called, to become a reality and at the same time opening a British technological lead over Germany that was never to be eroded.

Centimetric radar had many novel features. The very short wavelength meant that a small aerial could be used. By locating this at the centre of a paraboloidal reflector dish like that of an electric bowl fire, the emissions could be focussed into a narrow beam, thereby directing a high proportion of the total radiated energy out ahead where it was needed. Then so that the narrow beam could look in directions other than straight ahead, the dish was pivoted and mechanically driven in a preset pattern which gave scanning over a cone-shaped area ahead of the fighter.

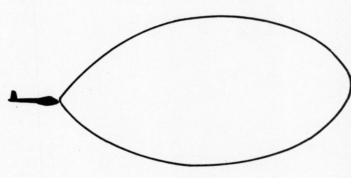

Centimetric AI scanned only ahead, in the typical pie shape of about 60 degrees to either side of the aircraft centreline. In elevation the scan was as shown, and ground clutter did not become a limiting factor until the fighter was low enough for the beam to touch the surface.

This was a tremendous advance. Not only did centimetric radar provide greater definition and angular accuracy, but by training the beam ahead, typically 45 degrees around the centreline, it ensured that ground returns would only be picked up from a relatively long way ahead. No longer would effective radar range be dependent on the altitude of the fighter. Finally the aerial and its reflector dish, from hereon called the scanner, were small enough to be enclosed in a streamlined nose cap made of dielectric (non–conductive, and therefore radar-transparent) material, reducing drag and improving aircraft performance.

Targets at a lower level than the fighter were still lost in the ground clutter, making low level interceptions no easier, but by eliminating the worst effects of clutter, reasonable detection ranges could be achieved at quite low altitudes. Of course, very low level targets, such as minelayers, were still undetectable unless the fighter could descend to a lower altitude than its opponent so that its radar was looking up against a clear sky background, but flying this low at night or in bad weather was a hazardous business.

The volume of sky scanned was also far less than the previous all-round coverage, even though effective range at normal operational altitudes was greater. A further failing was range reduction and inaccuracy at the outer limits of the conical field of view, but as the standard method of interception was to turn towards a contact, this was hardly serious.

A perennial problem with all AI radar has been sidelobes. As we have

A parabolic dish antenna provides a narrow, almost parallel, beam by emitting from a central feed onto the reflector.

seen, much of the radiation from early AIs went in directions which were not terribly useful. The scanner used by centimetric radar was far more directional, but still some radiation spilled over the edge of the dish, forming sidelobes. Although these were comparatively weak, they could be a cause of false returns, and under some circumstances ground clutter could sneak in through them. In later times they were also a source of vulnerability for jamming, permitting rogue returns into the system. Much later development work on scanners and antennas was aimed at minimising sidelobes, but they have not yet been eliminated.

The first American-developed centimetric radar was SCR-720, known as AI Mk X in British service. Whereas in the British AI Mk VIII the aerial was fixed and only the dish moved, in SCR-720 the aerial was fixed inside the reflector dish. The scanner rotated rapidly through 360 degrees in the horizontal plane, and the whole assembly was in turn gimbals-mounted underneath, which allowed it to "nod" up and down as it rotated – typically about 50 degrees up and 20 degrees down. The nod angle was adjustable in flight, and against low flying targets the down angle could be minimised to reduce the ground returns. Effective scan width was 75 degrees on either side of the centreline, the beam remaining constant throughout this arc, thereby providing the same limits of accuracy and range at the extremes as in the centre. It was thus a considerable advance on AI Mk VIII.

41

Another interesting feature was that later sets in this range could be operated with reduced scans. Once a target was detected, the scan width could be closed down initially to 20 degrees in azimuth, then to 10 degrees as the range closed for the attack phase. This concentration on one target allowed the blip to be painted far more often, making it easier to follow even in the presence of jamming.

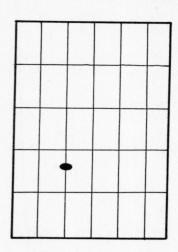

The B-Scope was introduced during World War 2 and remains in service today in the F-15, among other aircraft types. With modern radars a choice of range scales is available, but care in interpretation must still be taken, as lateral distances subtend increasing angles as the range closes.

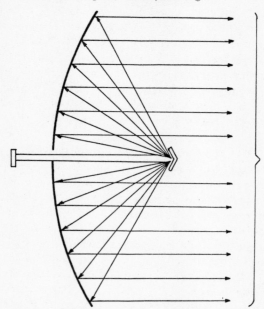

The advantage of a narrow beam is the ability to resolve closely spaced targets. If the beam width is less than the angular separation of the contacts, both targets can be detected; if not, they are likely to show on the scope as a single blip.

Another first was the introduction of what later became known as a "B" Scope. Most previous sets had used two circular scopes, one showing azimuth, the other elevation, and left the operator to interpret the raw data from the combination of the two. By contrast the B Scope was square and gave both azimuth and range, combined with a second scope showing both elevation and azimuth, although elevation was its primary function.

No military advantage is ever left unchallenged, and so it proved with radar. To counter it, a whole new science of ECM (Electronic Counter Measures) was created. Initially ECM took two main forms: noise jamming and window, or chaff as the latter is now universally called. Noise jamming produces "spokes" of light across the part of the radar screen in which the jamming aircraft is located, and also conceals other aircraft in this sector; chaff consists of metallic strips which, when dropped from the air, produce returns similar to those of a real aircraft, thus cluttering up the screen with multiple false contacts. Much later, deception jamming, the art of fooling the radar, was introduced.

The basic counter-countermeasure to noise jamming is to switch frequencies, but in the early days there were strict limitations to how often, or to what degree this could be done. Various forms of special circuitry were built in, and the ability of many AI radars to limit their scan and search a smaller sector of sky more often helped considerably, particularly in a chaff environment.

Closing down the scan area enabled the target to be painted much more often, which gave better results. The obvious next step was the "lock-on", which however did not enter service until after World War 2. In its earliest form, the scanner was controlled by the operator who pointed it directly at the target. This was done by projecting a small circle onto the display, then driving the scanner until the target was enclosed within it. The "lock-on" mode was then activated by means of a switch. This commanded the set to track the target automatically, by keeping the signal strength of the echo, which of course varied during the conical scan pattern, at a maximum.

It was the advantages of lock-on, also known as attack mode, that led to the development of deception jamming. Oddly enough lock-on mode made the radar easier to jam, as once it had been detected the full force of ECM could be brought to bear against it. If lock could be broken at a critical moment in the interception, say by range gate stealing or angular tracking deception, the operator was forced to start over again.

An interesting feature which emerged in the late 1950s was monopulse radar, which featured in the AI 23 radar of the English Electric Lightning. This consisted of splitting the beam into four overlapping lobes, which continuously sensed pointing errors about the boresight line – ie, the centreline of the aircraft. This allowed the antenna to be trained so as to reduce the pointing errors to zero. Monopulse operation not only gave extreme precision in following the movement of a target; it also proved virtually impervious to deception jamming.

For many years, making radar more capable involved making it bulkier and heavier. It needed more volume to accommodate it, more power to run it, and vastly more man hours to maintain it. With great numbers of thermionic valves, cooling also became a major problem. The situation was aggravated even more when the USA began to couple radar and fire control, to produce automatic interception systems.

The advent of the transistor changed all this. Invented in 1948, it was several years before it became available for operational hardware, but, when it did, results were remarkable. The ensuing miniaturisation allowed capability and reliability to be increased, and bulk, weight, and power requirements to be reduced. These advantages also spilled over into fire control computers, with similar results.

For many years the heart of most AI radars was still the magnetron. This had certain limitations. It was good for developing high peak power pulses, but could not generate a high average power level. Its pulse repetition frequency (PRF) limit was between 5,000 and 8,000 pulses per second, and any attempt to increase this led to a sharp drop in the peak power of individual pulses. Yet higher average transmitted power than this was obviously desirable.

For various reasons, the need to detect low flying aircraft assumed even greater importance from about 1960. A means had to be found of seeing aircraft through the ground clutter, and the obvious way of doing this was to utilise the Doppler shift. It had long been known that when the distance between two objects is changing, the frequency between them – whether sound, light, or radio waves – changes also, as is demonstrated in the well-known analogy of the variation in pitch of the noise of a train going through a station.

What was needed was to very exactly measure the Doppler shift from the ground passing under the moving aircraft, then filter out all echoes moving in conformity with it, within preset limits. Anything left over would almost certainly be a target.

The problem was one of precision. A basic weakness of the magnetron was that its pulses were slightly uneven – ie, no one pulse was exactly synchronised with its fellows. While the variations were miniscule, they were too large to allow the level of accuracy required to make use of the Doppler shift.

The solution was found in the travelling wave tube (TWT). This was not a new invention, in fact it dated from 1942, but its potential for AI radar only became possible when several other things, such as high speed digital computers, became available. Basically the TWT increases the power level of any signal fed into it. This made it possible to pulse it from a continuously running ultra-stable oscillator. This is called a continuous wave (CW) radar because the oscillator pumps out a continuous emission which, after amplification in the TWT, is switched on/off into a series of very precisely timed emissions. Each pulse was therefore exactly in phase with its fellows, giving what is known as a coherent radar, with sufficient accuracy to enable Doppler information to be extracted.

The other advantage of the TWT was that while it could not produce the high peak power of the magnetron, it could be run at a much higher PRF. By emitting far more pulses per second than the magnetron, it could therefore radiate higher average power, which as we have seen, gives much greater detection range.

Although detection range was increased, high PRF gave problems in measuring range because by the time that the first echo arrived from a distant target, several pulses had been emitted. The question then was which pulse had the echo come from? Was it pulse No 1 radiating from a distant target; pulse No 20 from a much nearer one; or anything in between? This was called range ambiguity. The solution adopted was to impress a low frequency modulation (FM) on each pulse, making each echo instantly recognisable from the others.

Ranging in this way is not as accurate as using low PRF, but it has its uses for long distance work. High PRF was also of limited use against targets with a low closure rate – eg, a target going in the same direction at a slightly higher or a slightly lower speed, or those with a head-on aspect. High PRF coupled with increased computer capacity allowed the radar to track targets while continuing to search for others. Previous to this, tracking involved keeping the antenna pointed at a single target, while using a reduced scan width, during which time the radar ignored all else.

In Track-While-Scan mode, the antenna continues to sweep through its search pattern. The range and angle of any contacts made are stored in a computer file, and their predicted positions compared with contacts on the next sweep. Files are continually updated, and new ones opened to the maximum limit of the system.

At this point AI radars combined the accurate frequency discrimination of high PRF with the accurate time discrimination and therefore ranging accuracy, of low PRF. The next requirement was for a waveform that combined both features. The adoption of medium PRF, between 6 and 16kHz, might look obvious, but it was only made possible by the digital signal processor, which greatly increased the number of filtering functions that could be carried out. This permitted a greater range of waveforms to be used. The higher the PRF the greater the detection range, while the lower the PRF the more accurate the velocity data obtained. A succession of medium PRF bands is used to provide high quality tracking data, while high PRF with FM can be interleaved with medium PRF for long range detection.

Perhaps the final advance that can be discussed without getting too technical is the programmable signal processor (PSP). Whereas previous processors were hard wired, the PSP works from software, giving it far greater flexibility. The PSP also allows a greater number of radar modes to be used. This takes complexity to the stage where the limiting factor becomes the speed at which the data can be processed. In this field, as in others, significant progress has been made with the recent introduction of the Very High Speed Integrated Circuit (VHSIC) – a microchip which speeds up the computing process and allows more information to be processed in a given time. Among other things, this allows high PRF to be used against nose or tail-aspect targets without interleaving with medium PRF, although it takes no less than 20,000 Doppler filters to do so. Another advantage is that under some circumstances, sufficient information can be extracted from the echo to give target identification.

A byproduct of greatly increased computer capability was synthetic cockpit displays. Whereas AI radars up to and including AI 23 showed raw analogue data, digital computers allowed this to be processed to the stage where it could be shown in a far more easily assimilable manner. Alpha-numeric formats could now be adopted, using symbols to show flight paths, velocities, and identities, together with relevant flight information for the fighter. Still later, these could be projected onto a head-up display. No longer did the pilot have to peer down at his instruments in the middle of a combat, it was all there in front of him.

Another advantage of synthetic displays was that even as ground clutter was filtered out, so too was jamming. The pilot now operated with a nice clean screen, unaware of any jamming coming his way. There was, and still is, just one problem. It is possible to produce jamming which conceals the target in such a way that the radar filters out both, the classic case of throwing the baby out with the bath water. This can produce a dangerous situation, as not only is no contact visible on the scope, but neither is there any indication of jamming which would make the pilot aware of something nasty lurking behind the woodshed.

Scanners, or antennas as they became known, had also seen considerable advances. The parabolic dish remained in widespread use well into the 1960s, and was hydraulically driven. The next step was a variation on a theme – the inverse-Cassegrain antenna. This was again a parabolic type, but with a sub-reflector placed in front of it. Sub-reflectors are of two shapes: hyperboloid, which presents a convex front to the emissions, and paraboloid, which is concave.

The emissions are directed at the sub-reflector which turns them back into the main dish which then reflects them forwards. Incoming returns get the reverse treatment. The main advantages of the inverse-Cassegrain type are that sidelobes are minimised, and that performance over a wide range of frequencies remains consistent.

The most common antenna in modern fighter use is currently the planar array. As its name implies, it is a flat plate and, without going into technicalities, it is so constructed that it emits through slotted apertures across its entire face. Its advantages are greater gain than a dish reflector, gain being the ratio of output to input. Almost all the radiated energy is in the main beam, with very small sidelobes. Disadvantages, apart from the specifically technical, are a relatively narrow bandwidth, which limits flexibility especially in multi-mode radars, and high cost. Often planar array antennas, or slotted waveguide antennas as they are sometimes called, are electrically driven, thus eliminating a great deal of weight and complexity.

Finally there is the phased array antenna. This is a fixed active array antenna, which means that the beam is pointed electronically and does not have to rely on mechanical movement of the scanner to find the direction of the target. This is called electronic scanning, which has many advantages over conventional antennas. The use of Gallium Arsenide Monolithic Microwave Integrated Circuits allows much smaller transmit/receive modules than was previously possible, with the result that more of them can be fitted into a given area. Each module can be individually controlled, with transmission and reception split 50/50, therefore multiple frequencies can be used simultaneously, with low power outputs and long wavelengths used in conjunction with adaptive digital beam forming techniques.

This gives little time transmitting, and a lot of time listening, giving a low probability of intercept, thus reducing the chance of being jammed. Active array radar has comparatively little thermal noise, which increases detection sensitivity and reliability. The scan can be stopped in a matter of microseconds, allowing the beam to check back on whether a contact is real or false. Finally, resolution is fine enough to use target motion to give non-cooperative target recognition, using inverse synthetic aperture techniques. Synthetic aperture is a technique whereby a picture of a target can be built up by using successive scans in very quick succession. It has been around a long time, but so far has only been used to identify ground targets.

A lot more could be said about radar but most of it would be beyond the scope of this chapter, which has necessarily been confined to basics.

4. The Catseye Fighters

Late in 1940, when Luftwaffe night attacks on British cities were at their height, a suggestion was submitted to RAF Fighter Command by a concerned citizen. Its message was simple: "Take cat in night fighter. Aim guns where cat is looking." This was not quite as half-witted as it sounds because at that time anything which would assist a night fighter pilot to penetrate the darkness was to be welcomed.

Radar was of course top secret at that time, and AI radar even more so. One thing was obvious, even to the man in the street. The success of the British fighter defences in the Battle of Britain the previous summer was not being repeated at night, and German bombers seemed to be reaching their targets virtually unhindered.

What was not so obvious was that the German fighter defences were having exactly the same difficulties, although as RAF Bomber Command lacked the radio target finding aids available to the Luftwaffe, raids on Third Reich targets were not as intense, nor as concentrated. For that reason, there was rather less urgency in building up a German night fighter arm.

It has been stated that the Luftwaffe had made no plans to counter the night bomber prior to the war, but this was not true. The rationale was as follows. The distances involved in raiding German targets were such that fighter escort, apart from that provided by the relatively low performance Blenheim Mk IF, was not possible. In daylight, the numerous high performance German fighters would be able to inflict unacceptable losses on British bomber formations. This being the case, it was extremely probable that if the RAF bombers came at all, they would come at night – a view reinforced by the number of squadrons that were nominally, at any rate, committed to night operations.

With this in mind the Technical Development Flying Unit at Griefswald, the Lehr Division, formed a Staffel to evaluate night defence in conjunction with searchlights. Then in 1939 the first night fighting Staffel, 10/JG 26, was formed under the command of Oberleutnant Johannes Steinhoff, later to become Chief-of-Staff of the postwar new Luftwaffe. This unit, with pilots drawn from several Jagdgeschwader, was equipped with Messerschmitt Bf 109Ds.

The Bf 109 had been designed as a fast and agile day fighter. As a night fighter it was almost totally unsuitable. It was not the most docile of aircraft and its frail, narrow track undercarriage was far from ideal for the heavy landings which so often attend night operations. Visibility from the tiny cockpit was poor, obstructed by heavy metal framing; the blind flying panel was inadequate, and night navigation aids non-existent. In effect this meant that it could only be operated on clear moonlit nights, although as these conditions were needed by the bombers to find their targets, this was thought not to matter too much.

Initial trials were not particularly promising. Often the Bf 109 pilot was blinded by his own searchlights, while flying accidents were common. Nevertheless the concept looked hopeful. At this time it was all the Luftwaffe had, and in February 1940 the first night fighting Gruppe was formed at Jever. This was IV/JG 2, commanded by Major Blumensaat, and was also equipped with the Bf 109. This unit scored one solitary victory on 9 July 1940, when Feldwebel Foerster blundered across a Whitley bomber. This success was far outweighed by operational losses, and IV/JG 2 was disbanded in favour of twin-engined aircraft units.

Meanwhile, on the other side of the North Sea, while the development of AI radar plus a suitable GCI set was being rushed forward at a tremendous pace, at squadron level things were not so good. The unreliability of the electronic components of the day, coupled with the difficulty of interpreting what was visible on the scope, and conveying intelligible steering instructions to an often unbelieving pilot, made progress slow. During the whole of 1940, only a handful of successful AI interceptions took place, and with the slow and inadequate Blenheim as the main AI carrier, these were often as much due to luck as to skill. The "catseye" fighters were thus left to hold the ring.

As had been the case in the previous conflict, operational accidents accounted for far more losses than enemy action. Night flying was still a hazardous activity, especially over a country with weather as unpredictable as that of England.

Accidents fell into five basic categories: taking off, loss of control, flying into high ground, mechanical failure, and landing. Of these, accidents on take-off were the most mysterious. Often they occurred in bad weather, when shortly after leaving the ground the nose dipped and the aircraft went in. While loss of power occasionally accounted for this, more often there was no apparent reason other than the blanket description of "pilot error". It took a long while to discover the root cause, which was a form of disorientation caused by acceleration.

As described by Roderick Chisholm in *Cover of Darkness*, the pilot could be likened to a man standing in a tube train. As the train leaves the station, the lights fail, while the man instinctively leans forward to counter the acceleration. Deprived of visual cues, his impression was that the train was going uphill, and that he was standing upright. In fact, the train was usually going downhill.

Taking off in a fighter at night, visual cues were quickly lost when the flarepath was left behind, while the acceleration all too easily gave the impression of climbing. In fact the pilot might not have been climbing, and would thus be deceived into flying straight into the nearest hill. Alternatively he might easily have felt that he was climbing too steeply, and pushed the stick forward to correct. At low altitude this gave little time to discover the error and correct it. There was only one answer, which was to ignore the view out of the window, and go straight onto instruments as soon as the wheels left the ground. Once the importance of this was realised, the number of take-off accidents was considerably reduced.

Loss of control was generally caused by disorientation, the basics of which were described in Chapter 1. Only on the clearest nights was the pilot able to see a horizon, which meant a lot of instrument flying, especially for the inexperienced. This was at the expense of keeping a lookout. Not that there was too much chance of seeing anything unless it was held by searchlights, but having to concentrate on instruments reduced the minimal to the miniscule.

"Bee" Beamont, later to become chief test pilot for English Electric, described a night sortie over Bristol in a Hurricane in which he had continually been "crossing his controls" and finding himself at all sorts of angles. Icing was an ever-present hazard, robbing the wings of lift and sending the aeroplane tumbling from the sky. Sometimes control could be recovered at lower altitudes; often it could not.

Flying into high ground accounted for many night fighter losses. It was all too easy to lose track of one's exact whereabouts at night. In fact, in poor visibility some single-seater pilots even managed to lose themselves in broad daylight. Often a sortie involved climbing through heavy cloud, to emerge into bright moonlight on top. Then when the patrol was over, the return to terra firma had to be made in the reverse direction. The pilot had to hope for two things: first, that changes in barometric pressure were not causing his altimeter to misread by a significant amount; secondly, that there was no high ground below. Of course, the letdown could always be made over the sea provided that the pilot knew for certain that he was over it.

Mechanical failure was an ever-present risk. Engine trouble was the most common cause. This was potentially lethal in a single-seater, as the chances of making a deadstick landing at night in open country were virtually nil.

Two engines gave an increased margin of safety, especially over the sea, but this was eroded in the landing phase by the problems of asymmetric handling, with one motor at full throttle and the other dead. This made turning into the dead engine while lining up on the runway a very sensitive business, while turning into the good engine was often all but impossible. Nor in the event of not lining up correctly was there much chance of going round again on one. It had to be right first time. All too often the crew were forced to abandon their aircraft and take to their parachutes.

Night landings were far from easy, and this was a common cause of accidents. Quite apart from the difficulty of judging the approach into an ill-lit airfield, a descent from high altitude would all too often cause frost to form on both sides of the windshield, completely obscuring forward visibility. Icing was often completely unpredictable, as Pilot Officer R. C. "Dickie" Haine of No 600 Squadron found out on one occasion during the winter of 1939-40.

"It was a very cold night, but funnily enough the aircraft (a Blenheim) was completely free of ice on the ground. Once we got airborne, everything iced up. The only clear vision panels we had were the side windows, but these were frozen up; I couldn't get them open. I called the ground, but they were very reluctant to put any lights on. The only thing I could see on the airfield (RAF Northolt) and that only vaguely, was the red flashing beacon. It was a most terrifying experience, but I finally got down all right, even though I went through the perimeter fence and ended on the main road."

Not all pilots were as lucky. The usual method of navigation was by dead reckoning, which became very inaccurate on a patrol in which the fighter was continually being instructed to alter course and change altitude. Radio homing was used, but it was primitive, giving direction but not distance. As Dickie Haine commented, the only way you could tell when you were getting close to home was when it got a bit louder.

Bringing the fighter back into the vicinity of its airfield was one thing but then the pilot's troubles were just beginning. Low cloud was the main enemy. Breaking cloud too late would force the fighter to go around again, frequently losing sight of the airfield lighting while doing so. At low level, the pattern of the airfield lights could often not be distinguished properly.

Even when the lighting pattern could be made out, the aircraft was often badly placed to make a landing. Few pilots were able to make hard turns at low level at night in order to line up correctly, and each failed attempt at landing eroded their confidence still more. A primaeval instinct to return to earth as quickly as possible sometimes bordered on panic, with the temptation to bang the aircraft down anyhow, over-riding reason. As the saying goes: Flak might rate five per cent, fighters might rate 15 per cent, but the ground always rates 100 per cent. It was the aerial equivalent of Russian roulette; all you could do was pull the trigger and hope for the best.

Only gradually was radio beam equipment installed to enable pilots to make blind approaches, letting down through the clag to emerge properly positioned off the end of the runway. Confidence that one was going to be able to land without problems after a long and exhausting sortie eased wear and tear on the nervous system, and made a valuable contribution to morale.

It should not of course be thought that all these problems were the prerogative of the RAF. The Luftwaffe also experienced them in full measure, with the possible exception of landing accidents, primarily because they had a radio beam landing approach system in service from an early stage. Be that as it may, the accident rate in the night fighter arms of both forces was appalling, and would not have been sustainable in peacetime. Only the exigencies of war made it more or less acceptable.

So far we have dealt with the means of getting the night fighters up, keeping them there, and recovering them safely. The next stage was enabling them to do something worthwhile. The first and most important thing was finding the enemy. Patrol lines 20 to 30 miles (32–48km) long were set up on likely avenues of approach, marked every few miles by groups of flares, each with its own distinctive pattern. Dickie Haine flew what was probably the first night patrol of the war, starting at 02. 00 on the morning of 4 September 1939. It was a strange experience as the blackout had come into force the day before. Not unexpectedly he and his crew saw nothing during a two-and-a-half-hour sortie.

A fighter would fly up and down its assigned patrol line, provided of course that it could see the markers, until directed to go chasing after a raider. The far from clear HF radio was still in general use, which was another handicap to overcome. Not until well into 1940 did the much better VHF radio come into widespread use. But despite the undoubted enthusiasm of the crews, sightings were few and far between, and interceptions almost nil. The early years of the war were marked by a feeling of total frustration for the night fighter crews.

The three variables in night interception were relative speed, distance, and time, and synchronising these in order to arrive in the right place was far from easy. To provide basic training, a sports stadium was used for simulation. Tricycles represented both bomber and fighter aircraft. The "fighters" were equipped with screens in front, so that the pilot could not see where he was going, while the rate of pedalling was strictly controlled to conform with scaled-down aircraft speeds. Observers high in the stands tracked the "aircraft" and passed positional information to the controller, who could not see what was going on. This worthy then radioed instructions to "crewmen" who were perched precariously on the back of the trikes, who in turn directed their pilots which way to steer and how fast to pedal. The benefit of this strange arrangement was that it enabled all concerned to fully appreciate the problems from both controllers' and pilots' viewpoints, at the same time refining the tactics of night interception. Nowadays they would have a very expensive simulator; in 1940 they had tricycles.

Co-operation with searchlights seemed to offer a far better solution. At first this was fairly haphazard, but later in the war a system of rectangular boxes was worked out. These used coloured searchlights, with a fighter assigned to a specific box. The colours didn't show up very well, and luminosity was reduced by the coloured filters. The idea was that the searchlights would then indicate the direction of incoming traffic. Once a bomber was illuminated, it would be coned by several searchlights. The night fighter would then call off the AA guns, a procedure unofficially called "crossing the Rubicon", then set off in hot pursuit until it eventually closed to firing range.

Theory was not borne out in practice. First, the early 90cm searchlights were not very effective above about 12,000ft (3,650m). If the bombers were much higher than this, they became practically undetectable. Secondly, cloud could all too easily get in the way. Thirdly, mist or haze diffused the beams so that no clear intersection was visible. Fourthly, the bombers tried to manoeuvre out of the beams, and often succeeded. Finally, only the underside of the bomber was illuminated. This may seem terribly obvious, but in practice it meant that the fighter could generally only see the illuminated bomber if it was looking up at it, unless the two were very close together. At any distance, a fighter with an altitude advantage was unable to see a bomber even though it was coned by searchlights. Sometimes a bomber would be seen from afar and the night fighter would set off in hot pursuit, only for the bomber to evade the beams and become lost in the darkness before it could arrive. These circumstances cruelly exposed the shortcomings of the Blenheim, which was demonstrably too slow for the task. Having to catch a bomber sighted several miles away was bad enough, but having in many cases to start from an inferior altitude due to the illumination problem aggravated the situation still more. A climbing Blenheim had little or no speed advantage even over a cruising bomber. As Dickie Haine recalled:

"I saw several aircraft shot down in the distance, but I was never in the right place to do the shooting. More than half of all the sightings I made were called off because there was no way that I was going to catch up with them."

After a brief and disastrous career as a day fighter, the Boulton Paul Defiant was switched to night operations in the late summer of 1940. The Defiant had many of the shortcomings of the standard day fighter, in that forward view from the cockpit was poor, and it lacked endurance and navigation aids, while sharing the Blenheim's fault of being undergunned. The sole armament of the Defiant was four . 303in Browning machine guns in a power operated turret. The absence of fixed forward firing guns had been its undoing in daylight, but at night this was no great problem. The pilot, free to concentrate on flying the aircraft, could formate with the bomber, holding a position which allowed his gunner a clear shot from an unexpected angle. A favourite attacking position was below and to one side, where the fighter was less likely to be seen by the bomber crew.

The Defiant was significantly faster than the Blenheim, and had a better rate of climb, therefore it was able to close to guns range more quickly. But once there, the gunner was faced with the problems of deflection, target precession, bullet trail, and being blinded by muzzle flash every time he opened fire.

The single-seat Hurricane and Spitfire lacked nothing in performance and firepower, but until October 1940 these were too heavily committed to the day battle to be much used at night, although often single aircraft were flown by experienced pilots. Of the two the Hurricane, with its sturdy wide track undercarriage and its better forward view, was most suited to night operations.

As the Battle of Britain drew to a close, several Hurricane squadrons were switched to the night role. The sole modification to these aircraft was the addition of a small metal sheet on each side of the nose to shield the exhaust flames from the pilot's vision. Of course these were no more effective than any other catseye fighter but, from a defensive point of view, the more fighters that were put up the better the chance of one or two stumbling across something in the dark.

It was at this point that another bright idea emerged. While the CH radar stations were too inaccurate to allow controlled interceptions, they did give a pretty good idea of the course, height and speed of incoming raiders. Could this not be used to lay a trap for them? The analogy was simple. A poacher does not run around a field at night trying to catch rabbits with his bare hands. He sets a few snares and sits back to await results. The snare in this case materialised as the Long Aerial Mine, or LAM. It consisted of a main parachute linked to a smaller stabilising 'chute below which was a bomb. Next came 2,000ft (610m) of piano wire, with a larger towing 'chute on the end. A line of LAMs dropped closely spaced ahead of the predicted course of the bombers would produce the equivalent of an aerial minefield.

When a bomber collided with the piano wire, the impact would sever a weak link with the support 'chute, while deploying the other two 'chutes, the lower of which, being the larger of the two, would pull the bomb down onto the bomber where it would detonate.

The idea was to drop a LAM barrier at 20,000ft (6,100m), the maximum operating altitude of the German bombers. Its rate of descent was about 1,000ft/min (5m/sec), which gave it an effective duration of nearly 10 minutes, allowing it to be dropped up to 30 miles (48km) ahead of the bombers. If the duration seems short, consider that the explosion of an AA shell lasts a mere one-fiftieth of a second.

One of the more interesting things about LAM was that it was small and light in weight, while the performance of the carrier aircraft was fairly irrelevant.

The obsolete Handley Page Harrow bomber could just about be coaxed up to the required height with 140 LAMs on board which, spaced at 200ft (61m) intervals, produced a screen more than five miles (8km) long.

The sowing of aerial minefields, codenamed Operation "Mutton" (guess why) began in December 1940. The sedate Harrows, seldom more than one at a time, were put up on patrol lines off the coast, after an unfortunate incident involving the death of a civil defence worker. Ground controllers then directed them where and when to release their LAMs, but difficulty was experienced in getting the lumbering Harrows to the right place at the right time. Although one or two successes were adjudged to have been scored, when a blip indicating a German bomber faded from the ground radar screen at the approximate position of a LAM barrier, it was soon recognised that they were not worth the effort.

By the beginning of 1941, the British night defences were beginning to get more organised, although they were not as yet terribly effective. Twin-engined night fighters prowled off the coast and Harrows laid their snares; while inland, AI equipped fighters stalked the bombers. As the GCI system grew, the catseye fighters tended to clutter up the radar scopes, and with ever greater numbers of friendly aircraft in the sky, own goals were increasing.

It was therefore decided to concentrate single-engined fighters over the target areas once these had become known. Between 12 and 20 single-engined fighters were put up per area, each being allocated a different height from which it was forbidden to stray. Altitude separation was typically 500ft (152m), although it could be more. With this system in operation, the AA guns were restricted to an agreed maximum altitude and the fighters operated above this. Results were not impressive. Sightings were rare mainly because the German bombers attacked from a lower level than the fighters, risking the none too impressive AA fire.

However, a handful of catseye pilots were better than the others. The most notable at this period was Flight Lieutenant R. P. Stevens of No 151 Squadron which operated Hurricanes, who over the next few months accounted for no less than 14 German bombers. His decidedly sporty speciality was to fly to where the AA and searchlights were thickest, there to search visually. Keen eyesight and accurate shooting did the rest. Stevens survived the friendly AA fire, only to be lost on an intruder mission over occupied Europe on 15 December 1941.

Pending the arrival of new GCI sets with 360 degree coverage, an experimental ground control system had been set up in 1940. This consisted of 10 gun laying radars spaced around the Kenley sector. With a slant range of about 40,000ft (12,191m), they had a useful radius of about five miles (8km). This was not really long enough; the maximum time that each radar could track a bomber was less than two minutes, but hopefully one radar could hand over to the next. Contacts were then relayed direct to the sector operations room where they were plotted, and fighters vectored against them. This system had a few successes, but its main failing was that the position of the fighter could only be determined by radio direction-finding, which involved a time lag, and therefore lacked sufficient precision.

One of the sillier schemes for employing catseye fighters was the Turbinlite Havoc. This was a revival of the World War 1 idea that night fighters should carry searchlights. The Turbinlite Havoc was equipped with AI radar, and carried a powerful searchlight in the nose. So far, so good. The effective range of the searchlight was far beyond that of normal visual detection and shooting distance, especially on a moonless night. This had three major operational effects. First, the interception could be carried out to much coarser limits from a ground control viewpoint. Secondly, the Havoc could close on the contact without fear of overshooting or collision. Finally it would reduce the possibility of faulty identification.

As the searchlight was to be switched on at ranges too long for effective shooting, the Turbinlite Havoc was accompanied by a Hurricane. Directly the target was illuminated, the single-seater would accelerate to close range and shoot it down.

What happened in practice was entirely predictable. On being suddenly lit up, the startled German bomber pilot would haul his aircraft violently around and out of the beam and once more would be lost in the darkness. Meanwhile the Hurricane pilot, his night vision impaired, was busy playing "dodge the Havoc", which was by now manoeuvring wildly in a vain attempt to keep the searchlight trained on the target.

It was fairly obvious that no-one had consulted Flight Lieutenant Guy Gibson, who in November 1940 had transferred to No 29 Squadron as a "rest" from bomber operations. No 29 was at that time re-equipping with Beaufighters, but a few Blenheims were still on strength. Towards the end of the year, Gibson crept up behind a bogey but was unable to identify it. Thinking it was a Blenheim from his own squadron, he crept in close and switched his landing light on, to get a brief glimpse of a large black cross before the German pilot wrenched into a screaming dive and vanished, never to be seen again. This was an indicator for the future of the Turbinlite scheme.

Twenty-five years earlier the Turbinlite Havoc would have been a wonderful answer to the Zeppelin, but it was never going to amount to much against an opponent with even a moderate amount of agility and performance. In service from late summer 1941 to early 1943 it achieved little, the only confirmed kill coming on 1 May 1942 when the accompanying Hurricane pilot sighted a Heinkel He 111 before the light was switched on. Requesting that it remained off, he closed to attack and shot the He 111 into the sea off Flamborough Head. In all, the Turbinlite Havoc was not a success.

So far it might appear that German night bombing was very much a one way street, but this was far from the case. Following the invasion of France on 10 May 1940, RAF bombers started to attack cities in Germany. The new radar-laid Flak batteries for defence against the night raider quickly proved to be less effective than expected. Nor were the handful of night flying Bf 109s able to achieve anything. Something better was needed, and quickly.

Luftwaffe requirements paralleled those of the RAF. They needed fighters suitable for night operations, flown by trained crews; they needed early warning detection with a comprehensive reporting, tracking and control system. Most of all they needed a night fighter able to find the bomber in the dark.

In many ways the German radar systems of the period were advanced, but they were not entirely suitable for the task which they were now called upon to perform, while the reporting system had to be developed from scratch. Most of all, the Luftwaffe needed a method.

Unlike the RAF, who had spent the years immediately prior to the war in developing defensive systems, Germany had to proceed with the utmost haste using what was to hand, however unsuitable. The result was inevitably a series of expedients, a situation that was to continue throughout the entire war as the Germans tried, but never quite managed, to catch up.

Like the RAF, the Luftwaffe had no purpose-designed night fighter in its inventory, and had to make shift with what was available. For home defence its choice fell on the Messerschmitt Bf 110, a twin engined two-seater. The Bf 110 was well suited to the task. Originally produced as a long range escort fighter, it was fast, with a significant speed advantage over the bombers which it was to oppose; it had adequate endurance, it was heavily armed with two 20mm cannon and four 7. 9mm machine guns in the nose, was docile to handle, and had a radio operator/gunner to assist with navigation.

The German night fighter force needed to expand rapidly, and a night fighter division was formed on 17 July 1940, under the command of Oberst Josef Kammhuber, who postwar was to rise to command the new Luftwaffe. Like their British counterparts, the German night fighter pilots scored only a few lucky victories in the early months. At first without even a rudimentary system of ground control, they did however have certain advantages. British bombers – Whitleys, Hampdens and Wellingtons, had rather lower cruising speeds than their German counterparts, while the distances to many of their targets were greater. This meant that they were at risk over enemy territory for considerably longer.

Initially the Luftwaffe relied heavily on searchlights to illuminate the raiders, but as most of these were grouped around cities, interceptions could only be made over the target area. This was undesirable for three reasons: first, the bombs were already going down; secondly, the fighters were often lit up by their own searchlights and shot at by "friendly" guns; and thirdly, it showed the bombers where the targets were. To eliminate this, Kammhuber moved his searchlights and sound locators into a continuous belt, stretching from Liege in Belgium to Schleswig-Holstein on the Danish border, leaving the Flak in place to protect the cities. This belt was patrolled by night fighters, each with its own sector. To ease the problem of identification, it was made a prohibited area to all other German aircraft.

While this was a step in the right direction, the system contained all the flaws of searchlight co-operation discovered by the British, including vulnerability to weather. In addition, the bombers tended to pour on the coals in the illuminated zone, crossing it as fast as possible and reducing the time available to the fighter to intercept.

The searchlight belt quickly proved to be only marginally effective, and it was soon obvious that something far better was needed. This was to be a radar detection and ground reporting system, coupled still later with AI radar. There was however an alternative course of action, which had been implemented earlier that summer.

There was one place where bombers would be far easier to find. This was over their own bases. They needed flarepaths to take off and land by, and would often have their navigation lights lit to reduce the risk of midair collision with their own kind. They would be at low speeds and low altitudes; on take-off they would be heavy with bombs and fuel; on landing the crews would be tired and less vigilant.

It was not enough merely to attack RAF bomber bases. What was needed was the ability to reach them, then loiter in their vicinity for extended periods, waiting for outgoing or incoming bombers. The Bf 110 lacked the necessary endurance, while the German bombers of the day lacked the firepower to be used as fighters. The answer was a compromise.

Kampfgeschwader 30 was a bomber outfit equipped with the Junkers Ju 88A, based in Norway. Unusually it contained a single Zerstorer Staffel, which flew the Ju 88C-2. The C-2 differed from the A model in having a solid nose which contained a single 20mm MG FF cannon and three 7. 9mm MG17 machine guns, and had been used in the anti-shipping role. Combining fighter firepower with bomber endurance and range, and able to carry a reasonable bomb load, it was therefore well suited to the intruder role.

Redesignated 4/NJG 1 in July 1940, this unit was transferred to Germany where it was joined by 5/NJG 1. This was a newly formed Staffel which was equipped with the Dornier Do 17Z-10 Kauz (Screech Owl) II. Together with 6/NJG 1, the Ju 88C-2s, which arrived a month later, they formed II/NJG 1, which was in turn redesignated I/NJG 2 in September 1940.

Like the Ju 88C-2, the Do 17Z-10 had a solid nose containing two 20mm MG FF cannon and four 7. 9mm machine guns. Interestingly it also carried Spanner Anlage, literally "Trouser Press" device. This was an infra-red detection system first flown in June 1940. In essence it was an infra-red searchlight which illuminated a target in front, which could be seen through the "Q-Rohr" screen in the reflector gunsight. But as its effective range was a mere 650ft (200m), it was of little practical value. Later still, experiments were made with passive IR detection, with little success. Passive IR gave no indication of distance, and it was too easily distracted by alternative heat sources (20 years later the emissions of a reciprocating engine were still regarded as a poor IR target). Only nine Kauz IIs were delivered.

German intruder operations began during August 1940. At first they were tentative, the crews were feeling their way. It was not long before they fell foul of the British defenders. In the small hours of 18 August, a Ju 88C-2 of 4/NJG 1 piloted by Oberfeldwebel Fritz Zenkel was sighted by a Blenheim Mk IF of No 29 Squadron about 15 miles (24km) southwest of Chester. A bright moon that night made visibility exceptional, and Pilot Officer Richard Rhodes firewalled his throttles in an attempt to catch up with what he thought was a He 111. This was just one of the many occasions when the limitations of the Blenheim were exposed. The raider flew south, then east, then north again, the Blenheim failing to close to firing range in a chase lasting 35 minutes. Meanwhile other Blenheims, directed from the ground, were trying to cut off the German, to no avail.

Finally the intruder crossed the coast near Spurn Head, and Rhodes, in desperation, opened fire from 1,200ft (366m), emptying his magazines in one long burst. Hit, the Ju 88 slowed down and vanished into thin cloud. By the time it emerged on the far side, the Blenheim had overshot, but Sergeant "Sticks" Gregory, later to become one of the top AI operators, swivelled his turret around and let fly with his single Vickers gun. With flames showing in the cockpit and on the starboard wing, the Ju 88 spiralled down into the North Sea.

It was not always thus. As the intruders gained experience they gradually built up a score. It was sometimes not even necessary to attack an aircraft directly. On 11 February 1941, a Hampden of No 144 Squadron was refused permission to land due to the presence of intruders, and was abandoned by its crew when the fuel ran out. Two months later, on 9 April, a Ju 88 intruder came close to scoring a famous victory when he caught the No 29 Squadron Beaufighter of Squadron Leader Guy Gibson in the landing pattern at Wellingore, wounding his operator and causing Gibson to swerve off the runway and hit some trees.

In all, results were not impressive. Just two RAF aircraft were lost to intruder action during 1940, and 52 up to October of the following year, when intruder operations were suspended, with an approximately equal number of aircraft damaged. Nor were the victims all bombers; they included a Tiger Moth and several Oxfords of Training Command.

On the other side of the balance sheet, six intruders failed to return during 1940, and a further 21 in 1941, two of which were believed to be "own goals". In addition there was the usual crop of operational accidents, and badly damaged aircraft which returned to occupied territory, if not to base, amounting to over 50 aircraft. Two of the handful of Do 17Z-10s were lost and others damaged, and the type was replaced by Ju 88Cs in the spring of 1941.

The Luftwaffe was not the first to initiate intruder sorties. As early as June 1940, Blenheims of Nos 600 and 604 Squadrons were trying their luck over northern France. Pilot Officer Alastair Hunter in a Blenheim of the latter squadron scored the first intruder victory of the war on the night of 18 June when he encountered a Heinkel He 115 floatplane at low level between Cap Gris Nez and Calais. On his return, excited squadron members wanted to know how he had found it in the dark. The answer was disappointing. The German, a rare genuine mug, had been flying with his navigation lights on.

The night blitz commenced late in 1940. London, the main target, was easy to reach from the Luftwaffe airfields in France and the Low Countries, and the German bombers were often able to make two sorties a night. In an attempt to curtail their activities, British intruder operations commenced in earnest.

No 87 Squadron and its Hurricanes flew many of the early trips. Using a forward airfield at Warmwell in Dorset, they set out in pairs, one aircraft to strafe aircraft on the ground while the other suppressed the defences. In practice, each did a bit of both. But good weather and a bright moon were needed to achieve results, and in a Western European winter, this combination was rare.

Just occasionally German aircraft were caught in the landing pattern and shot down. As is invariably the case in air combat, a few pilots were outstanding. The most successful Hurricane intruder pilot was Flight Lieutenant Karel Kuttelwascher of No 1 Squadron, who in three months from 1 April 1941, claimed 15 destroyed, including three He 111s over St Andre on the night of 4–5 May, and a further five damaged.

Blenheim and Havoc squadrons also flew intruder sorties, for which they carried bombs, but neither of these were equipped with AI radar, it being thought pointless to risk its discovery at this early stage. Then in late May 1941 the Luftwaffe moved east, ready for the invasion of the Soviet Union, and aircraft targets became less plentiful. Intruders had always been briefed to attack targets of opportunity, such as trains or barracks, and this now became their main activity.

By the spring of 1941, radar – both ground and airborne – was proving invaluable. Catseye fighters would roam the night skies for a while yet, but their day was fast drawing to a close.

5. Electronic Eyes

For the first nine months of the war, AI radar offered little but hope. The sets were unreliable; and even when they worked properly, squint remained a problem, particularly in the vertical plane. Sometimes the set just gave up, emitting what became known as "The Terrible Smell" before starting to burn, giving off clouds of acrid smoke which made the pilot unhappy until he knew the cause. Sometimes it pretended to work, showing spurious returns. More often it simply sulked and gave no useful results.

As if this wasn't bad enough, RAF Fighter Command contrived to shoot itself in the foot. The first radar operators were recruited from direct entry airmen, often with no technical knowledge and even less aptitude. Dickie Haine recalled:

"Apart from the set itself, we were badly handicapped by the operators in the early days. We had to put them in the Link Trainer just to get them used to the intercom. I remember telling the first one, 'This is a microphone, it's just like a telephone'. He said, 'Oh I've seen one of them, but I've never had occasion to use one!.'"

Common sense gradually prevailed, the more goonish were weeded out, a selection procedure with aptitude tests was introduced, and not before time the airman operators were promoted to Sergeant. Many of the AI-equipped Blenheims had their gun turrets removed, while the new Beaufighters entering service from September 1940 were turretless. In most night fighter squadrons, air gunners became redundant. While some transferred to Bomber Command, many trained as operators, two of the most outstanding being Jimmy Rawnsley and "Sticks" Gregory.

The first AI success was a long time coming. The Fighter Interception Unit (FIU) was set up in May 1940 to prove and iron the bugs out of new equipment while developing suitable tactics. Initially based at Tangmere on the south coast, the idea was that it would not only carry out theoretical exercises but fly operationally.

On the night of 23 July, the CH radar station at Poling detected a small group of German bombers leaving the Sussex coast at 6,000ft (1,830m). Patrolling at 10,000ft (3,050m) over base was a Blenheim Mk IVf of FIU, piloted by Flying Officer Jumbo Ashfield, with Sergeant Leyland as his radar operator and Pilot Officer Morris as observer. Following directions from the ground, Ashfield headed out over the sea to cut them off, trading height for speed as he went. About two minutes later, Leyland, crouching over his AI Mk III in the gloom of the fuselage, announced that he had a contact about a mile ahead, slightly low and to the right. Carefully he directed his pilot closer until Ashfield could see the bandit limned against the moon. It was a Dornier Do 17Z, later identified as belonging to KG3. Closing to about 400ft (120m), Ashfield fired a long burst, sending it down into the sea. AI had finally started to prove its potential, if not yet its worth.

If this was a start, it was a slow one, and the next kill by an AI-equipped fighter was long in coming. Even when the night blitz started in earnest, and the sky was apparently full of targets, successes were few and far between and most of those fell to catseye interceptions. The disgruntled night fighter crews dubbed AI radar "Magic Mirrors". Unserviceability, and this was a frequent event, was often greeted with a sigh of relief, and the operator would then clamber forward to provide a second pair of eyes on lookout.

AI Mk III was very limited, with a maximum range not exceeding two miles, and a minimum range of more than 1,000ft (305m). Minimum range was far too long on a dark night, but unless the fighter could be brought to within maximum range in the first place, this remained academic.

AI Mk IV was a considerable improvement. Maximum range was about four miles (6. 4km) with the aircraft at 21,000ft (6,400m), while minimum range was reduced to around 400ft (122m). Like the earlier model it suffered from squint, but was far more reliable. Its service introduction coincided with that of the Beaufighter Mk If, which far outperformed the Blenheim.

By comparison with its predecessor, the Beaufighter was massive. Drawn through the air by a pair of Hercules radial engines, it could achieve a maximum speed of 322mph (518kmh) at 15,000ft (4,572m), which was quite enough to overhaul any bomber likely to be encountered; it had quite a respectable rate of climb, and massive hitting power. The forward view from the cockpit was excellent. The pilot sat right up in the nose, with an optically flat bullet-proof windshield in front of him that was free from embarrassing reflections. The operator's position was mid-fuselage, under a transparent dome which gave him an all-round view when not occupied in peering into the hooded radar scope.

The Beaufighter gained a reputation as being tricky to fly. It would swing badly on take-off or landing if it was allowed to, and was unstable as a gun platform. As Dickie Haine recalled:

"In many ways it was a marvellous aeroplane. It was fast, and had tremendous firepower, but it used to wander laterally at all speeds. The more you tried to correct, the worse it got. In the end, you had to take your feet off the rudder pedals and let it damp out. But it was tremendously strong. I was halfway down my take-off run one night when a stick of bombs fell across the airfield. The blast stopped the engines and blew in the clear vision panels, but that was all. I didn't know what had happened. I thought I must have run into something!

"The Beaufighter Mk IIF, which I flew when I commanded an OTU at the end of the war, was not so good. It was powered by Rolls-Royce Merlins, which made it much smoother to fly. The absence of vibration was more like a jet, but even though they put some dihedral on the tailplane it was far more unstable. The fatality rate in training was terrible."

The service introduction of a faster, more heavily armed fighter carrying a better AI, at first made little difference. The AI operators were still feeling their way, while it remained very much a matter of chance whether the rudimentary system of ground control managed to place them within AI range, and if so, whether they were able to hold contact. There were however a few successes.

On the night of 19 November a Beaufighter of No 604 Squadron, flown by Flight Lieutenant John Cunningham with Warrant Officer Phillipson as his radar operator, was on patrol to the south of Birmingham. Spotting a cone of searchlights, Cunningham turned towards them and, shortly after, Phillipson picked up a contact on his AI. Slowly the range closed until the bomber, identified only as a "four-engined aircraft" was sighted dimly against the stars. Bringing his sights to bear, Cunningham opened fire, only to be dazzled by muzzle flash. Both visual and radar contact was lost.

Some 20 minutes later, a Ju 88 crashed in flames near the south coast. Interrogated, the crew said that they had been attacked by a night fighter at a time and place which tallied with Cunningham's combat report. Prior to this the lack of success had made the night fighter crews despondent. The effect on morale of Cunningham's victory was immediate. As Roderick Chisholm of the same squadron later wrote:

"For me it meant that the bombers we were sent to chase were really there, and that the cover of the dark was not absolute!"

The difficulty of placing the fighter in a position from which its AI could make contact was by now about to be solved. The Telecommunications Research Establishment (TRE) had commenced a crash programme in 1940 to develop a suitable ground radar. The basic requirements were adequate range, all-round coverage, and real time information for the controller.

The first of these became operational on 18 October 1940, and by 6 January 1941 a further five had been activated. A combination of high tech and Heath Robinson, they featured a large rotating aerial, described by one pilot as resembling a flattened birdcage. At first this was driven by two airmen, known as "binders", pedalling a tandem-type contraption. Only later were they powered. Range was 50 miles (80km), which meant that each set covered an area 100 miles (161km) in diameter, and they were sited to give overlapping coverage. Still later, when more became available, a network covering most of the British Isles was established.

To provide real time information, a rotating timebase was used, with a circular Plan Position Indicator (PPI) scope on which the controller could see instantly the relative positions of both bomber and the fighter. Height indications were provided by a separate gunlaying radar.

As the radar beam traversed, a bar of light swept around the PPI. Contacts were displayed as blips which lingered on the phosphor after the beam had passed, giving a clear indication of position before fading. At first a 360-degree sweep took eight minutes, but this was quickly reduced to just 65 seconds, so that each contact was redisplayed at frequent intervals.

Should the controller wish to concentrate on a particular area, the radar beam was steerable. The means of control was a simple bell push, which signalled the binders to stop, or even reverse the direction of their pedalling. The whole was housed in a collection of ramshackle huts.

The next problem to overcome was that of distinguishing who was who. This was theoretically solved by fitting RAF fighters, and later, all RAF aircraft, with Identification Friend or Foe (IFF) transponders. Triggered by the radar beam, these automatically modified the echo to give a distinctive blip on the PPI, but unfortunately they were not 100 per cent reliable, which was sometimes embarrassing for GCI.

The often confused situation did not help matters. German bombers, both incoming and outgoing, were often mixed with British bombers on operations and training aircraft on night cross-countries. One RAF fighter pilot recalled a single mission when he was vectored onto no less than three Wellingtons.

With practice the system became increasingly effective. The fighter pilots were encouraged to visit the GCI stations and talk over their mutual problems, and this gave confidence to both. One spin-off effect was that it was far harder for the fighters to get lost. Generally the controller knew the position of the fighter fairly precisely, and could talk them back to base.

The main shortcoming of the GCI stations was that at first, only one interception could be handled at a time. While this was in progress, a lot of bombers could pass unscathed through the area. This was later minimised by having a "cab rank" of fighters orbiting at known positions, then as soon as the fighter under control made contact with its AI radar, another could be launched in pursuit of a new target. Later still, two controllers were on duty at each GCI station, each able to handle an interception from the single PPI scope, but it was rarely enough. Spare night fighters were often sent to freelance across the main track of the bombers.

While GCI problems were being solved, the AI operators were on a steep learning curve. In daylight, the fighter pilot can see the position, aspect and heading of his target – where it is going and what it is doing. By contrast, AI radar shows only where the target is at any given moment in relation to the fighter. From these indications, which change as the spatial relationship of the two aircraft alters, the operator has to work out where the target is going and what it is doing, and having done that, direct his pilot to intercept.

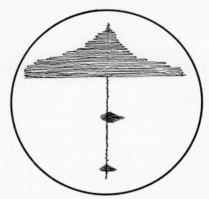 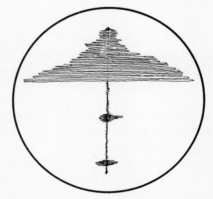

Two scopes were needed for AI Mk IV: one aligned vertically, the other horizontally. The thin fuzzy lines in the centre are timebases, with a small direct pulse at one end and a large fuzzy ground return at the other. From the position of the blips along the timebases and their relative movement, a skilled operator could determine whether the contact was to left or to right, above or below, how far ahead, and the relative speed compared to that of the fighter.

This was far from easy. AI Mk IV had two scopes, one with a horizontal, the other with a vertical time base, or trace. At the far end of the time base was the ground return, otherwise known as the "Christmas Tree", a bright, flickering mass of green light which advanced or retreated along the time base according to the altitude of the fighter. Below about 5,000ft (1,524m) the Christmas Tree would fill almost the entire screen, making detection impossible.

Nor were the time base lines very clear. They were hedged around with flickering spidery lines known as grass, caused by background radio noise. From these a contact would, if all was working well, emerge as a distinct hump on both scopes. From these blips had to be determined range, from how far it was down the trace, while relative height and azimuth indications were given by how far the blip extended on either side of the trace. Relative speed was determined by the rate at which the blip moved along the trace, if it did at all.

The task of an AI operator was twofold. First, he needed to correctly interpret what the radar scopes were showing, and secondly to direct his pilot accurately to within visual range. A great deal of skill was required; this could be acquired by constant practice, but even more valuable was natural flair. As in all forms of warfare, a few gifted practitioners emerged, and these were often snapped up by the more experienced (or most senior) pilots.

If a blip was faint, it was often hard to pick out from the surrounding grass. Having done that, was it ahead or astern? AI Mk IV gave all-round coverage, although range to the rear was limited. This gave rise to some amusing (in retrospect) incidents on exercises. If a fighter managed to get in front of its target without this being recognised by the operator, he would often identify it as being ahead and instruct his pilot to accelerate. Acceleration would open the range, and this would appear on the scopes as if the target was drawing away. The result was that the faster the fighter flew, the more the target appeared to out-accelerate it and draw ahead!

Something else which called for fine judgement was lining up astern. The amount the blip appeared on either side of the trace was far from precise. Inexperienced operators would call for a too radical change of course at close range and then have to correct in the other direction, causing the fighter to snake wildly from side to side without ever aligning correctly. Another potential source of interpretative error was that the scopes showed the target's position in relation to the fighter. If the fighter turned hard to engage a target at the same altitude but out to one side, as it banked, the target would start to appear as though it was ahead and above. Practice and still more practice was the only answer.

Most hazardous at night was the case of a target approaching from head-on. Typically the time between initial contact and collision was less than 25 seconds: several seconds could elapse before the sight of the blip racing down the trace was recognised and a warning issued to the pilot to take evasive action.

Perhaps the most difficult thing of all was bringing the fighter into visual range on a dark night. GCI would direct the fighter to a position from which the AI operator would gain contact at between two and three miles. With a speed advantage of up to 100mph (161kmh) in a straight tail chase, or frequently far more than this against a crossing target, the fighter had to dump its excess speed at exactly the right time. Too early and it might never to catch up; too late and it risked at best an over-shoot, at worst a collision. The margin for error was small.

The best operators were those who developed a technique of passing a con-tinuous running commentary to their pilots. Long silences were not conducive to efficiency, as the pilot, sitting in solitary state at the sharp end, quickly became restive if he was not being told what was happening. Teamwork between pilot and operator was the only answer; after long association the pilot could deduce a lot from the pitch of the operator's voice, which tended to rise in direct proportion to his level of excitement.

The Beaufighter was not fitted with airbrakes, but its gear limiting speed was 240mph (386kmh); provided that speed could be bled off to this level, it could be slowed by lowering the undercarriage. Another fault was common to all British fighters of the era. If throttled back hard, the engines would backfire and emit great gouts of flame, enough to warn alert German crewmen of its presence. German air-craft, with fuel injected engines, were not so prone to this.

Ideally then, the fighter should ghost up behind its quarry, slightly low, matching speeds as it came into firing range. Even on the darkest night, the sky was always a bit lighter than the ground. It was therefore easier to see an aircraft if it was outlined against the sky, and easier to remain undetected against the ground.

It was here that radar minimum range counted. On a very dark night, it was possible to get within the AI Mk IV minimum range of 400ft (122m) of an aircraft and yet be unable to see it unless its exhaust flames were visible. As these were shielded, this could only be done from certain angles. To drive on within minimum radar range without visual contact was to risk a midair collision. The correct tech-nique was to synchronise speeds and stay at the minimum limit of the radar while searching visually.

Even when visual contact was established, the bogey had to be positively identified as with friendlies and hostiles all mixed up, scoring an own-goal was an ever-present possibility. On clear moonlit nights there were few problems, but hazy starlight was another matter altogether.

In a way, pilots had to learn to see in the dark. This was done by exploiting the fact that the peripheral vision is more acute than direct vision. A pilot could become aware of a dark shapeless mass blotting out the stars in his peripheral vision, which would vanish when he turned his gaze directly upon it. The trick was to keep it in his peripheral vision while he closed the range a bit. At this stage it was more awareness than a sighting. At perhaps 300ft (91m) its silhouette could just be made out, but it would be two-dimensional, with little clarity and no depth.

In this situation, identification from astern was often unreliable and the best bet was to lose a little height and pull forward beneath the bogey, to try and make out the planform. Ross night vision binoculars were carried by some crews as an aid to visual identification, and these sometimes allowed the operator to confirm the pilot's sighting.

Having finally established that it was an enemy aircraft, the time came to shoot. The fighter dropped back and pulled up to bring the sights on. At this point there were two basic choices: whether to open fire in a slight nose-up attitude, or to

Right: The Avro 504C was a Royal Naval Air Service (RNAS) variant developed for anti-Zeppelin patrols with an auxiliary fuel tank replacing the front cockpit to increase endurance. The undercarriage was also revised, with V-struts, and the skid deleted. (P. Jarrett Collection)

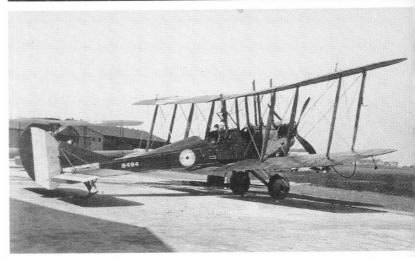

Centre right: The BE2C was widely used by the Royal Flying Corps (RFC) Home Defence squadrons and was flown against Zeppelins by many notable flyers, among them Leefe Robinson and John Slessor. (P. Jarrett Collection)

Below: The BE12B seen here was derived from the BE2C. A single-seater, it entered service with the RFC Home Defence squadrons in 1917 but its performance was inadequate for the task. This example is fitted with launch rails for Le Prieur rockets. (P. Jarrett Collection)

Left: Major G.W. Murliss-Green, commanding No 44 Squadron RFC, takes off from Hainault Farm in his modified night Camel. As can be seen the two Vickers guns are mounted above the top plane to prevent the pilot from being blinded at night by the muzzle flash, while the wing centre section is cut out to improve forward and upward visibility. (P. Jarrett Collection)

Left: Although tricky to fly, the Morane Saulnier L took part in some of the earliest anti-Zeppelin missions and night bombing raids. (FlyPast)

Left: After seeing action in the day fighter role during the last few months of World War 1, the Sopwith Snipe became the backbone of RAF Home Defence in the early post-war years. This example is seen in night colours. (Don Hannah Collection)

Above: The two-seat Bristol F2B combined the performance to catch Gothas with the docile handling demanded by early night operations. (FlyPast)

Below: The Bristol Blenheim Mk IVF with ventral gun pack. The transmitter aerial is in the nose; receiver aerials can just be made out above and below the port wing. (Alfred Price)

Left: A rather scruffy example of the Boulton Paul Defiant Mk II, the first AI fighter in service to have a pilot scope. Aerials can be seen on the fuselage just ahead of the cockpit, and on the port and starboard wings. (Alfred Price)

Left: The Bristol Beaufighter Mk IF had both the performance to catch the night bombers and the hitting power to destroy them with a short burst. (Don Hannah Collection)

Left: The Douglas Havoc Turbinlite combined a searchlight in the nose with AI Mk IV. It was modified from the DB-7 light bomber, as was the USAAF P-70 Nighthawk used in the Pacific. (FlyPast)

Right: The de Havilland Mosquito Mk II was the first fighter variant of this superb aircraft. It was developed throughout World War 2, and the final variant was the NF38, production of which ceased in November 1950. (Don Hannah Collection)

Right: The Mosquito Mk XIII, which entered service in February 1944, carried the centimetric AI Mk VIII radar, with a dish scanner enclosed in the nose. (Don Hannah Collection)

Right: The first really effective Luftwaffe night fighter was the Messerschmitt Bf 110. Bf 110Gs of III/NJG 5 are seen here at Konigsberg/Neumark in the summer of 1943. (Alfred Price)

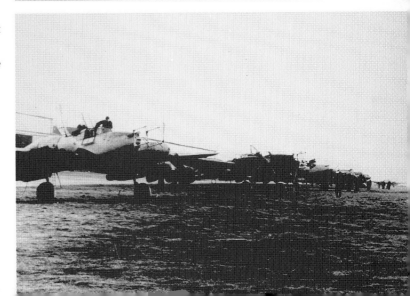

Above: The clumsy aerial array of Lichtenstein BC is seen here on the nose of a Bf 110G. The added drag reduced performance, while vibration caused problems with the radar. (Alfred Price)

Left: Despite its size, the Dornier Do 217J was quite effective in the night fighting role. Built in small numbers, it saw service from the early summer of 1942. (Alfred Price)

Left: The Junkers Ju 88 was, like the Mosquito, a remarkably versatile machine. This is a Ju 88G with the large SN-2 "antlers" radar antenna. The bulge above the cockpit houses the Naxos homing device. (Alfred Price)

Right: The twin barrels of "Schräge Musik" cannon can be seen here on this Ju-88G of NJG 102. The distance aft of the cockpit combined with the steep upward angle must have made aiming a neck-breaking operation for the pilot. (Alfred Price).

Right: The Heinkel He 219A was arguably the greatest German night fighter of the war, and certainly the only one capable of meeting the Mosquito on even terms. This one has two radars; SN-2 aerials surround the FuG 212 antennas. (Alfred Price)

Below: Focke Wulf FW 190A-5s were widely used in Wilde Sau operations over the Reich. (Ken Ellis)

Left: The Messerschmitt Me 262B-1a/U1 was the world's first jet night fighter, fitted with SN-2 radar, the antlers of which reduced maximum speed by 32kt (60kmh). Only about 10 ever saw action. (Don Hannah Collection)

Left The Northrop P-61A Black Widow was a purpose-designed night fighter for the USAAF, using British operational experience from 1940-41. (Don Hannah Collection)

Left: The Vought F-4U Corsair was modified as a night fighter with a radar pod on the starboard wing. Moderately successful in the Pacific, the -5N variant was the mount of the only Korean War night ace, Lieutenant Guy Bordelon. (FlyPast)

Right: The Grumman
F6F-2 Hellcat also car-
ried a radar pod under
the starboard wing, and
became the most widely
used carrier night fighter
of the Pacific war.
(Grumman)

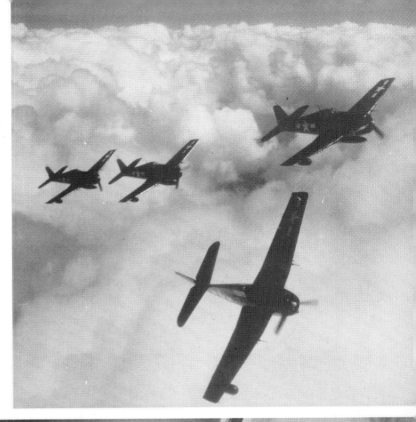

Below: Hellcat F6F-3N
cockpit, showing the
radar screen central. The
warning notice states
"Radar nacelle causes
airspeed to indicate
15-20 knots high in a
left sideslip".
(Grumman)

Left: Although designed as a long range carrier fighter, the Grumman F7F-3N Tigercat only operated from land bases. It saw considerable action in the Korean War. (Grumman)

Left: By carrying its AI radar in an underwing demountable pod, the Grumman F8F-2N Bearcat avoided the sideslip problems encountered by its Hellcat stablemate. (Grumman)

Left: The North American F-82 Twin Mustang consisted of two P-51 Mustang fuselages mated together with a common wing centre to give a two-seat twin-engine long range fighter. (FlyPast)

Above: The addition of a radar nose and an operator shoehorned in amidships produced the de Havilland Sea Hornet NF21, the highest performance carrier twin of its day. (FlyPast)

Right: Adopted as an interim measure, the de Havilland Vampire was essentially the standard day fighter with a Mosquito radar nose and cockpit grafted on. Identical to the NF10, this is an NF54 of the Italian Air Force. (FlyPast)

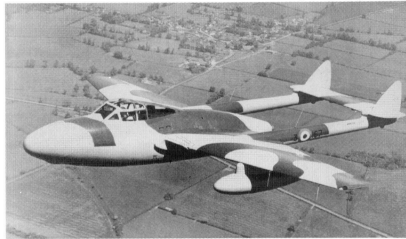

Right: Armstrong Whitworth were responsible for all four night fighter variants of the Meteor. This is the NF14, notable for its clear view canopy. (FlyPast)

Left: The McDonnell F3H-2N was the first really effective all-weather jet carrier fighter. Although it served in Korea, it was never engaged in air combat. (McDonnell Douglas)

Right: A Northrop F-89J Scorpion with two of the fearsome AIR-2 Genies and two AIM-4 Falcons. (Northrop)

Left: The most sucessful night and all-weather fighter of the Korean War was the Douglas F3D Skyknight. The variant seen here is the F3D-2M, armed with AAM-N-2 Sparrow beam-riding missiles. (McDonnell Douglas)

Right: The Scorpion was the most heavily armed fighter of its era. This view of an F-89H shows a battery of Falcons located around the vast tip tanks. (Northrop)

Left: A Lockheed F-94C Starfire lets fly with two pods of FFARs. Already the rockets are beginning to spread, giving some idea of the inaccuracy of this weapon. (Lockheed)

Left: Yakovlev's Yak-25, NATO reporting name "Flashlight", carried a large radar scanner as can be deduced from the size of the radome. Initially only carrying cannon armament, it would have been hard pressed to catch a Canberra let alone shoot it down. (P. Jarrett Collection)

Right: The Gloster Javelin was built in no less than nine variants. These are FAW8s armed with Firestreak AAMs. (Gloster)

Left: Guardian of the frozen north. An Avro Canada CF-100 Mk 4B of the then Royal Canadian Air Force takes off on a routine patrol. (Don Hannah Collection)

Right: An unusual feature of the de Havilland Sea Vixen was the canopy offset to port, leaving the radar operator buried in the "coal hole" to starboard. This is the FAW2. (Quarrie)

Left: The first single-seat collision course interceptor was the North American F-86D seen here. Despite its day fighter ancestry, it was purely a bomber destroyer. (USAF)

Right: The Vought F7U-3 Cutlass was the most radical fighter of its day, but it proved to be too much of a hot ship for night and all-weather carrier work. (Vought)

Above: Another hot ship was the Douglas F4D Skyray. Like the Cutlass it was a tail-less design, and its handling left much to be desired. (Jacques Naviaux)

Left: The Skyray "office", showing the radar scope in action. The steering dot can be seen within the ring, just to the left of the vertical bars. (Jacques Naviaux)

Below: The McDonnell F3H-2N Demon carried four small streamlined pods of FFARs to supplement its cannon armament. These were later supplanted by Sidewinders. (McDonnell Douglas)

pull right up to astern. The first option was often preferred. Not only did it bring the sight on quicker, but it gave a slightly larger target area, while keeping the fighter hidden against the dark ground below. The second option was more deliberate, and it allowed the pilot longer to aim. On the other hand, if the enemy gunners were alert they might return fire while the target aircraft was silhouetted against the horizon, the lightest part of the sky. Care had also to be taken not to drop back too far.

Another factor with the Beaufighter was that the guns were located low on the front fuselage. This had two effects. At very close range it was just possible that the shells might pass under the target, while if a long burst was fired, the recoil would cause the nose to pitch down a bit. Consequently it was advisable to aim at a point high on the target. The foregoing lessons did not all come together at once; they were learned over many months, as the night fighter crews gained experience. Some indication of increasing effectiveness can be seen in the figures for the first five months of 1941.

Table 1. Night Fighter Effectiveness, 1 Jan-31 May 1941 (Major Raids Only)

	Luftwaffe Sorties	RAF N/F Sorties	RAF/Luft Sortie Ratio	Contacts by N/F
January	1,444	486	1:2. 97	78
February	125	568	4. 54:1	58
March	3,128	1,005	1:3. 11	149
April	3,983	1,184	1:3. 36	172
May	2,441	1,988	1:1. 23	371

	N/F Sorties per contact	Combats per contact	Contacts	Claims
January	6. 23	11	7. 09	3
February	9. 79	13	4. 46	4
March	6. 74	56	2. 66	22
April	6. 88	94	1. 83	48
May	5. 39	196	1. 89	96

	N/F Sorties per claim	Contacts per claim	Combats per claim	Raiders % losses
January	162. 00	26. 00	3. 67	0. 02
February	142. 00	9. 79	3. 25	3. 20
March	45. 68	6. 74	2. 55	0. 07
April	24. 67	3. 58	1. 96	1. 21
May	20. 71	3. 86	2. 04	3. 93

Before going further, it should be stated that extremely bad weather in February 1941 severely curtailed bomber sorties, while in the latter half of May, movement of German units eastwards ready for Operation "Barbarossa" reduced the bomber force in the West. Having said that, what can we reasonably infer from these figures?

The first really significant point is that the number of contacts resulting in a combat showed a nearly four-fold increase, while the number of combats resulting in a claim almost doubled, giving nearly a 7-fold increase in the ratio of contacts ending in a claim. This demonstrates the increasing effectiveness of the AI-equipped night fighters and GCI, butit should be remembered that catseye fighters accounted for roughly one-quarter of the total. That the ratio of sorties per contact hardly varied merely underlines the ineffectiveness of the catseye fighters and Blenheims.

The steady increase in attrition of the Luftwaffe bombers pointed the way to the future had the blitz been continued, although by May it was still insufficient to make the raids unsustainable. But from this point on, large raids became far less frequent.

The learning curve of the British night fighter pilots was paralleled by their opponents who now expected to be intercepted, and took precautionary measures. Many bomber pilots took to flying through cloud rather than going over or under it. They could still be detected by radar and followed, but the chance of a visual sighting in cloud at night was virtually nil. Routine changes of course were also used to make the lives of the GCI controllers more difficult, and to throw off a possible pursuer. In the autumn of 1941, Bob Braham of No 29 Squadron encountered a further variation on the theme.

Flying from West Malling in Kent, Braham was scrambled to intercept a raider to the south of London. Vectored towards it by GCI, radar operator "Sticks" Gregory soon got a contact, but as they drew near it became apparent that they were closing much too fast. Throttled right back, and with wheels and flaps down, Braham sighted a Heinkel He 111 above and 300ft (91m) away. With barely 110mph (177kmh) on the clock, the Beaufighter was still overshooting and Braham weaved frantically to try and stay behind it, losing visual contact in the process. Radar contact could not be regained. As Braham later wrote:

"The German was a wily bird. He knew that by flying just about on the stall he was making our job almost impossible. As the night was so dark, he must have guessed that no night fighter pilot would see him until he was very close. Then he wouldn't have time to check his speed to get in a killing burst of fire."

After flying Blenheims and Beaufighters, young Dickie Haine was posted to No 96 Squadron at Wrexham, arriving there on 30 December 1941. No 96 flew Defiants and Hurricanes.

"At the time, we did not fly operational patrols, just exercises. After a while we got Defiant Mk IIs. These had a more powerful engine than the Defiant Mk I and were a bit faster. They were also fitted with AI Mk VI, with a pilot scope. As far as I was concerned, this was ideal. The pilot was responsible for the intercept, and the gunner for shooting.

"It was a single scope with a radial presentation and crosswires. The centre was blank and contacts appeared as curved 'worms' around it. The relative position of the contact had to be determined from the length and position of the 'worm' (if it was dead ahead this showed as a complete circle) and its distance out from the centre.

"As far as I was concerned it was ideal, because it was excellent for homing on beacons. (Radar beacons had by this time been established across England as a homing aid for night fighters.) The beacon would come up on the scope as a horizontal bar, the length of which would give you the distance to it.

"The scope was located low down behind the stick, which made it a bit difficult to see. I had no trouble in switching vision from the scope to outside, but then I had little difficulty with dazzle even when illuminated by searchlights. I may have been unusual in this, but not everyone's eyes are alike. My only problem was in seeing the scope in sunlight, which was hardly relevant to night fighting."

In all, six squadrons received Defiant Mk IIs, but they achieved little. Their performance, while better than that of the Blenheim, was inferior to the Beaufighter. A dozen Hurricanes were also equipped with AI Mk VI for evaluation. While reports on these were generally enthusiastic, the RAF was to stay with the proven two-seater formula, partly because of the difficulty of combining instrument flying with monitoring the radar scope, and partly because a truly exceptional night fighter was entering RAF service.

The de Havilland Mosquito was one of the outstandingly successful aircraft of the war. Originally designed as a fast light bomber with construction using a high proportion of non-strategic materials, its potential as a night fighter was quickly appreciated. Drawn by two Rolls-Royce Merlin inline engines, it comfortably outperformed the Beaufighter in all departments, while its handling was far more fighter-like.

The Mosquito Mk IIF was, like the Beaufighter Mk IF, fitted with AI Mk IV, although some early models carried AI Mk V, which differed in having a pilot scope in addition to those of the operator, and its armament consisted of four 20mm Hispano cannon and four . 303in Browning machine guns. The new fighter entered service in April 1942.

Earlier that year the Mk VII centimetric AI had commenced operational trials in Beaufighters of FIU. Unlike previous sets which produced an all-round signal, the new centimetric breed used a scanner dish which was highly directional. This minimised the effects of ground returns, which meant that it was effective at lower altitudes than hitherto.

Success was not long in coming. On 5 April, Pilot Officer Ryalls and Flight Sergeant Owen intercepted and shot down a low flying Dornier Do 217 over the Thames Estuary. The advantages of the new set were such that AI Mk VII, which was fairly much of a lashup, was refined and placed in large scale production as AI Mk VIII. This led to new variants of existing night fighters. The scanner dish assembly was housed in a dielectric thimble nose to produce the Beaufighter Mk VIF and Mosquito NF Mk XII, both of which entered service later in 1942.

Night raids on England continued after May 1941, albeit at a much reduced tempo, and night fighter scores continued to rise. In the following year, these were interspersed with occasional penetrations by daylight in weather conditions severe enough to make day

AI Mk VIII used a single scope with radial presentation. The central black spot is the zero ring. Three contacts are visible here: the short trace is an aircraft at co-altitude, half a mile away and 45 degrees to starboard; the middling one is dead ahead, about a mile and a half away, and roughly 20 degrees low; the long trace is about four miles away and 7 degrees up to the left. Interpretative skills were at a premium.

fighters ineffective, as we saw in the prologue. Night fighters were pressed into service to fill the gap. Even if they were unable to land at their home airfield, their range enabled them to divert to almost anywhere in the British Isles. The all-weather fighter had finally arrived.

Meanwhile the Luftwaffe night fighter force was laboriously tracing the same path as had the RAF before it. Searchlight co-operation proved inadequate, and steps were taken to produce a radar detection and reporting system, coupled with effective ground control. A German AI radar was still far in the future.

What was obviously needed was a radar similar to the British GCI set, but nothing like this was available. Haste being the order of the day, the Luftwaffe made do with what was to hand. The Freya set was adequate for early warning, but lacked the discrimination for interception, while giving no indication of altitude. The Wurzburg gunlaying radar could discriminate between targets that were quite close together, and provide altitude information, but had an inadequate range of just 21 miles (35km). Being highly directional, with a narrow beam, it was unable to follow two widely spaced aircraft simultaneously.

The solution was to combine the two types to form a night interception sector. Freya provided early warning, while one Wurzburg was used to track the bomber and a second the fighter. The problem then became to combine the information from the two Wurzburgs in a manner usable by the ground controller.

This resulted in the Seeburg Table, the top of which consisted of a frosted glass screen with a gridded map painted on it. Beneath it sat two men with coloured light projectors: red for the bomber, blue or green for the fighter. The courses of the coloured spots of light were plotted across the screen by a third man using wax crayons, and from this information the controller broadcast interception instructions to the fighter. Each system of three radars and a control centre, codenamed "Himmelbett" (Four-Poster Bed) formed a box patrolled by a single night fighter. The first few boxes were sited in front of the Ruhr, but gradually the system was extended to reach from Denmark to the Swiss border.

Despite the lack of a PPI and the timelag caused by Wurzburg operators reporting to the control centre, the Himmelbett system worked moderately well. Its greatest weakness was the short range of the tracking radars, which could only hold the bombers for about seven minutes at most. Often this was insufficient for the German night fighters to get into position, bearing in mind that they had to be directed to within visual distance from the ground. The Wurzburg Reise, or Giant Wurzburg, with a range of 36-42 miles (60-70km) was ordered to improve matters, entering large scale service in 1942.

The first German AI radar, codenamed "Lichtenstein", commenced operational trials in July 1941 installed in Bf 110, Ju 88 and Do 215 aircraft. Li, as it was commonly known, worked on a a frequency of 490MHz, with a wavelength of 62cm, which required an aerial length too large to be mounted internally. Four double pairs of dipoles were set vertically about the fighter's nose, causing a considerable amount of drag, with a consequent reduction in performance.

Li's maximum range varied between 10 and 18,000ft (3,000- 5,500m) and, like the British AI Mk IV, it was altitude-limited. Unlike AI Mk IV it was directional, with an angle of search of a mere 24 degrees. Minimum range was about 650ft (200m). Three scopes were used for ranging, azimuth and elevation indications. Like the early British sets, it suffered from squint, spurious returns, fading, distortion, and just plain unreliability. A third crewman was squeezed into the cramped confines of the Bf 110 to operate it. These factors, plus the loss of performance caused to the carrier aircraft, made it initially unpopular with the crews.

The first German airborne radar victory came on the night of 9 August 1941. Oberleutnant Ludwig Becker, with Feldwebel Josef Stauf as his operator, took off from Leeuwarden in Holland to patrol sector Löwe (Lion). Soon the ground controller was directing them towards a "courier", as the bombers were called. At last Stauf obtained radar contact at 6,500ft (2,000m) range, and Becker started to close on it. At some point the bomber became aware of its pursuer, and it took evasive action. Twice contact was broken, but by turning the fighter hard in the direction of the evasion manoeuvre, contact was regained. Finally Becker gained visual contact and opened fire.

By a strange coincidence, during the previous year Becker had scored the first German radar directed victory when flying a Dornier Do 17 of 4/NJG 1 during initial ground radar trials, shooting down a Wellington in flames on 16 October 1940. Now he persevered with airborne radar, and by the end of September had added several more to his score. His success was instrumental in persuading other pilots to keep trying, and gradually the radar-equipped night fighter gained acceptance.

In the early months of 1942, RAF bomber losses climbed steadily, reaching four per cent by April. In the main this was due to the increasing effectiveness of the fighter force. The bombers flew widely spaced in distance and time, each choosing its own route to and from the target. In effect this meant that a high proportion of Himmelbett boxes were in action during each raid, often several times in one night, and the patrolling fighters were able to concentrate on a high proportion of the bombers passing through them.

This all changed on the night of 30 May1942, when the RAF mounted the first 1,000-bomber raid on Cologne. For this the bombers were concentrated in space and time; advancing on a narrow frontage, few Himmelbett boxes were penetrated. Those that were found their radars swamped with contacts, causing difficulties in tracking. For each bomber engaged in a Himmelbett zone, dozens of others slipped past unmolested.

The rationale behind the idea of the bomber stream was twofold: concentrating damage in the target area while reducing losses to both night fighters and Flak. Certainly the swamping of the ever-increasing number of fighter boxes played a considerable part in keeping losses down. The Luftwaffe High Command called the bomber stream "alarmingly effective", while at the sharp end, Bf 110 pilot Wilhelm Johnen of 4/NJG 1 later wrote:

"The allied squadrons... flew at short intervals, almost goosestepping towards the weakest night fighter areas; then they crashed by sheer weight through this area like a broad stream driven through a narrow channel. Our whole night defence was crippled by these approach tactics."

The Himmelbett system had been designed to deal with a considerable number of widely scattered bombers, each flying its own route at its own time. Against the bomber stream it was far less effective, as a few fighters had too many targets to cope with, while the majority had no targets at all. Greater flexibility was needed, but until such time as more radar-equipped fighters were available, little could be done. The boxes were made able to control two fighters at a time, and their numbers increased to give an ever-deepening defensive belt, but with little effect.

Towards the end of 1942, almost all German night fighters carried radar and on 17 November Operation "Adler" (Eagle) was launched. This involved Staffeln of night fighters assembling en-masse over ground beacons near the projected track of the bombers. From these they were vectored into the bomber stream where they stayed, searching autonomously with Li.

With hindsight it seems obvious that this loose form of fighter control should have immediately superseded the fighter boxes, but Generalmajor Kammhuber, commanding the German night fighter force, was opposed to any change in his laboriously constructed defensive system. He remained unconvinced that the fighters could find the bombers without the aid of ground control, and was concerned about the dangers of uncontrolled fighters operating within his radar boxes.

There was, however, a silver lining for the Luftwaffe. The bomber stream would in future provide a target-rich environment for radar equipped night fighters provided they could be brought into contact with it.

There was in fact a parallel with the Battle of the Atlantic which was raging at this time: one U-boat commander commented that it was very convenient of the British to group their ships in convoys so that a lot could be sunk in a short space of time. Meanwhile the technical war was hotting up, with both sides trying to counter or exploit the electronic advantages of the other. The coming years would see the pendulum swing in both directions.

6. Night Victory

As 1942 neared its close, RAF bomber losses were again rising, testifying to the increasing effectiveness of the Luftwaffe night fighters. General Kammhuber's response to the bomber stream had been to expand his force and extend the Himmelbett belt, while adapting the GCI centres to handle two or more fighters each. At the same time, the German night fighter crews were being given plenty of practice in using their Li radar, and many grew very skilled. At this point the war entered a new phase. The idea of electronic counter-measures (ECM) was far from new. Both sides had employed ECM during 1940, Germany making a half-hearted attempt to jam the British CH system in the summer of 1940, while the British successfully interfered with German blind bombing systems from that autumn. One thing was obvious. Jamming was potentially far more important in the all-electronic night environment than in daylight operations. The electronic battle for Germany began in earnest.

The German night fighter crews now had to contend with various devices designed to lower their efficiency. Some of these were of course aimed at the ground detection and tracking system, but others were directed at the fighters themselves. The first of these was codenamed "Tinsel", which broadcast engine noise over the fighter radio frequencies, hindering or preventing the German crewmen from receiving instructions from the ground by hindering and interrupting communications. While it was close to impossible to completely block the German ground to air communications, anything which increased their "frazzle" factor impaired their efficiency. Over the next few years many other communications jamming devices would be introduced to confound the German night fighter crews.

It was not long before the hard worked Nachtjagdflieger were given yet another task. In January 1943, heavy bombers of the USAAF started to penetrate the airspace of the Third Reich. On 4 February, eight Bf 110s of IV/NJG1 were ordered to join the day fighters in intercepting them. Although three B–17s were claimed shot down, all eight Bf 110s sustained severe damage and as a result were unavailable for operations that night. The pattern was repeated during the days that followed. On 26 February, Hauptmann Ludwig Becker, at that time the leading German night fighter ace with 46 victories, was killed during a daylight engagement with American bombers near Emden. While machines were ultimately replaceable, men of this calibre were not.

Meanwhile RAF Bomber Command was being a mite too clever for its own good. Early in 1943 it introduced three new devices into service. The first was "Boozer", which warned when a bomber was being illuminated by radar. This was theoretically very handy, but when the warning light went off it might simply mean that the fighter had closed to visual range and switched its radar to standby, leaving the bomber crew with a false sense of security.

The second was "Monica", a tail warning radar with a range of about 3,000ft (914m) in a 45-degree cone astern. This was downright dangerous. Not only did it give far too many false alarms due to the presence of other bombers in the stream, but it was an emitter. Third, and most dangerous of all was H_2S, an early ground mapping radar used for navigation and blind bombing. Inevitably the Luftwaffe intelligence services discovered these items in shot down aircraft and after several months delay were able to deduce what they were and how they worked. It was not long before they had designed and produced receivers to home on them. The RAF was to pay dearly as a result.

Advances in blind bombing aids such as H_2S now enabled the RAF to attack accurately on moonless nights and in cloudy conditions. No longer did the bombers need good visibility, and this was to the disadvantage of the night fighters, which were forced to seek them under adverse circumstances. The Battle of the Ruhr opened on 5 March 1943, when 438 heavy bombers attacked Essen. Other raids on the main industrial area of the Third Reich followed thick and fast over the following months.

The night fighters did their best but were hampered by the adherence to the Himmelbett system, which typically allowed only 50 fighters to be launched out of roughly 300 available. Matters were aggravated still further by new British tactics. The bomber stream became concentrated even more: several hundred bombers now passed through the fighter boxes and over the target in between 30 and 40 minutes. At the same time increasing use was made of feints and diversions, making it harder for the Luftwaffe controllers to predict the target.

Between March and June 1943, a total of 18,506 bomber sorties were flown. Losses totalled 872, four-fifths of them by fighters, but this only gave an attrition rate of 4. 7 per cent – not nearly enough to stop the attacks. The fighters somehow had to do much better.

The freelance Bf 110 sorties of Operation "Adler" late in 1942 had been discontinued. Now they found a new champion in former bomber pilot Oberst Viktor von Lossberg, who pressed the case for their reintroduction, at first without success.

Another former bomber pilot with ideas of his own was Major Hans-Joachim Herrmann. Far more influential than his rank would suggest, Herrmann argued that single-seater catseye fighters could be used effectively over the target area, where the bombers would be lit up by searchlights, or silhouetted against the fires on the ground. A ceiling would of course have to be imposed on the Flak to allow the fighters to operate above it.

Why did Herrmann think that he could succeed where others, both British and German, had failed? Just two factors made a difference. First, Herrmann proposed to use ex-bomber pilots who were experienced in instrument flying. Secondly, the fires on the ground were far more extensive at this stage of the war than hitherto, often providing what almost amounted to an illuminated backdrop. This was especially the case with a thin layer of low cloud, which diffused the light from the fires.

Kammhuber was less than thrilled with this proposal, but was over-ruled from above. Permission was given for limited trials to be made, and the formation of Kommando Herrmann was authorised on 8 April. Equipped with a handful of Bf 109G-6s and FW 190A-5s, it flew the first mission on 20 April 1943 when, due to insufficient early warning, it failed to make contact.

Kommando Herrmann's first real chance came on 3 July, when the RAF raided Cologne. The Flak had not been warned, but Herrmann led his dozen fighters into the thick of it to seek out the bombers. This small unit later claimed 12 bombers destroyed, although this was naturally disputed by the local Flak commander. However, claims that the concept was now proven were premature.

The orthodox night fighters in service at this time were still upgraded variants of the Bf 110, Ju 88, and Do 217. Laden with aerials and equipment, they were too slow to intercept the Mosquito bomber, which at this time was roaming the skies over Germany in ever-increasing numbers with virtual impunity. The Messerchmitt Bf 210, which was intended to replace the 110, had simply horrible flying characteristics, and failed to enter service. Then in April 1943, a possible answer to the Mosquito arrived. This was the Heinkel He 219 Uhu (Owl).

The He 219 was large, roughly the size of a Ju 88, and had a tricycle undercarriage. It was fast, with a top speed exceeding 400mph (644kmh), very heavily armed with six 20mm cannon and rather more manoeuvrable than the new Ju 188S. Some of the evaluation flights had been made by Major Werner Streib, Gruppenkommandeur of I/NJG1. So impressed was he that he asked for a few preproduction aircraft for his Gruppe. Flying it on its operational debut on 11-12 June, Streib shot down no less than five Lancasters in 30 minutes. This promising start was rather marred when the flaps failed on landing and the aircraft was wrecked. This notwithstanding, the handful of Uhus of I/NJG1 went on to destroy a further 20 RAF aircraft in the following month, including six Mosquitos. The obvious next move was to place the He 219 in quantity production, but for various reasons, few of them technical and none of them operational, this was never done. In all less than 300 of these superlative night fighters were built before war's end. Meanwhile, back at the ranch, the British had a few nasty surprises in store for the Luftwaffe.

Until May 1943, RAF intruder missions had continued much as we saw in Chapter 4, but from the following month they began to be integrated with bomber operations, with patrols over known Luftwaffe night fighter bases timed to coincide with bomber raids. It was at this time that AI-equipped fighters were first released for operations over the continent, although the aircraft concerned carried AI Mk IV rather than the newer Mk VII and VIII.

Meanwhile, a device called "Serrate" had been developed which could home on Li emissions from up to 100 miles (161km) away. Like the radars of the period, it called for skilled interpretation. Two CRT displays were used, one for azimuth, the other for elevation. When a contact was obtained, "herringbone" bars stood out from either side of the traces, and the relative length and number of these indicated altitude and direction. As Serrate gave no indication of range, it could only be used in conjunction with AI. As with all new "black boxes", Serrate was temperamental.

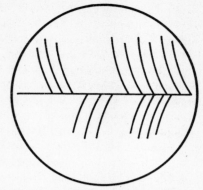

G1/G2) The British Serrate device to home on German radar needed two scopes - one vertical, the other horizontal - from which to deduce the direction of the emissions. The length and number of the "herring-bones" in the vertical display indicates a contact to starboard; those in the horizontal display indicate that it is above. AI radar still had to be used for ranging.

The unit selected to carry Serrate was No. 141 Squadron equipped with Beaufighters, which was to be based at Wittering. An intensive flying programme was needed to develop tactics for use with the new gadget and this took place at Drem in Scotland, where the Luftwaffe was least likely to learn of it. In June the squadron moved south once more. The first Serrate mission was to support a bombing raid on Oberhausen on 14-15 June. The plan was to mingle with the bomber stream at the same speed, so as to be indistinguishable from the bombers on German radar. Six Beaufighters refuelled at Coltishall to give maximum endurance, then set course at intervals for Germany.

In the lead was Bob Braham, No 141's commanding officer, with "Sticks" Gregory, by now a Flight Lieutenant, as his operator. Over occupied territory several Serrate contacts were gained, then quickly lost. It appeared that the German night fighters only used their Li for short periods.

It was in the target area that Gregory gained a really strong contact, and established on AI that the German night fighter was coming in from astern, about 6,000ft (1,800m) away. A continuous turn to port brought the Beaufighter around behind the German, who appeared to have lost AI contact, then Braham sighted it less than 1,800ft (550m) off to port in the bright moonlight. Closing, he opened fire at 1,200ft (366m), rolling in astern as he did so. Burning, the Bf 110 went down to crash northeast of the Ijsselmeer.

This was the only victory scored on that first mission, but others had been close to interception, only to have either the AI or Serrate fail at the critical moment. From this point on, the Nachtjadgflieger had not only to contend with the guns of the bombers, and intruders over their bases, but also hunters seeking them even as they sought the bombers.

It had long been known by both sides that radar could be jammed by aluminium foil strips cut to a length matching the characteristics of the hostile radar. Known as "Window" by the RAF and "Duppel" by the Luftwaffe, this was regarded as such a hot potato that both withheld from using it for a considerable period. In order to avoid retaliation in kind, the primary consideration for the RAF was first to introduce a radar which was less susceptible to jamming of this nature, prior to using Window over Germany. This duly arrived in the shape of the American SCR. 720, designated AI Mk X in RAF service, featuring a primitive lock-on capability which minimised the effects of Window. The first operational sortie with

AI Mk X was flown by a Mosquito on 4 May 1943, and it was rapidly brought into service over the following months.

In readying to use Serrate and Window, a great deal of effort had been expended in ascertaining the characteristics of Li, mainly by electronic reconnaissance, and deducing what was needed to jam it. Complete confirmation was however still missing. Then on 9 May an intelligence windfall came the way of the British. Oberleutnant Herbert Schmidt and his operator, Oberfeld-webel Paul Rosenberger, had flown many intruder sorties over England with 2/NJG2 in 1940-41, always

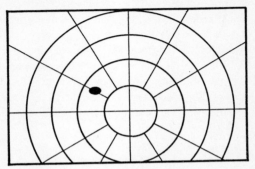

The C-Scope used in SCR-720 was used to give the relative position in the vertical plane, graduated in circles of 20, 40 and 60 degrees off boresight. This gave fairly precise steering information, although other scopes had to be used to determine range and relative speed. The contact shown is about 15 degrees to port and 30 degrees above.

without success. More recently they had flown defensive night fighter sorties with IV/NJG3, still with no result. This appears to have put them under a cloud, and they defected, landing their Li-equipped Ju 88R-1 at Dyce, near Aberdeen. Whether they were pro-British, as some accounts have stated, or whether their defection was an attempt to avoid an infantry posting to the Russian Front, has never been made clear. The important thing was that the RAF now had a fully operational German night fighter to evaluate. Trials were flown at RAE Farnborough, in which it was conclusively established that Li could not operate successfully in the face of Window. Shortly after, Bomber Command unleashed its secret weapon.

Shortly before midnight on 24 July 1943, German early warning radars detected a large build-up of RAF bombers far out over the North Sea. Slowly the plot neared the German coast, then turned southeastwards. Night fighters were scrambled, then the blow fell. The screens of the early warning and tracking radars filled up with contacts as over 700 bombers suddenly appeared to multiply into 11,000!

The confusion on the ground was only equalled by that in the air. The hapless Li operators picked up contact after contact on their screens, only to have them flash past at high speed as the fighter passed the Window clouds. Only when the bombs started to fall was Hamburg identified as the target, and by then the night fighters were thoroughly disorganised. The Himmelbett system had virtually collapsed, and all they could do was to search visually for the real bombers, with little success. Only 12 bombers went down that night to all causes; an attrition rate of just 1. 5 per cent. Over the next few days, three further night raids were made on the stricken city, and again Window kept attrition far below previous levels. This was a resounding defeat for the German night fighter arm.

Defeat by ECM did not, however, entail destruction; the night fighter units remained in being and new means of employing them effectively were not long in coming. Oberst von Lossberg's freelancing fighter proposal now found favour. On the approach of a raiding force, the night fighters were to take off and assemble over a radio beacon. As the general direction of the raid became known, the fighters would be shifted from beacon to beacon ahead of its track, until at last they could be fed into the bomber stream where they would stay searching visually, while petrol and ammunition lasted. While Window could hide individual bombers within the stream, it could not of course conceal the presence of the stream itself, although the use of diversions and feints could make life very unpredictable for the ground controllers.

This procedure became known as "Zahme Sau" (Tame Boar). What Wilhelm Johnen termed the Luftwaffe's "migratory period" had begun. Crews took off from their bases, flew and fought until low on fuel, then landed at the nearest airfield to replenish. If conditions allowed they would then take off for a second sortie, only returning home in the chill light of dawn. The already heavily laden Bf 110s were provided with external tanks to extend their endurance still more, further reducing their performance.

Meanwhile Hajo Herrmann's ideas on illuminated night fighting, codenamed "Wilde Sau" (Wild Boar), had also been given a sympathetic reception. Kommando Herrmann was expanded and redesignated JG300. One of the more interesting innovations of this unit was the suggestion that when a thin layer of cloud existed in the target area, searchlights should be played evenly upon it, silhouetting the bombers for the fighters high overhead. This was codenamed "Mattscheibe" (ground glass screen).

At first there were only enough aircraft to equip I/JG300, and I Gruppe was forced to borrow fighters from a day unit at the same base, which proved highly contentious. After a few successful operations, more fighters were made available, and a further two Wilde Sau units, JG301 and JG302, were formed in September.

The first major test of the new methods came on 17–18 August when the RAF raided the rocket development centre at Peenemunde, involving a deep penetration across Denmark and into the Baltic. The weather was clear, with few clouds, and the moon was full. Under such conditions the German fighters could expect to score heavily if they could bring sufficient force to bear, but the RAF had other ideas.

The first joker in the pack was Bob Braham's squadron, which was supporting the bomber stream. As the Beaufighter lacked the range to accompany the bombers all the way to the target, the squadron was divided into two – half covering the outbound leg, the rest taking off later to provide a reception force for the return trip. In a departure from previous practice, they were not mingling with the bomber stream, but patrolling its flanks, with four Beaufighters to each side. The aircraft on the southern, most vulnerable, flank were led by Bob Braham in person, with "Jacko" Jacobs as his operator. As Braham later commented, they hoped to persuade the Germans that they were stragglers from the main force.

This ploy worked only too well. The Luftwaffe detected a small gaggle of aircraft off the Frisian Islands and sent five Bf 110s of IV/NJG1 to intercept. The first to find trouble was Oberfeldwebel Georg Kraft. Closing on the bogeys, with his operator, Unteroffizier Dunger searching for Li contacts, he was suddenly hit from astern. A second burst set his aircraft on fire, and both crewmen bailed out as it went down into the sea. Kraft did not survive.

His assailant was Braham, who had been directed in behind by Jacobs and had opened fire at about 750ft (228m) range. Braham then climbed away and turned. As he did so, Jacobs warned him of yet another contact, very close. He reefed into a hard turn to starboard, to see another 110 also in a hard turn just above. The German gunner, Unteroffizier Gaa, saw the Beaufighter approaching from below, but was unable to bring his guns to bear. Closing fast, Braham gave a short burst from barely 150ft (46m), then broke hard to avoid a collision. The combined weight of fire from cannon and machine guns at such close range tore into the 110, which went down vertically in flames. Its crew succeeded in baling out but only the pilot, high scoring ace Feldwebel Heinz Vinke survived, after 18 hours in the sea.

Nor did things go well for the remaining Messerschmitts. A third fell to the guns of another No 141 Squadron Beaufighter; the fourth, piloted by the future ranking night fighter ace Leutnant Heinz-Wolfgang Schnaufer, was hit by "friendly" Flak but returned safely to base, while the fifth returned early with engine trouble. It was not an auspicious night for the fourth Gruppe.

While this small but vicious action was in progress, the Luftwaffe was reacting to the threat posed by the main force, or so they thought. Breaking away from the main stream, eight Pathfinder Mosquitos carried out a diversionary raid on Berlin, fooling the defenders into thinking this was the primary target. All available night fighters, 55 single and 148 twin-engined, were ordered to the capital where they were greeted by Flak which, hearing only engine noises, assumed they were hostile.

The bluff was only uncovered when target markers went down on Peenemunde, over 100 miles (161km) to the north. Those few fighters with enough fuel raced off to intercept. Catching the final wave of bombers, they shot down 41, seven per cent of the total. This was a grim portent of what might have been had the diversion not worked.

One of the successful fighter pilots that night was young Leutnant Dieter Musset flying a Bf 110G-4 of 5/NJG1, who claimed four heavy bombers before being shot down by the tail gunner of his final victim. This was a perennial hazard in night fighting. The standard approach was made from behind and below, but to shoot, the night fighter had to pull up astern, in full view of the tail gunner with his potentially lethal four-gun turret.

Some of the other night fighters did not have this problem. They carried "Schräge Musik" (Jazz), which consisted of guns fixed in the fuselage to fire upward at a steep angle, typically 65-70 degrees, aimed by a reflector sight on the cabin roof.

The first to score with this method was Unteroffizier Holker of 5/NJG 5, who claimed two bombers. He was quickly followed into action by Leutnant Peter Erhardt of 6/NJG5, who claimed four more.

The idea of upward-firing guns was almost as old as air combat. Major Lanoe Hawker of No 24 Squadron RFC had championed their use back in 1916, albeit by daylight. The RAF had tested the concept in Havocs in 1941. In the same year, Oberleutnant Rudolf Schonert fitted two upward-firing 7. 92mm machine guns in his Do 17Z-10. Trials proved successful and in December 1942, three Do 217Js were fitted with twin 20mm cannon mounted at an angle of 70 degrees. This installation was apparently seen by Oberfeldwebel Paul Mahle, an armourer with II/NJG5 who also often flew as a gunner, who introduced the idea to his unit.

In a Schräge Musik attack, the fighter could creep into the blind spot beneath the bomber, formating with it while taking careful aim at the vulnerable wing tanks, away from the bomb load which, if it detonated, might easily take the fighter down with its victim. As tracer ammunition was not used, there was nothing to give away the position of the fighter, and many months passed before Bomber Command realised the significance of this type of attack.

With the widespread introduction of Zahme Sau tactics, the Luftwaffe fighters were often held back until the route of the bombers became clear. The main German night fighter was still the Bf 110, albeit by now mainly the G subtype. Laden with black boxes, an extra crewman, external fuel tanks, and festooned with aerials, it had little enough margin of speed over the bombers to be able to catch them unless correctly positioned from the outset. Forward interceptions now became rare, and the modest-ranged Serrate Beaufighters found fewer opportunities to score, and were finally withdrawn.

Late August and early September saw three heavy raids on the German capital. Bomber attrition rose to 7. 5 per cent, a clear indication that the new Luftwaffe methods were working well. It had been assumed that the defenders would take up to a year to find a counter to Window, yet barely two months had elapsed.

In all, the final six months of 1943 were notable for the tactical and technical innovations introduced by both sides as each strove for mastery. The attrition rate inflicted by the defenders during the Berlin raids was not sustained. Over the next seven weeks Bomber Command raided Germany in force on 15 occasions, losing 260 bombers from more than 6,500 sorties, an attrition rate of just under four per cent. In part this reduction was accounted for by shorter penetrations, and darker nights as summer waned. At the same time, increasing use was made of course changes, feints and diversions, which wrong-footed the German controllers on many occasions.

Late summer also saw the introduction of the corkscrew as a bomber evasion tactic. Developed with the assistance of FIU, the corkscrew involved constantly changing altitude, aspect and heading along a mean course. It not only presented a very difficult target for the German pilots, but made the use of Schräge Musik almost impossible, as no fighter pilot in his right mind would attempt to fly close under a bomber manoeuvring in such a fashion. However, it was tiring to fly, it reduced the mean speed over the ground, and was therefore used only when fighters were known to be about. Consequently the Nachtjadgflieger were still often able to surprise bombers flying straight and level, and their score continued to mount.

The RAF had continued all this while to fly intruder sorties but without AI they had achieved little more than nuisance value. Bob Braham's Beaufighters lacked the endurance to be truly effective, and the obvious next step was to use the faster and longer-legged Mosquito.

The pioneering task fell to FIU, using a Mosquito equipped with AI Mk IV, modified with a rear-facing transmitter to increase range astern. The idea was to troll along, waiting for an unsuspecting German to intercept. Having permitted him to close to about 5,000ft (1,500m), a rate four turn would take the Mosquito out of the narrow Li coverage and into a position where the crew could get a forward contact in their turn.

In practice, few victories were gained in this manner, and it quickly became obvious that better results would be obtained by patrolling German night fighter airfields or radio assembly beacons. Be that as it may, radar and Serrate-equipped Mosquitos began to range the length and breadth of the Third Reich from this time, few at first, then gradually increasing in strength.

As the light nights of summer gave way to the darkness and bad weather of winter, the Wilde Sau units became ever less effective and suffered many losses due to accidents. A few did well, notably Hauptmann "Nasen" Muller, so called for his large proboscis, with 23 victories from 52 sorties, but they had been the exceptions.

In the autumn of 1943, the Luftwaffe introduced three new gadgets. The first was SN-2, an airborne radar unaffected by the Window then in use. Development of this had started the previous year, and unusually it used a wavelength even longer than Li, calling for another forest of aerials on the nose of the already overloaded night fighters. In many ways SN-2 was superior to Li, as it had a much greater scan of 120 degrees in azimuth, and +/- 30 degrees in elevation. Maximum range was about four miles (6. 5km), but minimum range was unacceptably long at 1,200ft (366m), well beyond the distance that the target could be visually acquired on a dark night. In normal times, this might well have caused SN-2 to be rejected, but with Li rendered virtually useless by Window, it was better than nothing.

The other devices were both homers. "Naxos Z" could pick up emissions from H_2S at about 10 miles (16km), while "Flensburg" could detect Monica signals from 130 miles (209km) with a high degree of angular discrimination. With these three items of equipment, Zahme Sau could be said to have come of age. Only a loose running commentary from the ground was needed; the night fighters could then find their own way.

By early 1944, when the new devices were reaching the Nachtjagdgeschwader in large numbers, the picture looked bleak for Bomber Command. It was however not all bad. New jamming systems had left German surface-to-air communications in total disarray, while spoofs and feints had considerable success.

As in any field of human endeavour, a minority performs outstandingly while the majority scratch around for little return. The target-rich environment of the bomber stream provided a happy hunting ground for the German experten who, when opportunity offered, racked up multiple kills.

The ranking experte at that time was Major Prinz Heinrich zu Sayn-Wittgenstein. His early victories had come on the Russian Front before being transferred west to NJG2. A legendary figure, he was reputed to have once made his operator stand to attention in the cockpit (how this was done was not explained) and confined him to quarters for three days for losing a radar contact. This was in the middle of the bomber stream! Resuming the mission, they then shot down three bombers, after which Wittgenstein pardoned the man and awarded him the Eisenkreuz First Class.

On the night of 21-22 January 1944, Bomber Command raided Magdeburg in force. Among the defenders was Wittgenstein, recently assigned as Kommodore of NJG2. After accounting for four four-engined bombers in the space of 40 minutes, he was hit by an unseen opponent, believed to have been a Mosquito, sending his Ju 88G down in flames. His operator, Feldwebel Ostheimer, baled out successfully, but the prince failed to get clear of his doomed aircraft. His final score was 83. Not far away, Hauptmann Manfred Meurer, Kommandeur of II/NJG5, attacked a Lancaster from below using Schräge Musik. Fatally hit, the bomber plunged into Meurer's He 219 and both aircraft plunged down together. Meurer's final score was 63. This double loss was a severe blow to the German night fighter arm.

The unjammed SN-2, combined with Flensburg and Naxos Z, gave excellent results over the next few months, provided that the German controllers could marshall their fighters at a spot from which they could be directed into the bomber stream. Sometimes the RAF spoofs and feints worked, sometimes they failed. When this happened, bomber losses were heavy. On 19-20 February, 78 bombers out of an initial 823 failed to return, an attrition rate of 9. 5 per cent. On other occasions losses were relatively light.

The climax came with the notorious Nuremberg raid on 30-31 March, when conditions combined with a succession of happy accidents to favour the Nachtjagdflieger. The bomber stream was scattered by unexpected winds, and contrails formed at lower than usual heights, making the bombers visible for miles in the light of a half moon. To make matters worse, the planned diversions were relatively ineffective that night. Finally, the German controller assembled his fighters quite fortuitously over two beacons right in the path of the bombers. Many fighters were therefore able to infiltrate the bomber stream at an early stage, which led to a protracted running battle.

This was Bomber Command's worst night, with 94 aircraft missing, plus one intruder Mosquito. Of these, the night fighters accounted for 79 and shared a further two with Flak. In all, roughly 250 fighters entered the bomber stream that night and, while several experienced pilots scored multiple victories, the majority achieved nothing. A notable failure that night was Heinz-Wolfgang Schnaufer. In an attempt to enter the bomber stream as early as possible, he had flown towards the coast from his base at St Truiden in Belgium, missing the bombers entirely. Most of the Wilde Sau fighters aloft were sent to the wrong areas; those few that did make contact may have accounted for five bombers only. Nor were the 17 Serrate Mosquitos out that night any more effective. Serrate could not home on SN-2 and they were left groping for unseen opponents. Just one Ju 88 fell victim to the intruders.

This was the most decisive night fighter victory of the war, and Bomber Command's attrition rate rose to an unsupportable 13. 4 per cent on this raid. It was perhaps fortunate that it was now switched to fly in support of the forthcoming Normandy landings. In any case, the shorter lighter nights of summer were coming, making deep penetration raids even more hazardous.

Luftwaffe raids on England had never entirely ceased, albeit at a much lower intensity than before, and the RAF night fighter squadrons found few customers. Gradually more Mosquito squadrons were formed, and centimetric AI Mk VIII entered large scale service. The much longer range of this radar brought one immediate benefit. Whereas with AI Mk IV, GCI had to direct the fighter in from astern to make contact, it could now bring it in from ahead, handing over as soon as contact was gained. GCI involvement was thus much shorter, enabling individual controllers to handle more interceptions within a given time span.

Early in 1943, the Luftwaffe started making daylight raids using FW 190 fighter-bombers, and it was not long before these also began to be used at night. In theory these were too fast to be caught by a Mosquito and, on 16 May, a flight of Typhoons from No 3 Squadron was scrambled to deal with them. These blundered around the night sky in vain and were finally ordered back to base, and the Mosquitos of No 85 Squadron scrambled in their place. Four crews intercepted the now homebound raiders, claiming four shot down and one probable. Inbound 190s were rather easier to catch; two drop tanks and a large bomb acted as a wonderful speed brake, while the high speed of the raiders greatly reduced the chance of the Mosquito overshooting.

German bomber losses during 1943 were heavy; at times the attrition level reached double figures. To reduce this it was only to be expected that the Luftwaffe would soon use Duppel to blind the defenders. This finally started on 7 October when about 35 aircraft raided Norwich. Although GCI was able to detect a few bombers on the fringes of the Duppel cloud, the rest were screened, as were the IFF returns from the defending fighters, making accurate control impossible. The situation was further confused by the presence of several RAF bombers returning from Stuttgart. The fighters scored only one victory that night when a Beaufighter pursued a bomber out to sea beyond the Duppel cloud.

Bomber Command's delay in using Window now paid off. New Window-resistant GCI radars were entering service, as were the first Mosquitos equipped with AI Mk X, although these did not become fully operational until January 1944. After the initial success, German bomber losses again started to rise. Between January and May, they totalled 329 – an attrition rate of nearly eight per cent and rising. With the Allied invasion of Normandy in June, the German bomber offensive fizzled out.

Centimetric AI was finally released for operations over occupied territory in May 1944 as part of a bid to attain absolute air supremacy over the invasion area. One of many Allied night fighter pilots taking part was Dickie Haine, now commanding No 488 (New Zealand) Squadron, equipped with Mosquito NFXIIIs:

"It was 4 August. I was on patrol near Caen, controlled by a radar picket ship. They warned us that bandits were approaching and vectored us towards them. Pete Bowman, my regular operator, got a contact and we came in behind and below to identify it. It was a Ju 88. I remember feeling surprised because I had got used to being sent to chase bogeys that turned out to be Lancasters! I pulled in close and fired a 3/4-second burst, and it went down east of Vire. We then went after another, but abandoned the chase due to friendly Flak.

"The Mosquito had no vices at all and really felt like a fighter to fly. If it had a fault, it was that it wouldn't slow down fast enough during an intercept. You needed a good operator to warn you to slow up in time. On 1 September we were vectored onto a bogey in the same area. We came up behind him very fast and I had to do a lot of juggling to avoid overshooting. Fortunately it was a very black night or he would have spotted us. I remember sitting right underneath him, putting down some flap to slow me. It was a Ju 188; I could see the pointed wings quite clearly. I finally managed to drop back a bit and shot him into the sea off Le Havre.

"Identification was always a problem. We were on patrol over Le Havre on 26 August when radar called and said that a friendly was being rather unfriendly, and suggested that we did a quick orbit. So we pulled on about 4g and went around. As soon as we straightened up there were a lot of very loud bangs; the starboard engine stopped, and the hatch came open. We flew back to base on the remaining engine with no problems; the Mosquito was brilliant on one. After landing, in addition to the engine damage, we found half a dozen shells in the dinghy, just behind Pete's head! He had been very lucky.

"The offender was a Captain Bennett, flying an American P-61 Black Widow. At the court of enquiry, when asked why he fired at a friendly Mosquito, he said he thought it was a Ju 88. When the prosecuting officer suggested that he should have known that a Ju 88 was much bigger than a Mosquito, he replied 'I guess I thought it was a little Ju 88!' I later heard they promoted him and sent him home."

With the Normandy beachhead established, RAF Bomber Command once more turned its full might against the Third Reich. The effectiveness of the German night fighters over the past months had made it obvious that they had some new means of detecting the British bombers, but so far all attempts to identify it and produce countermeasures had failed. This was hardly surprising. SN-2 worked on a very similar frequency to the latest Freyas, the emissions of which served to disguise the airborne radar, while Flensburg and Naxos Z were passive devices, and thus untraceable.

The breakthrough came on 13 July when a Ju 88G-7 of 7/NJG1 landed at Woodbridge, the pilot quite convinced that he was near Berlin. Its equipment was eagerly examined by British experts and countermeasures immediately put in hand. An active jammer, plus a new size of Window, took care of SN-2. At the same time, Serrate IV was developed to home on it. Severe restrictions were imposed on the use of H_2S, while the simplest countermeasure of all was used against Flensburg. The use of Monica by bombers was forbidden, but Mosquito intruders continued to use it.

The final piece of trickery to emerge was Perfectos. This device triggered the German IFF, and not only provided positive identification, but bearing and range indications also. Its benefits were however mainly indirect, as when its existence was discovered in a crashed Mosquito the German fighters took to keeping their IFF switched off, thereby putting themselves at risk from their own Flak.

These benefits took a little time to enter service, but when they did the effects were dramatic. Attrition due to fighter attack fell to 6. 6 per cent in October, 1. 5 per cent in November, and 0. 7 per cent in December. In this month, the night fighters claimed a mere 66 victories. Their own losses amounted to 114. They were never to recover.

The Luftwaffe was meanwhile giving the British night defenders one last problem. The Fieseler Fi 103, better known as the V1 or "Doodlebug", was a tiny pilotless aircraft. Powered by a pulsejet, it carried a large explosive warhead. The first V1 attacks on England were made on 13 June and over 2,000 had been launched by the end of the month.

Apart from a few jet Meteors, the only aircraft fast enough to catch a Doodlebug with ease was the Tempest day fighter. At night, gaining visual contact presented few problems due to the bright flame from the pulsejet, but judging range was another matter. Given the large warhead, which often exploded when hit with devastating results for the pursuing fighter, this was particularly critical.

An ingenious solution was devised to overcome this problem. A refracting system combined with a graticule was stuck to the inside of the Tempest's windshield, which produced a double image of the jet flame at long range, merging into one at 600ft (183m). The most successful Tempest pilot was Flight Lieutenant Joe Berry, who twice got seven in one night, and ended with a total of over 50.

The advancing Allied armies soon overran the Doodlebug launch sites, and the Luftwaffe resorted to air-launching them. Heinkel He 111s were modified to carry one Doodlebug under the starboard wing, inboard of the engine. They then flew very low over the sea, typically at 200-300ft (60-90m) at a speed of between 120-160mph (193-257kmh) before pulling up briefly to about 1,475ft (450m) to release the weapon before dropping down again to sea level to make good their escape.

The interception of ultra-low flying aircraft had always been a very sporty affair, as they were very difficult to detect on AI, while the possibility of misjudging altitude and ending in the sea was quite high even though very accurate radar altimeters were carried. The best chance was to catch the Heinkels when they pulled up to launch, but this took very fine timing. The Mosquito had too high a stall speed to be really comfortable in this role; the Beaufighter was rather better, but results were still meagre.

One possibility was to use an Airborne Warning and Control System (AWACS) to act as a mobile GCI station on the spot. The hardware already existed in the shape of a Wellington bomber kitted out with black boxes and with a dorsal mounted 360-degree rotating aerial. This aircraft had previously flown the world's first AWACS mission on the night of 19-20 May 1942, off the Norwegian coast, but further development had been protracted, both through technical problems and difficulties in finding a scenario where it could be consistently used.

It was now brought in as a possible answer to the Fi 103-carrying Heinkels, which regularly egressed the Dutch Coast off Den Helder. Operation "Vapour", as it was called, was flown on 14 January 1945. The Wellington, with civilian scientist E. J. Smith handling the black boxes, paraded up and down parallel with the Dutch coast at an altitude of 100ft (30m). A radio beacon enabled a handful of Mosquitos to take station on it in line astern and rather higher, without visual contact. Intelligence predicted a busy night and the stage was set for a turkey shoot.

Smith soon gained a contact and vectored the first Mosquito, flown by Dick Leggett of No 125 Squadron, towards it. Reducing altitude to 100ft (30m), Leggett struggled through darkness and broken cloud until his operator, Egbert Midlane, gained contact. It was flying at 250ft (76m) at a speed of 120mph (193kmh). The Mosquito eventually closed to about 300ft (91m) only to see that the bogey was in fact a Warwick of Coastal Command. The promised swarms of Heinkels failed to show. What could have been a historic addition to night and all-weather fighter capability failed to materialise. For whatever reason, the Heinkels never came again.

One of the outstanding fighters of the war was the German Messerschmitt Me 262 jet. While too fast to operate at night against heavy bombers, it achieved some success against Mosquitos. The first jet night fighter unit was Kommando Stamp, which later became Kommando Welter, and finally 10/NJG11. Its Staffelka-pitän, Oberleutnant Kurt Welter, had previously flown with II/JG302 on Wilde Sau operations. He was now charged with defending Berlin against the fast raiders.

For this, the old Himmelbett system of close ground control was brought back into action. This was necessary as the Me 262 did not at first carry radar. Then a few radar-equipped two-seaters appeared and these shot down at least eight Mosquitos. Welter, whose final score was believed to exceed 50, accounted for at least three of these. Exciting as the new jet night fighter was, it was a case of too little, too late.

The final year of the war saw the German night fighter arm in terminal decline. Operationally constrained by critical fuel shortages, they were hunted through skies that they no longer controlled by the ever present Mosquitos. To survive, they flew across country at very low level. With teutonic galgenhumor they called this "Ritterkreuz height". One pilot developed a technique of arriving over base at 10,000ft (3,050m), then diving steeply at the runway, pulling out hard at low level to mush off excess speed before landing.

The surviving experten were very good by any standards. Heinz-Wolfgang Schnaufer peaked in February, accounting for nine heavy bombers in one 24-hour period. His final score, which was never approached, stood at 121 at war's end.

As the war drew to its inevitable close, the Nachtjagdflieger took one last chance to bite back hard. Intruder operations over England had been halted by order of the Fuhrer in October 1941, and only small nibbles had taken place since. Then on 3 March 1945, Operation "Gisela" was launched. That night, as the bomber stream departed from Germany, 142 Ju 88Gs from NJGs 2, 3, 4, and 5, took off in pursuit. Crossing the North Sea at low level beneath the radar coverage, they caught the British defences napping. In all, the RAF lost 22 bombers and two Mosquitos to this attack. German losses totalled 22 Ju 88Gs, many of them due to running out of fuel on the homeward leg. One further intruder operation was carried out but this was even less successful. "Gisela" was the Luftwaffe's last fling.

7. Far East and Pacific Operations

The intensity of the night air battles over Western Europe was not matched in other theatres. Insofar as Britain and Germany were concerned, this was primarily because the best equipment was reserved initially for home defence, and only later was it made available for the Middle East and Italy, while one German pilot who had flown extensively on the Russian Front commented that night fighting was far more difficult there because the Russians were so backward that they had no radar emissions on which the fighters could home.

The early fumbling attempts of the RAF at providing an effective night defence in autumn 1940, had been witnessed by a team of observers from the United States Army Air Corps (USAAC). They were not terribly impressed, to put it mildly, by the ad hoc night fighters then in service (it should be remembered that the first Beaufighters were only then arriving at the squadrons). On their return to the USA they determined that a purpose-designed aircraft, equipped with AI radar, was essential for this very specialised role.

A specification was sent out to the manufacturers in October 1940, proposals were received on the final day of the year, and the contender from Northrop was selected on 11 January 1941, with an order for two prototypes. These duly emerged as the XP-61 Black Widow, the first of which made its maiden flight on 26 May 1942. The appearance of the Black Widow was strange, to say the least, rather like the proverbial horse designed by a committee which emerged as a camel! It was huge, dimensionally almost the same as the B-25 Mitchell medium bomber, and heavier than a fully loaded Heinkel He 111H. The nose had been left free to accommodate the AI radar; the main armament of four 20mm cannon was housed in a ventral bulge. The radar operator was seated in tandem behind the pilot in a stepped cockpit, while above and behind him was a remotely controlled and sighted dorsal turret with a 360-degree arc of fire, in which were mounted four 0.50in Browning heavy machine guns. The turret could also be locked in position and used as part of the fixed forward-firing armament.

The gunner was seated at the rear of the truncated fuselage, which in addition to the normal transparencies, ended in a large blown perspex cone. This gave the gunner an unprecedentedly good view to the vulnerable area behind and below, as well as sideways over the wings. To permit this arrangement the tail surfaces were carried on twin booms extending aft of the very powerful Pratt & Whitney Double Wasp radial engines.

Painted gloss black, the XP-61 looked imposing as it flew over Los Angeles during its flight test programme, so much so that an illustrator who saw it was sufficiently impressed to draw it in one of his comic strips. He was quickly visited by the "heavy mob", who were rather interested in why he was publicising a top secret fighter in this manner. (The author lived close to a Canadian army camp which was a fruitful source of American comics for the local schoolboys. He clearly remembers seeing the P-61 illustrated in this way; the Grumman Skyrocket was another aircraft to receive the same treatment.)

Development problems were encountered with the Black Widow. Among other things the turret disturbed the airflow when it was rotated, causing unacceptable buffeting to the tail surfaces, and was deleted after the first 37 production aircraft had been built. With hindsight, it seems more likely that troubles were encountered with the operation of the turret itself, because it was reinstated on the P-61B, which had no noticeable changes to the tail surfaces.

The entry of the USA and Japan into the war in December 1941 predated the operational debut of the Black Widow by 30 months. The Americans, like the British and Germans before them, were forced to use a variety of makeshifts during this time, including catseye fighters, searchlight co-operation, and converted light bombers.

Early night operations in the Far East and Pacific theatre differed from those in Western Europe quite considerably. First, bomber operations were tactical rather than strategic; the American homeland was never bombed, while night raids on Japan did not commence until 1944. Secondly, the numbers involved were relatively small. Thirdly, virtually all operations took place in what we might term undeveloped areas, like the Burma/Chinese border, Papua New Guinea, and the Pacific Islands, which precluded the setting up of permanent GCI systems. Finally, as much of the war involved control of the ocean itself, naval air power assumed at least equal and often greater importance to land-based air power.

In effect, this meant that worthwhile targets for night bombing raids were few in number, making it easier to place catseye fighters in position to intercept. This was the case with an action fought on the night of 29 July 1942.

The USAAF's 75th Fighter Squadron (FS), until the previous month part of General Chennault's "Flying Tigers", was based at Hengyang in China, which was frequently raided at night by the Japanese. Its Curtiss P-40Es were not equipped for night flying, but with a near-full moon due, the 75th decided to try and intercept. The only problem was whether the Chinese hill-watchers would be able to give them enough warning to enable them to climb high enough in time.

The warning duly came and a handful of P-40Es, led by Major John Alison, took off and raced for altitude. To reduce the chance of a mid-air collision, they climbed in a wide left hand spiral. As Alison reached 10,000ft (3,048m), Japanese jamming drowned out the radio messages from the ground. This was not a hopeful start.

At 12,000ft (3,657m), Alison levelled out and commenced to circle base. As he did so, a brief break in the jamming enabled him to hear that three bandits were approaching the field from the south. Scanning the sky below, he was unable to see them, but then he glanced upwards to see first six sets of exhaust flames, then three Mitsubishi Ki-21 bombers, almost immediately above.

Climbing to their altitude, he took station just outside the port side bomber, with the moon on the far side of them, only to be left floundering as the small formation swung hard starboard. Following the bombers through a full 180-degree turn, Alison again took station on the port side bomber and closed for the kill. This was a mistake, as now the moon was on the wrong side. He was sighted by an alert gunner on the far side of the Vic, who opened an accurate fire on him. Ignoring the hits, Alison let fly at the bomber ahead, which veered away, streaming smoke.

At this point Captain Albert Baumler came up fast from below and dropped in behind the stricken bomber, so Alison turned his attention to the aircraft with the troublesome gunner. A long burst, and a fuel tank in its wing erupted into yellow flame. As it went down burning, into the night, Alison eased his badly damaged fighter in behind the lead bomber, scoring hits on the starboard wing root. This aircraft too caught fire and rolled away out of control.

As Alison spiralled back down to the airstrip, his engine cut, then started to pour flame. With no other alternative open, he force landed in the Siang river, just avoiding a bridge in the attempt, and swam to safety.

In many ways, this was a classic catseye interception. Conditions were clear and the moon was bright enough to allow the bombers to fly in formation, and which of course they also needed to find their target. Alison attempted to use the moon to his advantage, but this was foiled by the bombers' change of course, and was then silhouetted in his turn. The combat then turned into a slugging match, both sides shooting it out, with the heavier firepower of the fighter giving it the advantage. The Japanese lost all three bombers; the 75th lost a single P-40E, although this was salvaged for spares after recovery from the river.

The first AI-equipped American night fighter was the P-70 Nighthawk which, like the Havoc in RAF service, was an adapted Douglas DB-7 light bomber. Entering service with the US Army Air Force (USAAF) – as the USAAC had since become – in April 1942, the Nighthawk was fitted with SCR-540, the US version of AI Mk IV. Like the Havoc, the Nighthawk was found lacking in speed, rate of climb and altitude capability, although with four 20mm cannon in a ventral tray it was more heavily armed. Many P-70s were used only for training.

Two six-aircraft detachments from US 6th Night Fighter Squadron (NFS) were however deployed to the Pacific in the spring of 1943: one to New Guinea, and the other to Guadalcanal. The night threat at this time was harassing raids by single aircraft, known collectively as "Washing Machine Charlie" from the sound of their engines. One of these, a Mitsubishi G4M bomber was shot down by a P-70 flown by Captain Earl Bennett with radar operator Corporal Edwin Tomlinson, on 19 April, for the first USAAF radar night fighter victory. This notwithstanding, victories were few and far between for the Nighthawk, mainly because its maximum patrol altitude was only 26,000ft (7,924m), and the raiders often flew higher than this.

To provide a higher altitude capability, both detachments took on charge a few Lockheed P-38 Lightnings. Those operating from Guadalcanal were used in conjunction with searchlights, with a modest amount of success, but the New Guinea detachment converted two P-38Gs in the field into two-seaters equipped with SCR-540 AI radar. Unfortunately these achieved nothing.

The USMC at first employed a night fighter converted from a light bomber that was just as unsuitable as the DB-7, the Lockheed PV-1 Ventura fitted with SCR-540. The only unit to see action with the night Ventura was VMF(N)-531, which deployed to the Solomon Islands in September 1943. To offset the inadequate performance of the PV-1, standard procedure was to patrol at maximum altitude in the target area. When GCI detected a bogey, the Ventura would be vectored directly towards it, then turned in astern, trading altitude for speed. Hopefully the AI operator would then gain contact and complete the interception. Remarkably this method resulted in 12 victories in five months, although it should be noted that just two pilots accounted for two-thirds of the total.

An interesting aside at this time was that whereas both British and Germans hesitated to use Window for some considerable time, the Japanese simply went ahead and used it. "Giman-shi", as it was called, was first used to jam American gun control radars during the Battle of the Solomon Islands in May 1943, thus predating the Hamburg raid in July of that year.

Whereas AI radar had typically been carried in large multi-seat aircraft, the USN now decided to acquire a single-seat night fighter. It could hardly be otherwise, given that it would have to operate from the limited accommodation provided by an aircraft carrier. Their initial choice fell upon Chance Vought's F4U Corsair.

The AI radar was designated AIA, neatly packaged in a pod installed on the leading edge of the starboard wing, where it displaced the outer machine gun. A neat feature of the radar was that by reducing scan width from 100 degrees in search mode to 15 degrees for attack, sufficient accuracy could theoretically be obtained to allow firing at an unseen target from up to 3,000ft (914m) away. For this, a continuous picture was fed to a CRT in the gunsight, the length of a horizontal bar extending on either side of the target blip indicating range.

In its early days, the Corsair suffered from "bounce" on landing and was therefore declared unsuitable for carrier use. Because of this, the first Corsair night fighter squadron, VF(N)-75, was deployed to Munda, in New Georgia, commencing operations in October 1943.

The fact was that Japanese night activity in the Pacific Theatre of Operations was on a very small scale, and this did not give the American GCI controllers sufficient practice to bring them to a high state of proficiency. The pilots of VF(N)-75 suffered considerably from this failing by missing interceptions, and it was not until the last night of October that Lieutenant Hugh O'Neill caught a G4M off Vella Lavella for the first USN night victory, thereby just beating the USMC Ventura outfit to the punch. The big fighter had just one problem: its high speed made it prone to overshooting its target. The answer was to come in low from astern, then bleed off the excess speed in a climb.

Operating from an aircraft carrier is a world away from flying from a fixed base on land. And carrier night flying is even more difficult. Back in 1943, some circles considered it a new experiment in suicide. To quote an American mess steward of the era: "Man was never made to fly, nohow. And if he was made to fly, he wasn't made to fly off a ship. And if he was made to fly off a ship, he sure wasn't made to do it at night!"

Carrier aircraft took off, sought a target somewhere out over the featureless ocean, then returned to their ship which was anywhere within 60 miles (97km) or more from where they had left it. There were no navigational landmarks out there; only the compass and a radio homing device which worked some of the time. This was difficult enough by day, but at night...

A certain amount of doubt existed whether a carrier night defence capability was worthwhile. It was considered that co-ordinated strikes against a task force would be very difficult to carry out at night, and that threats of this nature were best dealt with by radar-laid AA. Also a dedicated night fighter unit would occupy deck and hangar space far more usefully occupied by daytime fliers. A further consideration was that at sea losses were not easily replaced. All these factors combined to reduce daylight defensive and striking power, while increasing the load on an already hard worked crew.

On the other hand, there were plenty of islands to be retaken, which might require night operations, while in daylight, Japanese reconnaissance aircraft shadowing the fleet at the limit of visibility had proved amazingly elusive in cloudy conditions. AI-equipped fighters might well be the answer to these.

A tentative start was made late in 1943. The Grumman F6F Hellcat made its operational debut in August of that year. Then on 20 November, 16 G4M2s attacked Task Group 50.3 just after dusk, badly damaging the light carrier USS *Independence*. The need for night fighters to provide an outer defensive ring was thus confirmed. Following nights saw further raids, and an ad hoc force was put together to counter them.

On the night of 26 November, Lieutenant-Commander Butch O'Hare, commanding Carrier Air Group 6, led a section of F6F Hellcats from USS *Enterprise* off the deck to intercept a large inbound raid. Vectored towards the bombers by radar, the three F6Fs broke up and dispersed the Japanese force, shooting down two bombers in the process.

On the following night an even bolder experiment was tried. TBF-1C Avengers carried air-to-surface vessel (ASV) search radar, which at a pinch could also detect aircraft. The idea was that the Avenger would lead the fighters into position to attack the bombers. Like so many other good ideas, the execution of this plan left something to be desired.

Two Hellcats piloted by O'Hare and Ensign Warren Skon of VF-2 were catapulted off at about 1800 hours and were immediately vectored after bogies, but found nothing in the gathering gloom. After an hour of fruitless searching, they tried to set up a rendezvous with an Avenger of VT-6, flown by Lieutenant-Commander Phillips. The Avenger was otherwise engaged and its operator had meanwhile found a G4M and steered his pilot towards it. After making visual contact, Phillips shot it down in flames with his two front guns to record the USN's first carrier radar night fighter victory of the war. This was not quite what had been intended.

O'Hare called the torpedo bomber once more, requesting that it turn on its red station-keeping light so that the Hellcats could join up with it. Back came the reply that Phillips had latched onto yet another G4M. He flashed the red light briefly, calmly shot down his second bomber of the evening, then switched it on again.

The two Hellcats joined up, O'Hare taking the starboard position while the Avenger was in a turn to port. As they did so, the Avenger's gunner opened fire and Skon saw tracers apparently passing between him and O'Hare. A few seconds afterwards, O'Hare slid out of formation. Skon assumed that he was making an attack run on something and tried to follow, but quickly lost contact. O'Hare was never seen again and what actually happened remains a mystery. It is possible that a Japanese aircraft was involved, but if so neither Skon nor the Avenger crew saw it.

On 4 December USS *Lexington* was badly damaged in yet another night attack. As a temporary measure, the fleet carriers trained more "Bat Teams" of one ASV-equipped Avenger and two Hellcats, but these were quickly superseded by AIA-equipped single-seaters.

The Corsair had by now undergone modifications to its oleos which cured the tendency to bounce, and radar-equipped F4U-2Ns became the first true carrier night fighters when a four-aircraft detachment from VF(N)-101, a squadron formed using a nucleus of personnel from VF(N)-75, embarked on USS *Enterprise* in January 1944. A detachment was used rather than a full squadron for reasons stated previously. A second detachment from this unit reached USS *Intrepid* shortly after, while during February AIA-equipped F6F-3E Hellcats entered service, and detachments of these from VF(N)-76 were deployed on USSs *Yorktown* and *Bunker Hill*.

Experience in low level night operations was still lacking and on the night of 18 February half a dozen Nakajima B5Ns evaded the attentions of an F6F-3E from *Yorktown* and torpedoed *Intrepid*, damaging it so badly that it had to be withdrawn for repairs. With three carriers now out of the fray, it was obvious that the night threat needed far more effective measures to counter it. The idea of a complete carrier night air group now took hold.

The AIA radar was further developed to become APS-6 which was fitted to F4U-2N Corsairs and F6F-3N and -5N Hellcats, which were also equipped with APS-13 tail warning radar which covered an angle of 60 degrees out to 2,400ft (731m). The USN was reluctant to commit a fleet carrier for night operations and *Intrepid*, refitting at Pearl Harbor, was selected to carry Night Air Group (NAG)-41. This comprised VT(N)-79 with nine Avengers, and VF(N)-79 with 14 Hellcats. NAG-41 embarked during August and the first missions were flown in September. These were pre-invasion strikes in the Philippines, flown mainly by day because the Task Group commanders were reluctant to deprive themselves of the extra striking power. The radar pods were removed for operations over Japanese-held territory.

The first night victory for NAG-41 was scored by Lieutenant Bill Henry on 12 September when he detected a bogey at 21,000ft (6,400m) range. Closing, he identified it as a Mitsubishi Ki-46 which disintegrated under a hail of 0.50in bullets when he opened fire.

October saw NAG-41 Hellcats account for a further 10 raiders around Formosa and Luzon, plus two day victories. By the end of January, when NAG-41's five-month tour finished, it had accounted for 46 Japanese aircraft, the majority in darkness. The Night Air Group concept was proving itself and two more were formed, NAG-90 aboard *Enterprise* in January 1945, and NAG-53 aboard *Saratoga* the following month. These were, however, short-lived. *Saratoga* was badly damaged by Kamikazes on 5 February, as was *Enterprise* on 14 May, and thereafter carrier night air defence mainly reverted to detachments on fleet carriers.

In the crowded skies of Western Europe, where friend and foe were often inextricably intermingled, visual identification was an absolute requirement at all times. In the Pacific, things were different, particularly in fleet actions. Anything coming in over the search radar horizon was almost certainly hostile, while numbers were far less, allowing Fighter Direction Officers on the carriers to keep track of the situation more easily. To improve matters still more, a reliable IFF for the American night fighters became available from the summer of 1944 and this, combined with the blind firing features of APS-6, allowed attacks to be made without visual identification.

Its teething troubles over, the P-61A Black Widow finally reached the USAAF night fighter squadrons in the summer of 1944. Prior to this, units based in North Africa and Italy had had to swallow their pride and operate British Beaufighters and in one case, Mosquitos. In the Pacific they were only too glad to relinquish their inadequate Nighthawks in favour of the new fighter. The first unit in this theatre to see action was the 6th NFS, which sent a detachment to Saipan in the Marianas in June, notching up their first victories on the night of 6-7 July when they accounted for two G4Ms.

While generally effective against Japanese bombers, the Black Widow lacked speed and altitude performance and was not very manoeuvrable, although as we saw in the previous chapter, it could easily follow a cruising Mosquito through a 4g turn. But when the Japanese (like the Germans before them) began to use high speed fighter-bombers, the P-61A was rarely able to catch them. The 421st NFS, based at Leyte in the Phillipines, was replaced by a USMC Night Hellcat squadron in December 1944 for this reason.

It was not all bad news for the P-61; on 29 December 1944, Major Carroll Smith, commanding the 418th NFS based at Mindoro in the Philippines, accounted for no less than four Japanese aircraft, including one Nakajima Ki-84 "Hayate", a single-engined fighter generally considered too fast to be caught by the P-61.

Another factor was that while excellent for night patrol and intruder work, the Black Widow might also have to operate in the transition periods at dawn and dusk, or in daylight under conditions too bad for orthodox day fighters to be effective. At these times a considerable possibility existed of encountering a Japanese fighter or fighter-bomber under good visual conditions, when the Black Widow would be at a tremendous disadvantage.

A few P-38s fitted with APS-4(AIA) were used to offset this, but while these were fairly effective on intruder missions, the workload was far too high for defensive operations. A two-seater variant, the P-38M, was ordered, but entered service too late to see action. This was a pointer to the future. A dedicated night fighter of the period was unparalled in the purely defensive night role, but against fast fighter-bombers, or encountering fast agile fighters by day, it was inadequate. Whatever the disadvantages of the AI-equipped single-seaters, they were fast enough and agile enough to hold their own in visual conditions. But at this time the true all-weather fighter was still many years away.

The Japanese had been slow in introducing AI radar, although the means were to hand from quite early on. By 1944, ASV radar was carried by several types of Imperial Japanese Navy (IJN) aircraft, which accounted for the increasing accent on night attacks against the US Task Forces in that year. But well before this, the need for night fighters had been evident.

Like everyone else, the Japanese had made no provision for a specialised night fighter and were forced to use what was to hand. Catseye patrols were used on an ad hoc basis, with little success, while searchlight co-operation was virtually unknown. Then when in the first months of 1943 USAAF B-17 Fortresses and B-24 Liberators roamed the night skies above Japanese-held airfields in New Guinea almost unopposed, a sense of urgency was at last kindled.

As with other services, there was little choice. Nakajima's J1N1 "Gekko" was twin-engined and carried a crew of three. It had a reasonable turn of speed, an adequate ceiling, and a respectable rate of climb. More importantly it was already in service with the IJN, albeit as a reconnaissance aircraft, and based in the right area.

To adapt "Gekko" for the night defence mission, Commander Yasuna Kozono of 251 Air Corps based at Rabaul, devised (or more correctly, reinvented) a novel form of armament. This was a pair of fixed 20mm Type 99 cannon mounted amidships to fire upwards at an angle of 30 degrees. Presumably aware that upward firing cannon could possibly bring the bomber crashing down into its opponent, he added a second pair of cannon, also mounted amidships, to fire downwards at much the same angle. These would allow the "Gekko" to overtake the bomber from above, raking it as it went.

Two J1N1-Cs were returned to Japan for conversion in March 1943, where the IJN recognised their potential and began work on a dedicated night fighter variant. Returned to Rabaul in May, the two modified aircraft were soon in action, shooting down three four-engined bombers on two successive nights with their unorthodox armament. This incidentally predated the operational debut of the German "Schräge Musik" by three months, though not of course the upward-firing concept. Further victories followed and by August the J1N1-S night fighter variant was in full production. In the modified aircraft the gunner had been retained to change the ammunition drums of the cannon. In the J1N1-S, the guns were belt-fed, and the crew was reduced to two.

The "Gekko" equivalent in Japanese Army Air Force service was Kawasaki's Ki-45 "Toryu", which had also been designed as a long range day fighter. A night fighter variant was mooted at the same time and for the same reasons as "Gekko", but it became operational slightly later.

Rather faster, and with better altitude performance than "Gekko", night fighter Ki-45 "Kai-Cs" had their original forward firing armament deleted in favour of a single 37mm Ho 23 cannon. While one hit from a 37mm shell was normally enough to destroy a bomber, getting this one hit was not easy. Its rate of fire was a mere two shells per second (the German 30mm MK 108 could manage 11), while its low muzzle velocity gave a maximum effective range of little more than 600ft (183m); not that this mattered too much at night. This armament was augmented by two upward-firing 20mm cannon located just aft of the cockpit.

The later Ki-45 "Kai-D" mounted two 37mm weapons, coupled with two upward-firing 12.7mm heavy machine guns. One aircraft was experimentally fitted with a 75mm cannon, but reportedly its tail assembly failed during firing tests.

For the Japanese, the night air war changed in character on 15 June 1944 when 57 Boeing B-29s bombed a steelworks at Yawata, on Kyushu, the southernmost of the Japanese home islands. This was the first of many such raids.

The B-29 posed unusual problems for the night fighters. It flew high, typically at about 30,000ft (9,144m), and its speed in the target area was of the order of 260mph (419kmh). This combination made it difficult to intercept. Then even when (or more usually if) the fighter managed to scramble into position, the big bombers were defended by an unprecedented battery of remotely controlled guns, with not a single blind spot of which the night fighters could take advantage.

When late in 1944, bases in the Marianas became available, the bombing of Japan became much more intense, culminating on the night of 9-10 March 1945 when 334 B-29s raided Tokyo with napalm and incendiaries from less than 10,000ft (3,048m). So impotent were the Japanese night fighters at this time that they failed to make a single interception. The only B-29 losses were to AA fire, and even they were few.

The Japanese delay in developing AI radar and an effective system of GCI was now proving fatal, while even their ground-to-air communications were in chaos. A German Li had reached Japan by submarine in 1943, but it does not seem to have been developed further. The Japanese Army produced their E-1 set for the "Toryu", which operated on a wavelength of about 11cm, while the IJN introduced their own AI radar for the "Gekko", but neither reached service in any quantity before mid-1945.

Even with AI, the Japanese fighters scored few successes and these tended to be on clear nights in catseye conditions. Neither the "Gekko" nor the "Toryu" was really fast enough to be effective against the B-29, and various last ditch attempts were made to introduce a higher performance night fighter. Kawasaki developed the Ki-96 heavy fighter back in 1943, but indecision on the part of the High Command delayed progress. Eventually it was refined into the Ki-102, a fast two-seater with E-1 radar, armed with two forward firing 30mm Ho-105 cannon, and two slanting 20mm Ho-5s. But by the time that it was ready for production, the Japanese aircraft industry was rapidly being destroyed and it never entered service.

Other makeshift night fighters included the Mitsubishi J2M5 "Raiden", a single-engined single-seater used in the catseye role during the final months of the war, adapted to carry a single oblique 20mm cannon behind the cockpit; the Aichi D4Y "Suisei" adapted from a single-engined dive bomber and, perhaps the best of all, Kawanishi's rehash of Nakajima's P1Y1 "Ginga" bomber, the P1Y1-S "Kyokko", the nearest European equivalent to which was the Ju 88. It carried a radar derived from a proven ASV installation. But only a handful of "Kyokkos" saw action.

The war ended with a signal from Commander-in-Chief Fifth Fleet to Fifth Fleet Pacific: "THE WAR WITH JAPAN WILL END AT 12.00 ON 15TH AUGUST. IT IS LIKELY THAT KAMIKAZES WILL ATTACK THE

FLEET AFTER THIS TIME AS A FINAL FLING. ANY EX-ENEMY AIR-CRAFT ATTACKING THE FLEET IS TO BE SHOT DOWN IN A FRIENDLY MANNER." No doubt the American night fighters complied!

The night actions in the Pacific demonstrated some important lessons. Single-seat fighters could operate effectively at night using radar, and they could operate equally effectively from aircraft carriers without incurring prohibitive attrition. To neglect night defence, as Japan had done, was to risk paying a terrible price. Finally, the need for night fighters to be able to operate equally effectively by day, in visual conditions, had been emphasised. The signpost leading to the true all-weather fighter was quite clear, even at this stage.

8. The Road to Korea

The immediate postwar period was a time of taking stock and of assimilating the lessons learned. The most intensive night fighting had taken place over Western Europe, and conditions in this theatre had therefore been unlike those anywhere else. In the early days, catseye fighters operating in conjunction with searchlights had appeared to offer the greatest hope of intercepting bombers at night, and this method was widely used by both the RAF and the Luftwaffe. In the event, it was not to be; searchlight co-operation never came near to achieving anything like the attrition levels necessary to make night bombing prohibitively costly, even though later in the war searchlights became effective to well over 20,000ft (6,096m).

What quickly became apparent was that, as RAF Fighter Command had foreseen from the mid-1930s, there was no substitute for a specialist radar-equipped night fighter, operating under the control of an effective GCI system. This was borne out not only by the poor results achieved by the catseye fighters, but by the almost total failure of schemes like LAM and Turbinlite Havocs.

The importance of an effective GCI system had been amply proven at an early stage, and later events simply underlined this. Although not very effective at first, RAF night fighters had been rapidly gaining the ascendancy when the Blitz was wound down in May 1941.

Defensive action in any form of warfare has necessarily to be a response to a threat, and GCI was at its most effective when it was tailored to a particular pattern of raiding. This had been particularly true of the German Himmelbett system, which was designed to intercept RAF bombers flying singly to a variety of targets over a wide area. The introduction of the bomber stream in 1942 rendered it relatively impotent almost overnight, and new means had to be sought.

RAF raids on German targets prior to the late spring of 1942 were in the main ineffective. The bombers, scattered widely in time and space, attacked a number of targets on any given night. Far too many bombs were dropped more than five miles (8km) from their targets, and even when the bombing was accurate, little damage was caused. As the Luftwaffe had convincingly demonstrated against Coventry in the autumn of 1940, bombing could only be really effective if it was concentrated.

The RAF bomber stream, led by picked crews, was introduced primarily to concentrate the bombing in time and space, with the secondary intention of swamping the ground defences over the target. It also had the effect of swamping the rigid Himmelbett system, and thus ensuring that only a small proportion of the night fighters available could make contact. The Luftwaffe defenders were thus forced to become far more flexible.

The strengths of the bomber stream were in certain respects its weaknesses. By concentrating the bombers in time and space, it provided a target-rich environment for those fighters which managed to make contact, and the more able German pilots were sometimes able to notch up multiple victories as a result. Even the concentrated bombing afforded by the bomber stream was turned to advantage by the Luftwaffe. In conjunction with searchlights it created a large illuminated area in which catseye fighters could operate, and over which the bombers were forced to fly, although it must be said that this was unavoidable.

Flexibility was also essential where electronic warfare was concerned. Every method employed would in time be countered, and this area of the night air war turned into a race, the advantage going first to one side, then to the other. The RAF maintained a lead in technology throughout the war, but often this was not enough. For example, H2S and Monica were great ideas in theory, but they were misused, allowing the Luftwaffe to take advantage of them by using homing devices. The lesson here was that it is very difficult to use highly sensitive equipment over enemy territory without it being discovered and compromised, often very quickly.

Certain things were completely unpredictable. The use of Window was calculated to give an advantage for far longer than actually was the case. Who could possibly have expected that the Luftwaffe had developed a new AI radar with a longer wavelength than Lichtenstein? Allied research had concentrated on shorter wavelengths with higher frequencies, and it was only logical to think that the Germans would do the same. SN-2, coupled with passive homing devices such as Flensburg, enabled the night fighters to resume a high level of effectiveness far sooner than could reasonably have been anticipated.

Once the Luftwaffe night fighters had made contact with the bomber stream, little more could be done. The bombers had to look out for themselves. On the other hand, quite a lot could be done to prevent them making contact in the first place. There were two basic methods, the first of which was to sow confusion in the GCI system by using jamming screens to conceal the approach of the bomber stream. Then, when this was no longer valid, spoof raids were mounted and combined with radical changes of course by the main force.

These measures were often sufficient to mislead the German controllers, who were forced to guess at the eventual target and the course of the bomber stream to it. If they guessed wrongly, the night fighters would be ordered to assemble in the wrong place and would either not make contact at all, or perhaps only catch a few stragglers after a long chase, while distracted by having to keep a wary eye on the fuel gauge.

The second basic method was to exploit one of the weakest links in the Luftwaffe's defensive chain. Unless the fighters were directed accurately, they would be left floundering in the night sky, searching at random. To attain this, the Luftwaffe ground to air communications system was subjected to an intensive campaign of jamming, increasing in intensity until the end of the war.

While the combination of communications jamming, Window, feints and other expedients reduced the effectiveness of the night fighters by a tremendous amount during the final months of the war, it failed to prevent a handful of very

Above: Convair's F-102A Delta Dagger was the first semi-automated interceptor. Here it shows the long internal weapons bay and the unsightly yellow canary fairings. (GD)

Below: The F-106A Delta Dart is superficially similar to the F-102A, but close examination reveals many differences. The matt black screen down the centreline of the V-shaped windshield is clearly visible. (GD)

Below: The Pakistan Air Force used the Mirage IIIC at night in the 1971 war against India, with little success. (PAF)

Left: The MiG-21 has been used operationally at night by both India and North Vietnam, relying on close ground control to offset the limitations of the on-board radar. (HAL)

Right: Having for years insisted that a night and all-weather fighter had to be a two-seater, the RAF finally adopted the English Electric Lightning, with its AI 23 monopulse radar and two Red Top missiles. (MoD)

Left: The McDonnell F-101B Voodoo was used by USAF Air Defence Command to supplement the F-106A. The Canadian Armed Forces also found it useful for long range patrolling. (FlyPast)

Right: To provide greater all-weather capability, l'Armée de l'Air experimented with a two-seater powered by a single Pratt & Whitney TF30, the Mirage F2, the prototype of which is seen here. It was not adopted. (Dassault)

Bottom left: The McDonnell Douglas Phantom II, with its long range radar and up to eight on-board missiles, was the first true all-weather fighter to be able to take on agile lightweights in daylight and win. This is the F-4E. (McDonnell Douglas)

Right: Dassault's Mirage F1C was a more affordable single-seater scaled down from the Mirage F2. (Dassault)

Left: Tupolev's mighty Tu-28, also sometimes known as the Tu-128, is seen here with two huge AA-5 "Ash" missiles. The purpose of the ventral bulge is unknown, but is believed to house some form of radar giving all-round coverage. (via Salamander)

Right: The fastest interceptor ever to enter service was Mikoyan's MiG-25 "Foxbat", seen here with afterburners lit, making an enormous infra-red target. (AirForces Monthly)

Left: A Sukhoi Su-15 "Flagon-F" over the Baltic, armed with two AA-3 "Anabs" and two AA-8 "Aphids". This type is notorious for the shooting down of two Korean airliners. (Swedish Air Force)

Right: The fastest and longest ranged interceptor of all would have been the Lockheed YF-12A which was designed for speeds of up to Mach 3, but it never got past the trials stage. (Lockheed)

Left: Although the B-70 Valkyrie failed to enter service, the Mach 2-capable Convair B-58A Hustler posed a difficult challenge to the Soviet air defences. (GD)

Left: The numerically most important Soviet tactical all-weather fighter was for many years the Mikoyan MiG-23, seen here over the Baltic. (Swedish Air Force)

Left: Although the design is over 20 years old, Grumman's F-14 Tomcat still retains an unparalleled long range kill capability with its combination of AWG-9 weapons control system and AIM-54C missiles. (Grumman)

Left: The Tomcat rear cockpit, dominated by the circular tactical information display with the detail data display above it and multiple display indicator to the right. (Hughes)

Right: AWG-9 contains a lot of black boxes. In the left foreground is the IRST sensor, for long a feature of the Tomcat. (Hughes)

Below: Two F-15C Eagles of the Bitburg-based 36th TFW patrol over the broken land-scape of western Germany. In the Beka'a action of 1982 and the Gulf War of 1991, the Eagle proved itself an unsurpassed fighter by day and by night, in fair weather and foul. (McDonnell Douglas)

Left: With its plethora of dials, the instrument panel of the F-15 is the last of the dinosaurs. The radar B-scope is crammed into the top left-hand corner, while targetting information is displayed on the HUD. (McDonnell Douglas)

Left: In modern fighters, air combat information is displayed on the HUD in alpha-numeric format. (Northrop)

Left: The F-16A Fighting Falcon was developed as an austere agile fighter, then criticised for lack of all-weather capability. That it has been improved is demonstrated by this dramatic shot of a night Sparrow launch. (GD)

Right: Four F/A-18C Hornets of VFA-15 Valions in formation above broken cloud. Given the range and capabilities of modern radars and missiles, a traditional day fighter would fare badly playing hide and seek around a cloudscape such as this. (McDonnell Douglas)

Below: The Hughes APG-65 radar was arguably the most capable and flexible of its era. Its black boxes are pull-out modules which can be replaced in minutes, even with ease by groundcrew wearing arctic gloves. (Hughes)

Above: Tornado F3 is a dedicated interceptor designed to operate autonomously far out over the North Sea, in all weathers, and in the face of intensive ECM. (BAe)

Left: Tornado rear cockpit showing three displays. As with the Tomcat, the Tornado backseater acts as a battle manager. (Panavia)

Below: Seen here armed with two Matra Super 530Ds and two R550 Magic 2 missiles, the tail-less delta Mirage 2000C is a very capable interceptor, especially against high and fast intruders. (Dassault)

Above: The RDY radar in the latest Mirage 2000 is seen here demonstrating the steerability of its antenna. (Thomson-CSF)

Right: The Mirage 2000-5 has a "glass cockpit", with no less than four multi-function displays plus a wide angle HUD. Of particular interest is the "look-level" display just beneath the HUD. (Dassault)

Below: The MiG-15 was used at night in Korea. Working with GCI and searchlights, it achieved some success against USAF bombers but proved vulnerable to the radar-equipped F3D. (FlyPast)

Left: The MiG-29 "Fulcrum" was the first of the new generation of Russian fighters using an advanced combination of radar and infra-red detection and tracking. (AirForces Monthly)

Right: The MiG-31 "Foxhound" combines "Zaslon", the first phased radar to be fitted to a fighter, with four AA-9 "Amos" long range missiles and four underwing AA-12s. (AirForces Monthly)

Left: Planar array antenna of the "Zhuk" radar fitted to the MiG-29, showing the IFF dipoles.

Left: The Vympel AA-12 "Amraamski" is a launch-and-leave weapon which adds even greater capability to the MiG-29S seen here.

Right: In the Gulf War of 1991, the Iraqi air defences proved incapable of detecting the angular Lockheed F-117A. Low observable technology poses a whole new problem for the defending fighters. (Lockheed)

Left: The latest "Flanker" derivative is the canarded Su-35. The huge radome and IRST seeker just in front of the cockpit, dominate from this angle.

Left: As technology gets more complex, so costs increase. Saab's JAS39 Gripen is a worthy attempt to squeeze a lot of capability into a small and affordable aircraft. (Saab-Scania)

Left: Eurofighter 2000, seen here in mockup form, is to be the future fighter aircraft for Britain, Germany, Italy and Spain. (Alenia)

Right: Rafale M is catapulted from the deck of the aircraft carrier *Foch* during trials in April 1993. Rafale M is a single-seater for l'Aéronavale, while l'Armée de l'Air Rafales will be two-seaters. (Dassault)

Right: The Northrop/McDonnell Douglas YF-23 was the losing contender in the USAF's advanced tactical fighter contest. Stealth was obviously one of the main considerations at the design stage. (McDonnell Douglas)

Above: Combining speed, stealth and agility, the Lockheed/Boeing F-22A is to replace the F-15 at some future date. It is the ultimate fighter for the foreseeable future. (Lockheed)

Right: One final question remains: how would the ultimate fighter fare against what appears at the moment to be the ultimate bomber, the Northrop B-2A? (Vought)

experienced flyers from adding significantly to their scores. Providing the bomber stream could be located, ranking experte Heinz-Wolfgang Schnaufer specialised in heading for where the jamming was heaviest, there to search visually. How effective this could be was demonstrated during a 24-hour period in February 1945 when, with the jamming campaign at its height, he brought down no less than nine heavy bombers. The dual lesson here was that while ECM was invaluable, it could never be guaranteed to provide complete immunity and, while offering local concealment, served as a positive indicator that something was around which might repay closer investigation.

At the end of the war it was found that the Luftwaffe had finally developed centimetric AI radar, with many sets powered by magnetrons taken from shot-down British bombers (machined from a solid block of copper, the magnetron was notoriously hard to destroy), plus a communications system that would have been very hard to jam. Had these devices become available in quantity six months earlier, the pendulum might well have swung in the other direction for a while. No technological lead is ever certain for any length of time. In the event, it was a case of too little, too late, for the Luftwaffe.

High speed raiders posed a difficult problem for both sides. At home, Mosquito night fighters were sometimes but not always able to catch the fast FW 190 and Me 410 fighter-bombers; while in the other direction, Mosquito bombers ranged the length and breadth of Germany, challenged only by the few He 219s and even fewer Me 262 jets. The Bf 110s, Do 217s and Ju 88s, bristling with drag-inducing aerials and laden with black boxes, "Schräge Musik", and extra fuel, had little enough margin of speed over a cruising four-engined bomber, let alone anything faster.

Once the night fighters had penetrated the bomber stream, they could fly along with it, gradually overhauling and attacking the heavies one by one. It is an interesting point that had the RAF traded bomb load for fuel and adopted a higher cruising speed, the work of the Nachtjagdflieger would have been made far more difficult. Less time would have been available for them to reach the bomber stream, while once there, interceptions would inevitably have been far fewer.

While a significant speed advantage was essential in reducing the time taken for the fighter to reach the whereabouts of the bomber stream, or to overhaul a contact in minimum time, it could be altogether too much of a good thing. Unless excess speed could be dumped quickly, an overshoot – or worse, a mid-air collision – could easily result. During the war, the minimum safe flying speeds of night fighters increased more or less in proportion to their maximum speeds, and if a slow flying target was below their limit, it was practically uninterceptable. By the same token, while the speedy Me 262 could intercept Mosquitos at night, it was simply too fast to be used effectively against heavy bombers. Performance and technical mismatches were to remain a bugbear in combat for many years, as we shall see later in this chapter.

The effectiveness of intruders in the night air battles was difficult to assess with any degree of precison. In purely numerical terms, they achieved barely enough to justify their own attrition levels, which were high, although this is not taking into account the results achieved against targets other than enemy air assets. It does however appear that the halting of Luftwaffe intruder operations at a time when RAF Bomber Command was finally getting into its stride was a bad error. Equally serious was the German failure, with one or two isolated exceptions, to intercept forward over the North Sea.

On the other hand, there can be no doubt that when Mosquito night fighters began bomber support missions in 1944-45, they had an effect on Nachtjagdflieger efficiency out of all proportion to the number of victories they scored. The number of bombers saved cannot be assessed; nor can the number of Luftwaffe fighters that crashed while out of fuel, trying to evade, or landing on unlit airfields. What is known is that a great morale ascendancy was gained. In the minds of the German night fighter pilots, the Mosquito became a real bogey, and they credited it with powers far beyond those it actually possessed. Their prayer was supposed to be "Dear Hermann, please give me a Mosquito!".

The intensity of the night air war in the Far East and Pacific was far less than in Western Europe, the level of Electronic Warfare (EW) technology was basically lower, and the main lessons learned were those concerning carrier operations. First it was established, as much due to operational necessity as anything, that fighters could not only operate from carriers at night, but also from the quite modest decks of escort carriers. Attrition due to operational accidents was high, but not unbearable.

Experiments with airborne early warning, in the shape of ASV-equipped Avengers, were generally inconclusive, although they pioneered the way for this new form of control. The main advance in the Pacific was the use of single-seat fighters with AI radar, which demonstrated conclusively that they could be moderately effective. The RAF, which had experimented with AI Hurricanes in 1942, and a solitary Typhoon in 1943, rejected the concept for three reasons. A two-man crew was deemed preferable to share the workload; longer endurance was wanted than was available; the range bar which grew out of the target blip was sometimes mistakenly used by pilots as an artificial horizon. Against a target taking evasive action, this was distinctly unhealthy.

The USN had little choice in the matter, as no two-seat carrier-compatible aircraft was available at that time which had the desired level of performance. The other great advantage of an AI-equipped single-seater was that it could also operate by day. This made it particularly useful during the transition periods at dawn and dusk, when it was possible that a hostile day fighter might be encountered in visual conditions. This was not the case with a twin-engined two-seater, which was far too vulnerable in these circumstances. In this connection, it should perhaps be noted that RAF night ace Bob Braham was shot down in daylight over Denmark in 1944 by German experte Robert Spreckels and became a guest of the Third Reich for the duration. His Mosquito was no match for Spreckels' FW 190 in daylight.

Confirmation that the USN was not entirely satisfied with the single-seat night fighter concept came in the summer of 1944. The Grumman F7F Tigercat was a large single-seat aircraft powered by two massive Pratt & Whitney R-2800 radial engines producing 2,100hp each, designed to provide close air support for the US Marines. It was fast, it climbed well, was heavily armed with four 20mm cannon and four 0.50in calibre heavy machine guns, and it had adequate endurance. It was hoped that it would eventually be carrier-compatible, despite its size.

In October 1944, production switched to the F7F-2N, a night fighter variant fitted with APS-6 radar – which incidentally displaced the heavy machine guns – and a second seat for the operator. Deliveries reached VMF(N)-533 during 1945; the squadron hurried through its conversion and operational workup period, and set course for Okinawa, only to arrive the day before the cessation of hostilities. It was thus deprived of what might have been an outstanding operational debut.

Further AI Tigercats were the F7F-3N, with an extended nose housing the far more capable SCR-720 radar, and the F7F-4N, which was strengthened for carrier operations, and featured a catapult attachment and a tail hook. This final variant eventually became carrier qualified, although it was never operated as such.

When at the end of the war, the Nachtjagdflieger records became available to the Allies, one of the more remarkable features was the high scores of the German experten compared with their British and American counterparts. This was all the more remarkable in view of the technical disparities in their respective equipments. The three Allied top scorers were all RAF: Bransome Burbridge with 21, all on offensive operations; Bob Braham, with 20 at night out of a total of 29, split between offensive and defensive operations; and John Cunningham with 20, all on defensive operations. By contrast, two Luftwaffe pilots topped 100 at night: Schnaufer with 121 and Helmut Lent with 102, while a further 22 had scores of 50 or more. Even more remarkably, 17 of them survived the war, even though nearly all at one time or another were shot down, baled out through fuel shortage, or were involved in serious landing accidents. Lent was killed in a landing accident in October 1944 while, as we saw earlier, zu Sayn-Wittgenstein and Meurer, respectively the third and fifth ranking experten, both went down on 21 January 1944. This made the achievements of Schnaufer, whose final total was nearly double that of Werner Streib, the next highest scoring survivor, all the more remarkable. Especially when one considers that he was a comparatively late and slow starter, and gained many of his victories at a time when the star of the Nachtjagdflieger was on the wane.

The difference between the German and Allied aces can primarily be accounted for by sheer opportunity. Exceptional pilots existed on both sides, but the German pilots operated in a target-rich environment, with far more chance to hone their skills. By comparison, opportunities for the Allied pilots were few and far between, as equally they were in the Pacific.

The years following the end of the war saw the piston-engined night fighter reach its zenith. In Britain, the final night fighter variant of the ubiquitous Mosquito to see action in World War 2 was the NF30, faster, and with a higher operational ceiling than its predecessors. Although production was severely curtailed at the end of the war, two further variants were introduced after this time. These were the NF36 and NF38, the latter of which was fitted with the British AI Mk IX rather than the American AI Mk X. Not until November 1950 did production of night fighter Mosquitos cease.

AI Mk IX radar had been a long time in entering service. First mooted in 1941, it was a considerably developed Mk VIII with one or two radical new features. A primary requirement was that it had to be able to operate in the face of Window; to do this it was given a "lock-on" feature enabling it to look directly at the target and not be distracted by other returns. It was also proposed to project the display onto the fighter's windshield. The first experiments with windshield display projection had been made in 1942, but difficulties were experienced in obtaining the right degree of brightness, while focussing at infinity had proved unattainable at that time.

In one of those disastrous accidents too often found in war, the trials aircraft was shot down in error in December 1942, by an inexperienced Spitfire pilot, destroying the experimental radar and killing one of the leading scientists on board. As the American SCR-720 (AI Mk X) became available shortly after, work on AI Mk IX was suspended for a considerable time. As finally developed, AI Mk IX had partially overcome these problems, although unlike the modern HUD, only raw data could be displayed.

The Fleet Air Arm finished the war with just one type of carrier-borne night fighter, the Fairey Firefly. A single-engined two-seater of lower performance than contemporary single-seaters, the Firefly had a chequered history in this role. Intended to replace the even lower performing Fulmar, the Firefly NFII carried AI Mk X, but with separate scanner and receiver dishes housed in pods inboard on the wings. For technical reasons this proved unsatisfactory, and a few Firefly Mk Is were adapted to carry the American ASH (British Mk XV) radar.

Not until 1949 did the Fleet Air Arm get a really capable night fighter, the Sea Hornet NF21. Very similar in appearance to a scaled down Mosquito, the Hornet had been ordered by the RAF as a long range single-seat fighter for the Pacific theatre, but entered service too late to participate. Extremely fast, agile, and with exceptional endurance, the Hornet was an obvious choice for the Fleet Air Arm and, modified for carrier operations, entered service in 1948 as the Sea Hornet F20. By this time, the Royal Navy was thinking more in terms of all-weather operations, and with ASH (Mk XV in British service) radar in the nose and an operator's cockpit set amidships, the Sea Hornet NF21 entered service in January 1949, retiring from front line squadrons when superseded by jets in 1954.

Interestingly, the world's first purpose-designed AI radar-equipped night fighter, Northrop's P-61 Black Widow, was already obsolescent at the end of the war, thus proving less durable than some of the compromise aircraft which preceded it. It would appear to have suffered from too much theoretical input at the design stage, backed by too little practical experience. It was too big, too heavy, and possibly a mite too clever for its own good. Despite the use of more powerful engines in the later P-61B and C, the Black Widow lacked speed, manoeuvrability, and high altitude performance. Production ceased at the end of 1945.

Like most night fighters of the era, the immediate successor to the Black Widow in USAAF service was a modification of an aircraft designed for something else. A fighter had been required to escort ultra-long range bombing missions in the Pacific and which could yet hold its own against the Japanese fighters in service. The North American P-51 Mustang was by far the best long range fighter of its day, but it did not quite have the endurance required, while such long missions were exhausting for single-seater pilots. Something better was wanted, and urgently.

The solution adopted was simple, if hardly original. Two P-51H fuselages were mated with centre wing and horizontal tail sections to produce a high performance twin-engined two-seater, in far less time than it would have taken to develop a completely new aircraft. One interesting feature was that the engines were "handed" to rotate against each other, which not only cancelled out torque but in the event of an engine failure minimised the worst effects of asymmetric handling. As the P-82B Twin Mustang, it entered production in 1945, but was too late for the war against Japan.

The Twin Mustang was an obvious choice for the night role. Whereas the escort fighter carried two pilots, the starboard cockpit was fitted out for the radar operator, and a radar pod was suspended beneath the central wing section, protruding far enough forward to bring the scanner ahead of the propellers. In all, three night fighter variants entered service. The P-82F carried AN/APG-28 tracking radar and the P-82G and H both had SCR-720C search radar. The latter differed from the G only in being optimised for cold weather operation in Alaska.

Having proved unsuitable for carrier operations, the USN introduced a new night fighter into service in the early postwar years to replace the F7F Tigercat. This was also a Grumman product, the F8F Bearcat. A stubby single-seater, it was essentially a replacement for the Hellcat in the day fighter role, but like it, a few were fitted with a radar pod on the wing leading edge. But the Bearcat was a bit of a handful for night carrier use and only 15 F8F-1Ns and 12 F8F-2Ns were built.

The surrender of Germany and Japan in 1945 left a vacuum. With no major threat in the offing and industry reverting to more peaceful pursuits, the development of radar and ECM suffered accordingly. Not until 1948 did the Soviet Union begin to cast a long shadow over world peace.

During the Great Patriotic War, the Russians had made little progress in radar, and none in AI. In March 1942 they requested details of radar from the British Government, but when during the following month the RAF sent a mission to Moscow, with mobile GCI units and other equipment (although not including AI, which at that time was too secret to be allowed over occupied Europe), little interest was shown. Nor was there any response to an invitation to visit London to discuss AI radar. If Stalin disapproved of a tacit admission that the Soviet Union was far behind the decadent West in this field, we shall probably never know.

Be that as it may, such Soviet night fighting as took place was of the cateseye type, with and without searchlight co-operation. The aircraft employed were usually single-seaters, such as the Yak-9B, although a number of twin-engined heavy fighters which had been modified from Pe-2 dive-bombers, were also used. Some Pe-2s and SB-2s were also fitted with searchlights to illuminate the night raiders, to little effect.

The Russians did however score one notable first. The 586th Fighter Regiment was equipped with Yak-9Bs flown almost entirely by women. Over Stalingrad on 24 September 1942, Olga Yamshchikova destroyed a Ju 88 to become the first ever female fighter pilot to record a night victory.

Early in 1944 came the first recorded use of radar by the Soviet Air Force, when primitive mobile stations entered service. Then after the German surrender, heaps of information plus radars and scientists fell into their hands. Aware of their deficiencies in this field, they commenced an all-out effort to catch up. Over the next 40 years they never quite succeeded.

The piston-engined fighter reached its peak in the immediate post-war years, but the writing was already on the wall. Even more significant than the AI-equipped Me 262 jet had been the Arado Ar 234 Blitz, which entered service late in 1944. The jet bomber, with its unparalleled combination of altitude and speed, was the threat of the future, and the only effective counter would be the jet night fighter. Without the imperative of war, or the threat of war, to act as a spur, initial progress was slow. The first British jet night fighter prototypes did not fly until 1950, a full year behind the Canberra jet bomber, and both were modified day fighters. The French had to build their aircraft industry and air arm from scratch, and their Vautour IIN did not appear until mid-1953. It was therefore left to the United States to pioneer the dedicated night and all-weather fighter, working to requirements drafted in 1945.

Two types were ordered initially: the Northrop F-89 Scorpion for the USAF (as the USAAF became in September 1947) and the Douglas F3D Skyknight for the USN and USMC. Although designed to do much the same job, they could hardly have been more different. First flown on 23 March 1948, the Skyknight was entirely conventional in appearance. The two-man crew sat side by side as in the Mosquito and, like that aircraft, an optically flat windshield was fitted. To keep weight down, a ventral chute was provided for crew escape, and these features gave it a rather portly appearance, to the degree that in service it rapidly became known as "Willie the Whale". Radar was the Westinghouse APQ-35, and a tail warning system was fitted. Armament consisted of four 20mm M2 cannon mounted beneath the nose. With the aid of external tanks, the Skyknight could stay airborne for seven hours. Its one weakness was the pair of Westinghouse J34 turbojets which provided a thrust/weight ratio of only 0.35 on a fully laden F3D-1, reducing to 0.29 on the heavier F3D-2. Although intended as a carrier aircraft, the Skyknight was never operated as such, and most went to USMC squadrons, entering service in 1951. Although underpowered, it was pleasant to fly and was to remain in front line service until 1970, albeit in the EW role in the latter years.

The F-89 Scorpion, which first flew on 16 August 1948, was altogether much larger and heavier than the F3D. The two-man crew was seated in tandem on ejection seats, but much of the rest was innovatory. With a thickness/chord ratio of just nine per cent, the broad wing was very thin for the time and featured decelerons – split ailerons which could be opened above and below the wings to form speed brakes. The wing itself was mounted in the mid-position to allow access to the mid-set engines. This posed two problems: the first was that the main gear had to retract into the wings, and to fit the limited space, large diameter narrow wheels with little thin tyres were designed. On a warm day, even taxying was enough to overheat them. The other was that the intakes were set very close to the ground, where they ingested all sorts of small objects, with dire results.

The initial armament requirement was for four flexibly mounted 20mm cannon to be carried in a remotely controlled turret in the nose, but common sense soon prevailed and four, and later six, fixed 20mm M2 cannon were adopted. The fire control system (FCS) was the Hughes E-1, incorporating the APG-32 radar, and service entry took place in June 1951. Like Skyknight, the Scorpion was grossly underpowered, even though from the F-89C model the two Allison J35 turbojets were fitted with afterburners, giving an extra 44 per cent of thrust.

During its gestation period, the F-89 had been viewed rather dubiously in many quarters and at one point the USAF looked likely to buy the F3D. But as the acquisition of a Navy fighter by the Air Force was looked at askance, a decision was taken in October 1948 to develop the Lockheed T-33 jet trainer as an interim all-weather fighter until such time as the bugs had been ironed out of the F-89.

The prototype T-bird, a development of the F-80 Shooting Star day fighter, had first flown seven months earlier. All it needed was the installation of the Hughes E-1 FCS, six (later reduced to four) 0.50in heavy machine guns, an after-burner for the Allison J33 to compensate for the increased weight, and some minor equipment and structural changes. These changes were quickly accomplished, and the F-94 Starfire prototype made its maiden flight on 16 April 1949. Production began shortly before the end of the year and the first unit to be equipped with the type, the 319th All Weather Fighter Squadron, became operational in June 1950.

It was at this point that war broke out in Korea. The country had been partitioned into north and south on either side of the 38th Parallel, and communist-dominated North Korea invaded to try to unify the country. For once the United Nations acted promptly and sanctioned action to repel the invaders. The USA bore the brunt of the air fighting, although other countries, Great Britain, Australia and South Africa, provided sizeable contingents.

The small North Korean Air Force (NKAF) had no night capability, and the early clashes all took place in daylight, although often in appalling weather. The first aerial victory of the conflict fell, as it happened, to an all-weather fighter.

On 27 June, 11 F-82G Twin Mustangs of 68th and 339th Fighter (All Weather) Squadrons, based at Itazuki in Japan, were tasked with covering the evacuation of American civilians from Kimpo and Suwon airfields, near Seoul. Orbiting at less than 1,000ft (305m) they were attacked by NKAF fighters which emerged from low clouds and latched onto the tail of a Twin Mustang flown by Lieutenant Charlie Moran. Moran broke hard, stalled and, on recovering, found himself astern of a Yak 9, which he promptly overhauled and shot down. Meanwhile Lieutenant Skeeter Hudson hauled hard around after a single-engined two-seater, later identified as a Yak 11. The North Korean pilot saw him coming and pulled up into cloud to evade, but Hudson was by this time so close that he maintained visual contact. Two short bursts, and it went down in flames. In the same engagement Lieutenant Walt Hayhurst was credited with a probable.

At first the war went badly for the United Nations forces who, although they controlled the air, were rolled back into a small area around Pusan. During this period, the Twin Mustangs and USMC Tigercats were employed mainly on night interdiction of North Korean supply routes. Finally the tide was turned and the

North Koreans were chased back up the peninsula, almost to the Chinese border. Then in November the People's Republic of China joined the fray, using overwhelming numbers on the ground, and a new threat, the MiG-15 jet fighter, in the air. Once again the tide of battle reversed, as the United Nations forces were pushed back into the south. Not until February 1951 did the situation stabilise more or less along the line of the 38th Parallel.

One of the features of the Russian front in World War 2 had been the intensive use by the Red Air Force of nuisance raiders. Dating from 1926, the Policarpov Po-2 was a two-seater light biplane designed for liaison tasks. Pressed into service against the Wehrmacht as the Legkii Nochnoi Bombardirovshchik (Light Night Bomber), painted black and fitted with a silencer on the engine, these antiquated aircraft were able to penetrate German-held territory at low altitude with little risk of interception. While they rarely caused much material damage, the disruption factor was high. In June 1951, these open cockpit museum pieces began to appear in the night skies over Korea where they were collectively dubbed "Bedcheck Charlie". They posed a unique problem for the American flyers. The harassment they caused ensured that they could not be ignored, but countering them was another matter altogether. They sneaked in very low under the ground radar coverage, and at this altitude were very difficult for AI fighters to detect against the clutter. Their cruising speed was well below the minimum flying speed of the night fighters in the theatre, which posed enormous problems when closing to visual range on a dark night, while if they knew a night fighter was around, their turning ability made keeping AI contact almost impossible.

The first Po-2 to be shot down in air combat fell to the guns, not of a night fighter, but to a B-26 Invader of the 8th Bomb Squadron. Encountering it by accident, the 14 0.50in calibre machine guns of the intruder shot it to pieces. This first victory over Charlie was followed swiftly by one almost equally fortuitous. The only American night fighter units in Korea at this time were the USAF F-82s of 68th NFS, and the USMC squadron VMF(N)-513, equipped with a mix of F7F-3N Tigercats and F4U-5N Corsairs. As the Twin Mustangs were scheduled for replacement in the near future, they were restricted to night interdiction missions. Consequently it was the Marine squadron that was to see most of the action.

On 30 June, radar operator Warrant Officer Robert Buckingham picked up a contact north of Kimpo and directed his pilot, Captain Edwin Long, towards it. The Po-2 was flying far too slowly for the traditional stern attack to be feasible, but visibility that night was good enough for the North Korean biplane to be sighted from quite a distance. Twice Long dived his F7F-3N to the attack, but each time the Po-2 evaded, its observer returning fire with a machine gun. On the third run, Long's 20mm shells finally found their mark, sending the Po-2 down in flames.

The problem of countering Bedcheck Charlie was never really resolved, in spite of numerous attempts to do so, although a few victories were scored. The next decisive encounter came on 12 July, when Captain Donald Fenton despatched a Po-2 with his F4U-5N Corsair. This was followed by a lull and not until 22 September was another Po-2 shot down, by Major Eugene Van Grundy, in what was to prove the final Tigercat kill of the war, and only the second of its career.

Another anti-Charlie measure was a quartet of armed T-6 Texans which was kept on strip alert at Suwon for some months. Possessed of a lower minimum flying speed than the dedicated fighter types, they were in theory more capable of dealing with the slow Po-2s, but without radar and sophisticated navigation aids their difficulty was in finding them.

The night air war entered another phase in December 1951, when very fast and high contacts were picked up on radar, penetrating as far south as Seoul. These could only be jet fighters, almost certainly MiG-15s, which had previously only been encountered by day. While they posed no initial threat, it seemed only a question of time. The AI-equipped fighters in theatre were too slow to catch the jets, and at the same time were vulnerable in the clear visual conditions often found above the weather. It was obvious that jet night fighters were needed.

At Itazuke, the USAF 68th NFS was in the throes of converting from F-82s onto F-94B Starfires. As an interim measure they detached two aircraft to Suwon until March 1952, when they were replaced by the 319th Fighter Interceptor Squadron (FIS), also with Starfires. But by this time the MiG-15 incursions had ceased.

Heavy losses in a daylight action during October 1951 forced the USAF B-29 force to switch entirely to night bombing. Without AI fighters, the communists were forced to use the MiG-15 in a catseye role with GCI, using searchlights and flares for illumination. A Polish defector was later to state that the majority of these night flying MiG pilots were Russians.

Progress was slow. Enemy fighters were sighted by B-29 crewmen on several occasions during April and May 1952, but it was not until 10 June that they made a serious effort. On that occasion, four B-29s were held by searchlights, while an estimated dozen night fighters attacked, shooting down two and badly damaging a third. From this point, VMF(N)-513 were called upon to provide bomber support, patrolling ahead of the bombers. At first this was done by Tigercats, but their performance was inadequate against the much faster jets. Re-equipment with F3D-2 Skyknights became urgent, and this took place in the second half of 1952.

Skyknights were used to set up barrier patrols between the MiG bases and the bombers. Their first victory came on 3 November 1952. Patrolling near Sinuiju, Master Sergeant Hans Hoglind obtained a radar contact flying at 320kt (593kmh) and 12,000ft (3,657m), and steered his pilot, Major William Stratton, towards it. Contact was briefly lost, then regained, and Hoglind directed his pilot gently in astern of his unsuspecting opponent. Finally Stratton made visual contact and fired three short bursts, hitting the port wing, fuselage and tailpipe. The enemy aircraft, provisionally identified as a Yak-15, went down trailing smoke.

As this was the only reference to a Yak-15 during the Korean War, this identification seemed suspect. Then at Farnborough in 1992, Yakovlev OKB chief Alexsandr Dondukov categorically stated that the only Yak aircraft in Korea were piston-engined. This made it almost certain that Stratton's victim, which in any case was the first jet ever to be shot down at night by another jet, was a MiG-15. Just to prove it was no fluke, a second Skyknight, crewed by Captain Oliver Davis and Warrant Officer Dramus Fessler, shot down another MiG-15 just five nights later.

At about 0130 hours, Davis and Fessler were patrolling at 19,000ft (5,791m) when ground control notified them of a bogey (unidentified aircraft) 10 miles (16km) ahead and at 12,500ft (3,810m). Davis commenced to lose altitude, and as he passed 14,000ft (4,267m) he opened the throttle to full military power. Fessler gained AI contact, and directed Davis into a gentle turn to starboard. Contact was immediately lost, but GCI had been following events and once more steered the Skyknight in the right direction. Fessler regained contact, and Davis put the F3D into a 30-degree bank to starboard to follow.

By now the Skyknight had accelerated to 430kt (797kmh) indicated, a true air speed of almost 525kt (604mph/973kmh), which was decidedly on the fast side for the circumstances. In order to gain a visual without risking collision, Davis and Fessler came in astern and offset about 10 degrees to port of the bogey, gaining visual contact at half a mile or less. GCI was then requested to identify it as friendly or hostile. He replied, "Bag it. Bag it!"

The Skyknight was closing rapidly and Davis momentarily deployed his speed brakes to slow up a bit. The jet exhaust of the bandit was very bright, making it hard to discern the outline of the target, who at that moment, possibly warned by his own GCI, commenced a hard turn to starboard. Hauling around with him, Davis fired a short burst of less than half a second, just 20 rounds in all, causing an explosion in the area of the tail pipe. Bits flew back past the F3D, which by this time was dangerously close, and Davis hauled hard back on the stick, overshooting the MiG to starboard. Flames and smoke poured from the fuselage of the stricken fighter, which was seen to impact the ground one minute later.

Up to now, the USAF Starfires had been limited to defensive sorties rather than risk having their E-1 FCS compromised by losing an aircraft over enemy territory. Then in November 1952 they were finally released to operate over the North, at first with little result.

On completely dark nights, visibility was insufficient for the elusive Bedcheck Charlies to contour chase, forcing them to fly rather higher than usual. These were the conditions on 10 December when GCI detected a Po-2 and vectored a Skyknight crewed by Lieutenant A. Joseph Corvi and Master Sergeant Dan George towards it. At minimum range Corvi was still unable to obtain visual contact and, aware that he must still be closing, opened fire using the radar information presented on his gunsight. The effect of four 20mm cannon on a flimsy biplane was devastating, and pieces of Po-2 came back past his aircraft.

Corvi and George were immediately vectored after another Bedcheck Charlie, once more obtained radar lock without being able to make visual contact, and again opened fire on spec, this time without visible result. The contact faded from the radar screen, but whether it was hit and went down, or simply took refuge in the ground clutter, could not be determined.

January 1953 saw a change in tactics. Monitored radio transmissions led the US forces to believe that some communist night fighters were being used to draw off the barrier patrols while a second force intercepted the B-29s from above. This was countered by Starfires taking over the barrier patrols while Skyknights flew top cover to the bombers in the target area.

This got immediate results. On 12 January a Skyknight crewed by Major E.P. "Jack" Dunn and Master Sergeant Larry Fortin, flying bomber escort, gained a contact which evaded downwards and was lost in the ground clutter. After the B-29s had unloaded and departed the area, it, or possibly another aircraft, was again picked up on AI. It was patrolling in a figure of eight pattern which made it difficult to follow, but after about five minutes, Dunn succeeded in getting on its tail. In all he fired six short bursts with no apparent result, and the MiG-15 started to climb away. Pulling up after it, Dunn fired a final burst, and was rewarded by the sight of it catching fire and diving into the ground.

F3Ds accounted for two more MiG-15s during the month and on 28 January the F-94 at last opened its account. Captain Ben Fithian and Lieutenant Sam Lyons of 319th FIS were vectored onto a contact flying at 5,000ft (1,524m) west of Pyong Yang. Coming in astern and well throttled back, Fithian, like Corvi a few weeks before, was unable to make visual contact. He therefore opened fire using the information presented by his E-1 FCS, which of course was intended for just this purpose.

The first two bursts drew no result, but with the FCS still locked on, Fithian "stirred" the control column during the next, to spray a wider area. The impact of his 50-calibre API rounds was clearly visible and he concentrated his fire on that spot. The enemy aircraft, probably a Lavochkin La-11, caught fire and was seen to crash.

F-94 attrition was high, and no less than 28 were written off to various causes, mainly accidents, while claiming only four victories, two of which involved the loss of a Starfire. On 3 May an F-94B crewed by Lieutenants Stanton Wilcox and Irwin Goldberg gained radar contact on a low flying Po-2. Throttling back to minimum flying speed to stay in position, Wilcox opened fire and shot it down, only to have the recoil from his guns cause him to stall. With insufficient height to recover, he went in beside his victim. Then on 12 June, Lieutenant-Colonel Robert McHale and his operator, Major Samuel Hoster, misjudged their attack run on a Po-2 and collided with it.

The re-equipment of VMF(N)-513 with Skyknights had left the land-based forces without a suitable means of countering Bedcheck Charlie, who was becoming a real nuisance in the final months of the war. The night jets were unable to fly slowly enough to be effective. Piston-engined night fighters seemed to offer the only solution. It so happened that these were available. USN Composite Squadron VC-3 was carrier-based, flying night attack missions for Task Force 77 with F4U-5N Corsairs.

A four-aircraft Corsair detachment was therefore borrowed from USS *Princeton* – "Sweet Pea", as she was more usually called – and commenced land based operations on 27 June. Three nights later, Lieutenant Guy Bordelon shot down two Yak-18s, followed by two more on 1 July and finally a La-11 on 17 July. This quick-fire series of victories made him the only night ace of the Korean War.

Even before the VC-3 detachment, Marine Air Group 1 had produced a couple of extempore night fighters. These were Douglas AD-1 Skyraiders, with adapted bombing radars and an operator's position behind the pilot. In addition to tracking aircraft, the radar provided a crude picture of the terrain ahead. Directed by the operator, the pilot therefore had an elementary terrain avoidance system which was a great comfort when flying over the mountains of North Korea, although he was of course reliant on the skill of his operator in interpreting the scope.

The Skyraiders managed just two combats before the Corsairs of VC-3 became available. On 15 June, Major George Linnemeier shot down a Po-2, while on the following night Major Robert Mitchell damaged a second before breaking off to avoid a collision.

The problem of Bedcheck Charlie was never satisfactorily solved. The mismatch between high and low technology was to cause many further problems during the coming years. This was most dramatically shown nearly 40 years later when a young German pilot in a light aircraft evaded the entire Soviet air defence system in daylight, and landed in Red Square, Moscow!

To summarise, night fighter action in Korea was of low intensity and accident attrition was higher than could be justified by the number of victories scored. On the other hand, not one B-29 was lost to enemy fighters when barrier patrols were flown by Skyknights and Starfires, and their effectiveness must be judged in this light. Be that as it may, neither the Skyknight nor the Starfire was a match for the MiG-15 in visual conditions.

In conformity with Oswald Boelcke's first dictum "try to secure advantages", Navy and Air Force jet fighter pilots were justifiably cautious in bright moonlight and clear visibility, preferring to make use of darkness and cloud cover when the higher performing Russian fighters were about. Nor would they continue their mission unless their radar and fire control systems were working 100 per cent, as it was these that gave them the advantage. The all-weather fighter had yet to come of age.

9. The New Threat

Two factors helped shape the postwar world. The first was Operation "Barbarossa", Hitler's invasion of the Soviet Union in the summer of 1941. This left lasting scars on the Soviet High Command which were to influence their thinking for more than four decades. The second was the paranoid nature of the Soviet leader. Iosip Vissarionovitch Stalin ruthlessly suppressed all dissent to his regime from the moment he assumed supreme power, purging all whom he regarded as a threat, whether this was justified or not.

These two factors combined to make the Soviet Union hostile towards the West, mistrusting its motives and intentions. The vast amount of aid supplied during the Great Patriotic War did nothing to allay these fears and from the early postwar years the Soviet Union adopted an increasingly intransigent attitude towards its former allies, finally culminating in the Cold War.

From the Soviet viewpoint, the main threat was the USA, which combined a huge strategic bomber fleet with the possession of nuclear weapons. The night capability of RAF Bomber Command appears to have been regarded as less of a threat. The Soviet response was twofold. As the US Air Force (the USAF was formed from the US Army Air Force as a separate air arm in 1947) normally operated in daylight, a primary requirement was a defensive force of high performance jet fighters able to intercept the B-29; the second was a strategic bomber force of their own.

The means were already to hand. A few B-29s had landed in Soviet territory late in 1944 and, with these as a model, the Tupolev OKB set out to reverse engineer the type, which emerged as the Tu-4, first flown in 1946. At the same time, efforts were made to produce nuclear weapons. Night and all-weather fighters were for a time relatively neglected, despite the vast amount of German radar equipment and the many German electronics scientists that had fallen into Soviet hands at the end of the war.

The Soviet move towards obtaining nuclear weaponry was not unknown to the Western nations, who estimated that the chances of an early success were very high. To counteract this, Britain took the decision to develop her own nuclear weapons in 1947, followed shortly after by France. To the Soviet Union this appeared to be an escalation of the threat, and she redoubled her efforts. The first Soviet nuclear test was carried out in September 1949. Western intelligence forecast that by mid-1950, the USSR would have about 25 A-bombs and 200 bombers capable of delivering them, rising to 75 bombs and 500 heavy bombers over the next two years. While the main threat was considered to be daylight raids, the possibility of devastating night raids could not be discounted.

Specification 4/48 had been formulated for a new RAF night/all-weather fighter to replace the piston-engined Mosquitos in the mid-1950s, but as relations between East and West worsened it became obvious that an interim jet fighter was needed as a matter of urgency. In typical British fashion, three lashups were hurriedly produced and in 1951 these were evaluated by the RAF Central Flying Establishment (CFE).

The Vampire was a single-seat, single-engine design, with tail surfaces carried on twin booms. The NF10 variant produced by de Havilland as a private venture in 1949 was basically an FB5 with a Mosquito NF36 cockpit and AI 10 radar grafted on to give a side-by-side two-seater configuration, and driven by the slightly more powerful DH Goblin 3 engine.

CFE reported that acceleration was sluggish at 35,000ft (10,667m), and it was reluctant to go up to 40,000ft (12,191m). Time to 35,000ft was 13½ minutes. Although performance was lower than the Venom NF2 and Meteor NF11, it was expected to cope with targets flying at up to Mach 0.70, and had a handsome speed margin over the Tu-4. Not unexpectedly, it was described as a vast improvement over the Mosquito, although the lack of ejection seats and poor crew escape facilities were criticised.

The Venom NF2 was similarly derived from a single-seat day fighter with the same layout as the Vampire, but with thinner wings and other aerodynamic refinements, and the much more powerful Ghost engine. The cockpit layout was similar to that of the Vampire NF10, but with a larger roof hatch to facilitate baling out. With no ejection seats, the crew had still to avoid hitting the horizontal tail after abandoning the aircraft.

CFE reported that time to 40,000ft (12,191m) was 9 1/2 minutes; service ceiling about 45,000ft (13,715m); critical Mach number at altitude was 0.87, and maximum speed at sea level was 525kt (604mph-973kmh). Its manoeuvrability was also praised, although this hardly squares with a later statement that rate of roll was sluggish.

The third interim type was derived from the Gloster Meteor single-seat twin-engined day fighter, which had first entered service in 1944. A two-seat conversion trainer was produced in 1948 as the T7. Fitted with AI and with a radar operator in the back seat, this was an obvious choice.

The conversion was undertaken by Armstrong Whitworth and entailed quite radical revisions. A lengthened nose was introduced to accommodate the radar and to offset the instability this caused, F8 tail surfaces were adopted. However, the revised nose displaced the four 20mm Hispano cannon which were relocated in wide-span wings outboard of the engines. This was hardly the best place for them as, when they were fired, the recoil force caused the wings to flex, with a subsequent loss of accuracy.

CFE reported quite favourably on the handling qualities of the Meteor NF11, even though performance was inferior to that of the Venom. Time to 35,000ft (10,667m) was 11½ minutes, and it could reach 40,000ft (12,191m) even at maximum all-up take-off weight. Limiting Mach number at altitude was 0.8, although below 10,000ft (3,048m) it was structurally limited to 435kt (806kmh).

On the other hand, visibility from the cockpit was poor. The hood had a surplus of heavy metal framing. At high altitudes the perspex over the pilot's head became thickly encrusted with ice, making him blind to any target more than 25 degrees above. Finally, landing in rain was unduly hazardous because the windshield became obscured and there were no direct vision panels.

In the event, all three interim types entered service. Of these, the Vampire NF10 was chosen almost by default, as it happened to be available sooner. Deliveries commenced in 1951, and it was phased out in 1954. The Venom NF2 proved initially disappointing, as operating restrictions prevented it from achieving its full potential. Entering service in 1953, it was followed later that year by the NF3, which stayed in service until 1958. But this was not to be the end of the road for the Venom. Adapted for carrier operations as the Sea Venom FAW20 and FAW21, fitted with ejection seats and American AI radar, it remained in Fleet Air Arm service until 1960.

Most successful of all was the Meteor, which went through four succesive variants, ending with the NF14, which had a clear canopy, improved environmental control in the cockpit, more powerful engines, and the Westinghouse APS-57 radar, known as AI 21 in British service. The Meteor NF13 was a tropical version which ironically was used in action against RAF Canberra bombers during the Suez campaign of 1956. Although a few Canberra pilots sighted Egyptian night fighters, the performance of the Meteor was inadequate to allow it to intercept. As luck would have it, the only night air combat victory by the type came in the same conflict.

The Egyptian Chief-of-Staff was visiting Syria and he, in company with various senior officers and journalists, was due to leave Damascus to return to Cairo on the evening of 28 October, travelling in two Ilyushin Il-14s. Israeli intelligence got wind of this, and decided to ambush him with a Meteor NF13, a type in Israeli service as well as that of Egypt. The task fell to Chato Tsidon, commanding officer designate of No 119 Squadron.

The cruising speed of the Il-14 was 175kt (324kmh), while the stalling speed of the Meteor NF 13 was 140kt (259kmh). This immediately posed problems. The high angle of attack at this low speed would make aiming difficult, while the recoil from the four 20mm cannon could easily slow the Meteor enough to cause it to stall. Undaunted, Tsidon and his operator, Alyasheeb Brosh, spent the afternoon practicing low speed interceptions.

It was a dark and moonless night as Tsidon and Brosh headed out over the Mediterranean at 10,000ft (3,048m). Soon GCI vectored them towards a target and at a range of three miles (5km) Brosh gained AI contact and directed his pilot to it. A visual was only obtained at 650ft (200m) and, under strict orders to make positive identification, Tsidon closed right in and flew alongside for 10 minutes before he was certain. Dropping back with lowered flaps, he opened fire, hitting the port engine. Only three of his four wing-mounted guns worked, and the asymmetric recoil caused the Meteor to stall and spin off. Recovering, he regained visual contact with the Il-14 which, with one engine burning, had slowed, compounding the difficulty of attacking. Once more he attacked, closing to an estimated range of 66ft (20m), relying on the spin which would ensue on firing to enable him to avoid colliding with his target. Again his shells struck home; again he stalled and spun down, this time recovering only 300ft (91m) above the sea. His fire had been fatal, and the Il-14 also went down, engulfed in flames.

Unfortunately for Tsidon and Brosh, it was the wrong Il-14. The Egyptian Chief-of-Staff normally travelled in the lead aircraft, but on this occasion he had been delayed and the take-off order had been reversed.

Night interception with guns was only effective using a pursuit course, ending with an attack from astern. The emergence of high flying jet bombers would compound the problems immensely. In the thin air of the stratosphere, manoeuvra-

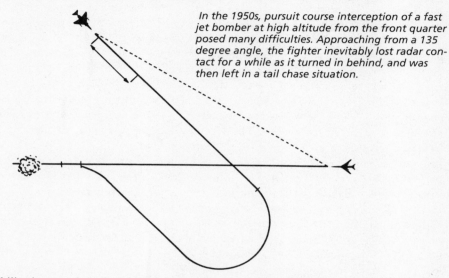

In the 1950s, pursuit course interception of a fast jet bomber at high altitude from the front quarter posed many difficulties. Approaching from a 135 degree angle, the fighter inevitably lost radar contact for a while as it turned in behind, and was then left in a tail chase situation.

bility is severely reduced, and turn radii were correspondingly wide, giving no margin for error. In addition, the significant speed advantage needed by the fighter to catch the bomber might become unacceptably eroded. Finally, as the Luftwaffe had discovered in World War 2, longer ranged weapons with greater hitting power were needed against heavy bombers.

For various technical reasons, a larger and longer ranged aircraft gun was impracticable. On the other hand, sufficient range and hitting power could be achieved by quite a small rocket projectile. Starting from the German R4M, the Americans developed Mighty Mouse, a folding fin aircraft rocket (FFAR) of 2.75in (70mm) diameter. The FFAR was theoretically effective out to 9,000ft (2,743m) range, although it was far from accurate. In order to overcome this, FFARs were to be fired in a salvo, blanketing a fairly large area of sky in the region of the target, giving a good chance of obtaining at least one hit. And just one hit by an FFAR was devastating. Initial trials indicated that the optimum firing range was in the order of about 4,500ft (1,372m).

While FFARs had both the necessary range and destructive power, the problem remained of bringing them to bear. If attacks could be made from ahead or abeam, the stately jockeying for the astern position and the long tail chase could be eliminated. The Hughes Aircraft Company, virtual newcomers to the electronics field, now refined their E-1 fire control system to allow attacks to be made from any angle. What was more, they made the interception semi-automatic. This was a revolutionary step. Historically, up to and including the Korean War, just five per cent of fighter pilots accounted for 40 per cent of all victories, demonstrating conclusively that pilot quality was the dominant factor in air combat. Of the rest, something like 50 per cent achieved nothing, while the remainder brought home just the occasional kill. The problem had been how to make the low-achieving 95 per cent more effec-

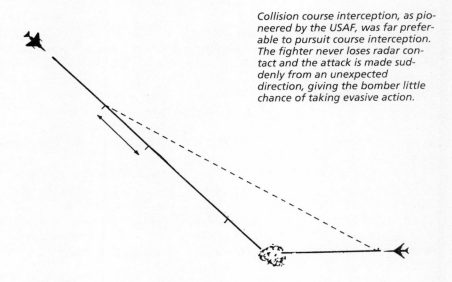

Collision course interception, as pioneered by the USAF, was far preferable to pursuit course interception. The fighter never loses radar contact and the attack is made suddenly from an unexpected direction, giving the bomber little chance of taking evasive action.

tive. Until this point, the only answer had been better training, but now clever electronics appeared to offer an alternative solution. The new semi-automatic interception and Fire Control System (FCS) was the first move towards making every pilot an ace via technology.

The Hughes E-4 FCS consisted of a computer which linked the Westinghouse APG-36 radar to the automatic pilot. Once the radar had acquired the target and started to track it, the FCS would continuously calculate speeds, distances and angles, then fire the rockets at the optimum moment. What was more, the E-4 could be used in a single-seater. The pilot's task was to centre the target blip in a ring on his scope, then draw the search to the automatic position. Clever electrons would do the rest. The fast attack from the front quarter would almost eliminate the risk of being hit by defensive fire from the bombers, while this angle would also give a larger presented area of target, and thus a better chance of a hit, than the traditional stern aspect.

To carry the E-4, North American adapted their successful F-86 Sabre. In order to fit the radar in the nose, a chin inlet was adopted, giving the F-86D a very distinctive appearance. Twenty-four FFARs were carried in a ventral tray which, when the time came, dropped down, fired, and was immediately retracted. The FFARs, radar and associated black boxes significantly increased weight, and to offset this, an afterburning J47 was fitted.

The first F-86D trials were carried out in 1950. It had been intended that the FFARs could be fired in salvos of six, 12, or all 24, but it was soon realised than even 24 rockets were not really enough. The most optimistic estimate of kill probability with all 24 fired together was 60 per cent. This made the F-86D very much a "one-shot" fighter, and a lot of them would have been needed to deal with a massed raid.

In spite of assertions to the contrary, the Dogship Sabre, as it was known, was never intended to operate in daylight in the presence of enemy escort fighters. Although developed from the most successful fighter of its era, its armament was unsuitable for fighter combat, while the pilot, unable to look around because his head was firmly in the radar scope, would have been extremely vulnerable. All that can really be said is that the F-86D would have had a better chance of eluding enemy fighters in daylight than any other all-weather aircraft then in service.

Both USAF night fighters then in service, the F-94 and F-89, were also developed with collision course FCS and FFAR packs, the two-seat configuration allowing greater radar capability than was possible with the F-86D.

Although the F-94C was unmistakeably still a Starfire in appearance, it was to all intents and purposes a new aeroplane, and was originally designated F-97A. The wing thickness/chord ratio was reduced to 10 per cent to increase the limiting Mach number to 0.87, and to offset the inevitable weight growth an afterburning Pratt & Whitney (P&W) J48-5 engine was installed. The F-94C was remarkable in being stressed for 8.67g, and for having the extraordinarily high wing loading of 115lb/sq ft (563kg/sq m).

The FCS was Hughes' E-5, and an annular ring of 24 FFARs was inserted around the radome. When fired, these gave the pilot the impression that he had blown up by covering the front of the aircraft with flame and smoke. As with the F-86D, 24 rockets were found to be insufficient, and later this total was doubled by fitting two pods of 12 FFARs to the wing leading edges.

One of the basic requirements of a night and all-weather fighter is endurance, and this was lacking in both Sabre Dog and Starfire. In this respect the Scorpion was much better. The F-89D carried two enormous wingtip pods, each with 52 rockets in the front and extra fuel in the rear. The guns were removed from the nose to make room for yet more fuel, and two drop tanks could be carried beneath the wings giving the enormous total of 18,421lb (8,356kg). FCS was the Hughes E-6, which combined APG-40 radar with the F-5 autopilot and APA-84 ballistics computer. Allison J35-35A afterburning engines were fitted, giving a thrust/weight ratio of a mere 0.34 at maximum take-off weight. First ordered in April 1951, the F-89D was bedevilled with engine and structural problems, and did not reach the squadrons until January 1954.

Still later, streamlined pods were developed which could be carried on underwing pylons, allowing many USAF, US Navy (USN) and US Marine Corps (USMC) fighters to be armed in this way. Official reports on the efficacy of the

FFAR were generally optimistic, but what was the opinion of the man at the sharp end? A young Lieutenant, Jacques Naviaux, joined the USMC all-weather squadron VMF(AW)-542, equipped with Douglas F4D-1 Skyrays, in 1961. He later recalled:

"A working radar, which was not all that rare, could detect a fighter at 24nm (44km), and track it at 20nm (37km). The plan was to fire a salvo of four 19-shot pods on a 110-degree lead collision course, with a firing range of 1,500ft (457m). Whether or not we would have hit anything on a regular basis is a matter for conjecture, but I think not, although I did manage to shoot down a drone at Point Mugu for one of the only recorded kills.

"We flew practice firing runs using rockets against a Delmar towed target. The firing aircraft carried a Delmar Scorer, a combination radar and a 35mm camera. Only once while reviewing Delmar runs did I see both a rocket and a target in the same frame."

This does not exactly inspire confidence in the FFAR as a weapon, especially when one considers that a salvo from the Skyray consisted of no less than 76 rockets, and that the firing range by 1961 had been reduced to one-third of the previously considered optimum. Perhaps it was as well that the FFAR was not called upon to go to war.

One final attempt was made to produce an unguided rocket that was a real bomber killer. If lots of little rockets could not guarantee a hit, perhaps one big one, with a really effective warhead, might succeed. A Douglas product, this duly emerged as the AIR-2 Genie. Genie was huge. It was 9.67ft (2.946m) long, with a body diameter of 17.5in (44.5cm), and weighed 822lb (373kg). All-burnt speed was Mach 3.3 and range was 5.4nm (10km). The warhead was a 1.5-kiloton nuclear weapon with a lethal blast radius exceeding 1,000ft (305m), making extreme accuracy unnecessary. In theory the FCS tracked the target, commanded the pilot to arm the missile, launched it when firing parameters had been achieved, immediately afterwards pulling the fighter into a hard turn away from the target; then, after a precisely calculated interval, it detonated the warhead and destroyed the target.

In practice things were not quite like that. Munitions carried on the underside of an aircraft have to be ejected through the disturbed air of the slipstream before the motor ignites. Motor ignition on Genie was by means of a nylon lanyard, which pulled a pin when fully extended. The force thus exerted on the big missile did nothing to ensure that it went in the desired direction. Jack Broughton in his memoir *Going Downtown*, recalled being with a squadron tasked to use up some Genies (without warheads) that had reached the end of their shelf life: "...we saturated the Gulf of Mexico with every Genie that we could get to accept the fire signal and leave our aircraft. They took off in all directions, but very rarely toward the target drones."

It is very easy to be critical of attempts to produce a weapons system based on unguided rockets. Guns were demonstrably inadequate at night by virtue of their too short range and lack of hitting power against a superheavy bomber. The development of air-to-air guided missiles had begun during World War 2, but they were a long time in maturing and an interim weapon was badly needed. What alternative was there?

115

The shortest route for Soviet bombers raiding the USA lay over the North Pole, which meant that they would first have to traverse Canadian air space. The air defence of Canada posed difficult problems. With a population of little more than one-tenth of the USA, but a land mass rather greater, resources were lacking and defence assets had therefore to be spread thinly. It did however offer a unique opportunity for forward defence. What was needed was a very long range fighter, capable of operating in darkness and very severe weather conditions, from short, austere landing grounds.

The Royal Canadian Air Force, as it then was, had always maintained close ties with the RAF, but now their ways were to diverge. The defence needs of Canada differed widely from those of the mother country. With no suitable British aircraft under development for the task, they set out to provide their own. The result was the Avro Canada CF-100, unofficially called the Canuck. The Canuck, which first flew on 19 January 1950, was a twin-engined two-seater of orthodox appearance with unswept wings. However, it did have some interesting features. Instead of locating the engines out on the wings like the Meteor, or tucking them under the wing roots like the Scorpion, they were placed alongside the fuselage, passing above the low set wing. This configuration conferred several advantages. It allowed short main gears; it left most of the fuselage behind the tandem cockpit available for fuel; and it made the width across the engine/fuselage area extremely wide, providing a significant amount of body lift in manoeuvring flight.

The CF-100 Mk 2 was powered by two non-afterburning Canadian Orenda 2 engines rated at 6,000lb (26.7kN). Thrust/weight ratio was 0.375, rather better than that of the contemporary F-89A, while the large wing gave the moderate loading of 59lb/sq ft (289kg/sq m). Initial armament consisted of a belly pack of eight 0.50in Colt-Browning heavy machine guns, matched to the Hughes E-1 FCS and APG-33 radar.

The Canuck was remarkably agile for such a big aircraft, and further variants were produced. The main versions were the Mk 4B, with the guns replaced by a retractable pack of 48 FFARs, Hughes collision-course FCS with APG-40 radar, and Orenda 11s rated at 7,275lb (32.3kN). Still later the Mk 4B was fitted with wingtip pods, increasing its firepower by a further 60 FFARs. Tip pods were also a feature of the "big wing" Mk 5, with span increased from 52ft (15.95m) to 58ft (17.68m), which increased the service ceiling from 47,000ft (14,325m) to 54,000ft (16,458m).

Although designed specifically with Canadian air defence requirements in mind, the CF-100 also saw service in Europe. Operation "Nimble Bat" on 4 November 1956 saw the arrival at Merville, on the Franco–Belgian border, of No 445 Squadron RCAF, with Mk 4Bs. They were followed shortly after by three more squadrons of CF-100s. For the first time, NATO had in Europe an all-weather fighter with the endurance to allow effective standing patrols to be mounted. Impressed by its capability, the Belgian Air Force acquired a batch of 47 Mk 5s in 1957-58, for the only export sales of the type.

With the Skyknight unsuited to carrier operations, the USN was reduced, like the RAF and FAA, to adapting conventional day fighters by giving them a modicum of night and all-weather capability.

In 1945 the young McDonnell Aircraft Company had produced the first ever jet carrier fighter, the FH-1 Phantom. This was quickly superseded by the far superior F2H Banshee, which became carrier-qualified in May 1949. The "Banjo", as it became affectionately known, was a single-seat fighter, powered by two small Westinghouse J34 engines in the wing roots. Standard armament was four 20mm cannon in the nose. To fit a search radar was the obvious next step, but this could only be done by lengthening the nose to take the APS-46, a 3cm radar derived from the wartime APS-6. Designated F2H-2N, and first flown on 3 February 1950, this became the first jet night fighter to operate from carriers. The type was active over North Korea, flying night patrols, B-29 escort and intruder missions, although no air combat successes were recorded.

The F2H-2N was followed by the -3, a dedicated all-weather single-seater with a longer fuselage, the cannon moved aft and greater internal fuel capacity. The APS-46 radar was replaced by the totally different Westinghouse APQ-41. The final variant was the -4, with uprated engines. Handling of all types was docile, and the Banshee remained in service well into the 1960s.

The acquisition of German aerodynamic research in 1945 had stimulated Western aircraft design and over the next 10 years many new shapes appeared. Swept wings and deltas, flying wings, tail-less configurations and variable geometry were all explored, although most got no further than the experimental stage. The quest was for ever greater speeds and climb rates, and higher ceilings. Performance now moved into the transonic region.

In many ways this was a step in the dark. The aerodynamic forces involved were not at first fully understood. As speeds neared Mach 1, compressibility effects caused strong buffeting. In the same regime, the aft movement of the centre of lift could cause a violent uncommanded pitchup. Transverse flow across a swept wing could result in tip stalling as the speed of sound was approached, with the same result. Swept wings also caused dutch roll (yaw combined with roll), and whereas in traditional straight-winged aircraft the wingspan exceeded the fuselage length, with swept-winged designs the reverse was often true. This gave rise to a new bogey – inertia coupling – and in some cases this resulted in loss of control and catastrophic structural failure. At high angles of attack the tail surfaces could become blanketed by the wings, which rendered them ineffective, often ending in a locked-in deep stall from which recovery was impossible. Nor were the problems all at the high speed end of the envelope: low speed handling was also adversely affected. These factors bedevilled progress and took many years to overcome.*

As we have seen, the early jet fighters were, with two notable exceptions, straight-winged. The exceptions were of course the F-86 Sabre and the MiG-15. These, the first transonic fighters, led the way into a new era of high performance and inevitably others followed.

---

* Another factor that emerged at about this time among the English speaking nations was the increasing use of nautical miles in lieu of statute miles, and knots in lieu of miles per hour. Naval air arms had always used these measures, and their adoption by land based air forces was to ease navigational problems rather than any need for consistency. A nautical mile is 1.1515 statute miles, and 500kt = 576mph (927kmh).

In the F-86D, the USAF was the first in the field with a transonic all-weather fighter which, as we have seen, was a development of the F-86 Sabre day fighter. The USN followed the same line, adapting single-seat day fighters to suit the night and all-weather role, while the RAF and FAA both ordered a bird optimised for the task. Given the pace of technical progress at that time, it is hardly surprising that all encountered severe problems.

The first swept-wing aircraft to be operated from a carrier, and the first fighter ever to have afterburning built in from inception, was Vought's F7U Cutlass. Completely unconventional in appearance, it was a tail-less aircraft with very broad chord wings, on which were mounted twin fins and rudders. After a protracted development period, the Cutlass finally entered service in 1953. In service it proved to be a very hot ship and after a brief and accident-prone career it was retired in 1956.

Marginally capable of all-weather operations, and almost as exotic in appearance was the Douglas F4D Skyray, which first flew on 23 January 1951. The "Ford", as it was generally known, was designed to meet a 1947 specification calling for an interceptor able to reach 40,000ft (12,191m) in five minutes or less – a seemingly impossible feat at that time. Impossible or no, legendary chief designer Ed Heinemann set out to meet it.

Initially the design was strongly influenced by the tail-less delta configuration pioneered in Germany during World War 2 by Dr Alexander Lippisch. What finally emerged was a single-seat single-engine tail-less layout, with a wing that was not quite a delta but a thin, broad chord, low aspect ratio wing swept at 52.5 degrees on the leading edge with a much shallower sweep on the trailing edge, combined with large rounded tips. An interesting feature was what was possibly the earliest example of wing/body blending.

This unique wing configuration combined a huge (557sq ft/51.75sq m) lift area with the very low aspect ratio of 2.01, a figure only surpassed many years later on a service fighter by the Saab J35 Draken. Wing loading, at 41lb/sq ft (198kg/sq m), was incredibly low for the time, while the afterburning Pratt & Whitney J57-8B gave a thrust loading at combat weight of 0.71 – far in excess of any contemporary fighter. These factors combined to give sparkling performance. Angle of climb was a staggering 70 degrees and rate of climb far exceeded the specification. The icing on the cake was an incredibly fast rate of roll which enabled the Ford to change direction very quickly. Primary armament consisted of four 20mm cannon located in the wings, with 65rpg; four 19 shot-pods of FFARs were also routinely carried. Collision course interception was provided by the Aero 13F FCS, incorporating the Westinghouse APQ-50 radar.

One major shortcoming was lack of internal fuel. Endurance was very limited and the Ford became known as the "10-Minute Killer" as a result. External tanks were routinely carried to make up the deficiency, but the weight and drag of these reduced performance. Like the F7U, its unconventional layout gave rise to some nasty handling characteristics, as Jacques Naviaux recalled:

"When transitioning from subsonic to supersonic flight, the centre of pressure shifts, producing a nose-down tuck with a stick force of 25-30lb (11-14kg). This was not a problem; that came going the other way. Decelerating from supersonic to subsonic produced an eye-watering 4.5g pitchup. For the pilot who was already in a high-g turn the result was cumulative, resulting in instant overstress! The engineering solution was the transonic trim compensator, but like many of the cockpit systems of that era, it usually did not work!"

Commenting on the FCS:

"Once locked on, the pilot's task was to fly the steering circle and the steering dot, keeping the latter centred in the former and holding down the trigger until the rockets fired. I looked at a lot of radar scope film and only once saw the dot inside the circle on firing. It just wasn't that easy to do!"

This comment of course applied to the system. This difficulty was not confined to the Skyray.

As we saw earlier, icing on the cockpit canopy transparencies was a problem with the Meteor NF11. The Ford, with its incredibly fast rate of climb, often followed by an almost equally precipitous descent due to fuel shortage, also suffered. Although the windshield contained an electrical heating element, this did nothing for the canopy and quarterlights. A revised cockpit environmental control system was fitted in later models, but even this was far from foolproof. Under certain circumstances, fog could form in the cockpit thick enough to obscure the instrument panel. Icing could also affect operation of the engines. Jacques Naviaux again:

"The twin spool compressor had a bleed air valve which was prone to icing. Under that condition, use of the afterburner, or even full power, would result in a compressor stall. This could be really spectacular at night, when flames came out of the intakes! In the winter months in Japan, it was not uncommon to have a cloud deck from 200ft (61m) up to 40,000ft (12,191m). I launched more than once with the goal of reaching VMC conditions on top, only to have the power limited by bleed air icing, which limited me to 35,000ft (10,667m)."

"Given its low fuel capacity, and the overall state of carrier operations in that era, which did not include in-flight refuelling as a backup on every recovery, the Ford was not very suitable for carrier operations, and thus had a limited life in the fleet."

The third, and probably most suitable transonic type to reach the USN was the McDonnell F3H Demon. Far more conventional in appearance than either Cutlass or Skyray, the Demon was a single-seat, single-engined fighter with 45 degree swept flying surfaces, with the tail surfaces mounted on a boom above the engine nozzle. First flown on 7 August 1951, the Demon had a troubled gestation period. Handling was inferior, with pronounced dutch roll; the rate of roll was too slow, endurance too short, and the Westinghouse J40 turbojet proved a major area for concern. Demonstrating a previously unsuspected sense of humour, the USN now decided to make the Demon an all-weather fighter.

The fuselage was redesigned and various structural changes were made to accommodate a larger engine, extra fuel and the Westinghouse APQ-50 radar. Unusually, the cockpit was given a one-piece wrap-around windshield. The once sleek fuselage now took on a distinctly portly aspect. Armament was four 20mm cannon with 150rpg, and four 19 shot-pods of FFARs.

The F3H-1N failed to enter service due to the unreliability of the J40 engine, and most of this model were carted away to become instructional airframes or gunnery targets. The new powerplant selected for what became the -2N was the Allison J71-2, which gave far more thrust than the J40.

Even with the new engine, the problems were not over, the most serious of which was distortion of the wings during rolling manoeuvres at high speeds. This was caused by the torsional forces exerted by the ailerons, which permanently deformed the wings. This was a measure of how little was known about the aerodynamic forces involved in high speed flight at that time. The cure was to add spoilers for high speed rolling manoeuvres.

The Demon remained short on endurance, and the obvious cure was to add drop tanks. This became the classic example of not taking anything for granted. With an extra 512 US gallons of fuel carried in two slender tanks beneath the fuselage, the Demon was actually found to have less range and endurance than in the clean condition, due to higher than predicted interference drag. The eventual solution was a bolt-on flight refuelling probe.

Short-legged and always underpowered, the Demon was never an outstanding performer, but handled pleasantly and was well suited to carrier operations. It was not finally replaced until 1965; a year later than the Skyray.

The British transonic fighter equivalents were the DH110, first flown on 26 September 1951, by none other than John Cunningham, who had become de Havilland's chief test pilot after the war; and the Gloster GA5, which took to the air for the first time on 26 November of the same year. Both were twin-engined two-seaters designed to specification F4/48, and there the resemblance ended.

The DH110, later to become the Sea Vixen in FAA service, combined the twin-boom layout of the Vampire and Venom with a 40 degree swept wing. As the horizontal tail surface could not be swept to match the wing, it was given a very thin section which produced the same aerodynamic characteristics. That this worked was attested by the fact that the DH110 reached a speed of Mach 1.11 in a shallow dive on 9 April 1952 – the first two-seater to exceed Mach unity.

Power was two Rolls-Royce RA7 Avons, each rated at 7,500lb (33.3kN), and armament consisted of four 30mm Aden cannon located beneath the cockpit floor. One very unusual feature was the crew layout. The pilot's cockpit was offset to port, initially with a single piece wrap-around windshield, later replaced by a V-shape which was far better at clearing rain and spray, while the radar operator was buried in the nacelle to starboard, with a small vision port in the side. This arrangement gave two advantages. The radar scopes of the day were difficult if not impossible to see in bright sunlight, and the "coal hole", as it became known, kept light levels down. It also reduced drag. Be this as it may, it was not very popular with those who had to fly in it.

Official dithering, assisted by a very public crash at the Farnborough Air Show in September 1952, caused development to be held back and the RAF ordered the rival GA5, later named Javelin. This left the FAA as the sole customer. Navalisation took further time and not until March 1957 did the first Sea Vixen FAW1 take to the air.

This was equipped with the GEC AI 18 radar; the guns were replaced by two FFAR launchers each with 14 2in (51mm) rockets, while the main armament was four Blue Jay homing missiles. Creeping weight growth was offset with Rolls-Royce Avon 208s, each rated at 11,230lb (49.9kN). Service entry was not until 1959, several years later than originally intended. From 1963, the FAW2, with more comprehensive electronics and much more fuel, entered service.

In the air the Sea Vixen FAW1 was a lively performer, with a wing loading of 58lb/sq ft (283kg/sq m) and a thrust loading of 0.60 at maximum take-off weight, combined with the rather high aspect ratio of 4.01. On the ground, it had foibles. Even with throttles at idle it accelerated while taxying, and after touchdown, aerodynamic braking was used by raising the nose until the tail booms scraped the runway (they were fitted with ablative shoes for protection). Had it entered service in 1954, it would arguably have been the best all-weather fighter in the world at that time. But it was not to be. The Sea Vixen was finally phased out in 1972.

Specification F4/48 also gave rise to the Gloster Javelin, which was about as different to the Sea Vixen as it was possible to get. It had a broad fuselage, with two widely spaced Armstrong Siddelely Sapphire turbojets running down its sides; not quite to the same degree as the CF-100, but not far off. Pilot and operator were seated in tandem under a two-piece canopy. But the wing was something else: a true delta with rounded tips and a 10 per cent thickness/chord ratio, it was enormous, both in area and in depth. Wing loading of the first production aircraft in clean condition was barely 34lb/sq ft (166kg/sq m), far less than even the Skyray, although the thrust loading of 0.51 failed to match that of the USN fighter. Proportionate in size to the wing was a massive fin, capped with a large delta tailplane.

The RAF selected the Javelin rather than the DH110 for its supposedly greater development potential. In a way this was correct, as the Gloster fighter certainly had the volume to contain anything that they could dream up. They then proceeded to gild the lily by developing the Javelin through no less than nine different variants in a total production of only 385.

Modifications during production included changes of radar, all-moving tailplanes, additional internal fuel, more powerful engines, kinked and drooped leading edges, afterburning engines, missile armament, vortex generators – the list is endless. If only the bugs had been ironed out in the development stage, the RAF could have had a pretty good fighter fairly quickly, but instead chose to muddle on with interminable extras. The one variation which might have produced an outstanding fighter was a supersonic version with a thin wing, but this never got past the paper aeroplane stage.

The main fault of the Javelin was that it was larger than it need have been, with a thicker wing and more wetted area than was necessary, calling forth the soubriquet of "Dragmaster". Speed bleed-off in hard turns was really quite spectacular. The high set tail was easily blanketed by the vast wing, causing a deep stall, and its early development was marred by a series of fatal crashes. Only later was it found that a deep stall could often be recovered by spinning, then recovering from that.

It had its good points. The speed brakes were outstanding, controlling speed well during very steep descents. It was pleasant to fly and at high altitudes could match the higher wing-loaded Hunter day fighter. At the time of the Rhodesian crisis in the late 1960s, No 29 Squadron with Javelins was deployed to Ndola in Zambia when the Rhodesian Air Force had Hawker Hunters. Fortunately they never clashed. The Javelin was finally phased out in 1968.

Meanwhile the USSR had been taking its first faltering steps into the radar-aided night and all-weather field. In some ways, the air defence of the USSR is similar to that of Canada with vast, sparsely populated areas to cover; with appalling weather, few facilities, and darkness for many months of the year north of the Arctic Circle. The need for long range and endurance determined that their night and all-weather fighters would be large and heavy, and would need two engines. Optimised for bomber interception, they also needed extra heavy armament and AI radar.

Very little is known of early Soviet radar development, but it appears that they had produced at least two workable types by 1948-49. In true Soviet fashion, one was very small, the other very large. The small one was the forerunner of the "Izumrud" (Emerald) series, which became very widely used to give day fighters a limited – or perhaps more correctly, marginal – amount of all-weather capability. The large one was the first "real" night fighter radar, with more than one mode offering a large scanner, high transmitted power, and reasonable range.

"Izumrud" operated in S-band. Initially it had just one mode, and for this reason was given the reporting name of "Scan Fix" by NATO. The scanner dish was very small and the receiver aerial was separated from it. Range and general performance were reportedly modest. The large radar could operate in three different modes, and for this reason was given the reporting name of "Scan Three" by NATO. It used X-band, at about 3cm wavelength, had a large (30in/76cm) diameter scanner, and was in many ways similar to, although larger than, the APS-6 of the USN. With AI radar developments looking promising, the Soviet Air Defence Force requirement was issued in 1948.

The influence on aircraft design of TsAGI, the Soviet Aero and Hydrodynamics Institute, has often resulted in competing aircraft having similar layouts. This was very noticeable with the three contenders for the night and all-weather fighter which, apparently in an attempt to eliminate asymmetric handling problems while reducing drag, had two engines mounted in tandem in a staggered configuration with the leading engine exhausting amidships and the second beneath the tail. Then whereas the Western nations had built interim night fighters with straight wings before progressing into the aerodynamic hinterland of unconventional shapes, the Russian designers went immediately to swept wings.

First to fly, in January 1949, was the Sukhoi Su-15, not to be confused with the much later Su-15 "Flagon". A single-seater with the wing set in the mid position, the cockpit was offset to port above the inlet duct for the rear engine. A huge pitot nose inlet was used, bifurcated to feed both engines individually, with a small radome above it. Armament consisted of two massive 37mm N-37 cannon with 110rpg. The Su-15, also known as "Samolet P", lasted only a few months before breaking up in the air during a high speed run.

Very similar in appearance and configuration was the I-320R, although this was a two-holer with pilot and operator side by side and set well back. Like the

Su-15 it was powered by two RD-45 turbojets (Rolls-Royce Nene derived), while armament consisted of no less than three N-37 cannon installed beneath the nose. The radome was, like that of the Su-15, set above the intake.

The final aircraft of the trio was Semyon Lavochkin's La-200 which first flew in September 1949. The layout was basically very similar to the I-320R, with a two-man crew side by side level with the wing leading edge, but with a circular intake with the radome set in the centre of the splitter. Armament was again three N-37 cannon.

None of the three were taken up, primarily because it was found that the small "Izumrud" radar could be fitted to the MiG-17. In an attempt to offset this, the La-200 went through one very interesting transformation. A whole new nose and intake system was grafted on, consisting of a huge radome apparently capable of accommodating "Scan Three", and a unique triple-intake system – one in the chin position feeding the front engine, while two high-set cheek intakes supplied air to the rear engine. First flown in 1952, the La-200B was dropped in favour of the more orthodox Yak-25.

The advantages of the tandem engine layout have already been stated, but it seems reasonable to speculate that in practice it had many disadvantages. The leading engine had to be tilted down at a shallow angle and the exhaust would cause ground erosion; it would be difficult to achieve a satisfactory position for the centre of gravity; then, with engines and inlet ducts occupying most of the fuselage, space for fuel was at a premium; and finally, the long ducts to the rear engine would be prone to choking and duct rumble.

By contrast, the Yak-25, later given the NATO reporting name of "Flashlight", was far more workmanlike. For a start the engines, two slim axial flow Mikulin AM-5s, were set in nacelles beneath the 45-degree swept wing which was unusual in having the same chord from root to tip. The nose was occupied by a large bluff radome housing "Spin Scan" radar, while the two-man crew sat in tandem beneath a two-piece canopy with the pilot forward of the leading edge. Armament was two N-37 cannon. Some sources have stated that it also carried a battery of 55mm FFARs, but this seems unlikely.

The only really unconventional feature was the landing gear which consisted of a single-leg, twin-wheel arrangement on the centreline just aft of the centre of gravity, supplemented by a small nose gear and wingtip outriggers.

Like most Soviet designs, the Yak-25 went through a series of modifications during its service life. These included more powerful AM-9 turbojets (later redesignated RD-9s when Mikulin fell from favour and Tumansky took over), an extended wing root and wingtips, and a more streamlined radome.

"Flashlight" would have been hard-pressed to intercept a Canberra and stood little chance of catching a V-bomber or B-52. Maximum speed was in the region of 615kt (1,140kmh) and ceiling was 45,600ft (13,900m), which was not aided by the heavy wing loading of 880lb/sq ft (431kg/sq m). The one thing in its favour was its range, officially stated to be 1,620nm (3,000km). Given the thirsty engines of the period this seems high but as most of the fuselage volume was available for fuel, it is not impossible. In addition, stated empty and take-off weights appear to indicate a fuel load in excess of 12,000lb (5,443kg) which would give the high fuel fraction of 0.33. "Flashlight" remained in production until 1958 by which time an estimated total of 1,000 aircraft had been built. It was not phased out of frontline service until well into the 1960s.

Developed more or less in parallel with "Flashlight" was the French foray into the night fighter field, the SNCASO 4050 Vautour IIN. Configurations of the two were very similar. Two SNECMA Atar turbojets were housed in nacelles beneath a 35-degree swept wing which was tapered and mounted in the shoulder position, while the main gear was a true twin-wheel bicycle type, supplemented with outriggers which retracted into the sides of the engine nacelles.

The two-man crew were seated in tandem beneath dual clamshell canopies and the slim nose held a French CSF search and tracking radar. Armament consisted of four 30mm DEFA cannon with 100rpg, fitted with flash suppressors to reduce dazzle at night, supplemented by up to 240 68mm SNEB rockets internally.

While the stated maximum speed of 594kt (1,100kmh) was rather less than that of "Flashlight", the wing loading was lighter at 68lb/sq ft (333kg/sq m) and rate of climb and ceiling were both superior. Later in its career, Vautour was adapted to carry AAMs. Entering service in 1956, the Vautour was replaced by the Mirage F1 after some 20 years with the l'Armée de l'Air.

10. Technology Takes Over

Historically, the trends in aircraft development had been ever higher, ever faster. The decade following the Korean War saw maximum speeds and rates of climb more than double, while ceilings increased by about 50 per cent, stretching well into the stratosphere. Developments in aircraft armament had not kept pace with performance. While batteries of unguided rockets had provided a certain amount of extra range, they were only of use against a non-manoeuvring target. The time was ripe for the emergence of the air-to-air homing missile.

The requirements were simple: a considerably greater effective range than the FFAR, preferably higher speed, a warhead large enough to kill a bomber with a reasonable degree of certainty, and the ability to home on a target. The first three were relatively easy to attain. Getting the missile to manoeuvre accurately towards the target was the main problem. There were three possible methods: beam riding, infra-red, or heat-homing, and radar.

With beam riding, the fighter used a simple ranging radar which sent out a narrow "pencil" beam which the missile would follow. Launch range was typically about 2nm (3.7km) and the pilot had to hold his aim on target to within one-quarter of a degree during the full duration of the missile's flight, about eight seconds. Although effective against non-manoeuvring targets, the aim limitations were beyond the abilities of the average squadron pilot if the target attempted even quite gentle evasive manoeuvres.

British experiments with Fireflash were abortive, but in the USA a beam rider actually entered service. This was the AAM-N-2 Sparrow I, which was carried by Skyknights, Cutlasses and Demons from July 1956. However, the limitations of beam riding were such that new forms of guidance were developed for this big missile.

Active radar seemed an obvious choice, but in the pre-microchip era the difficulty of producing a set small enough to fit into a missile with a body diameter of just eight inches (203mm) was extreme, while range was severely limited by the size of the antenna. A simpler alternative was semi-active radar homing (SARH), in which the fighter illuminated the target with its onboard radar and the missile homed on the returns. The first guided missile to become operational, the Hughes GAR-1 Falcon, used SARH homing. After launch it accelerated rapidly to Mach 3, by which time the rocket fuel was expended, after which it would coast out to an effective range of just over 4nm (8km).

Good though it was, Falcon was overshadowed by the much longer ranged AIM-7 Sparrow family, the later variants of which all used SARH and, using a sustainer motor, reached out to between 22nm (40km) and 54nm (100km). The extended range of the Sparrow did however introduce a new dimension to air combat. First, it theoretically allowed attacks to be made from far beyond visual distance even in clear weather. Secondly, it greatly extended the range at which shots could be taken at a fast-moving retreating target.

The third guidance system used was infra-red, where the missile homes on heat emitted by the target aircraft. This is a far simpler and more reliable system than radar, and very short wavelengths in the IR spectrum (even shorter than those of visible light) give far greater accuracy than radar IR missiles do however have certain disadvantages. They are easily distracted by alternative heat sources such as the sun (although no-one has yet hit it!), or hot spots on the ground, for which reason they were of little use below 5,000ft (1,524m). Early models could only be used from the rear quadrant, thus perpetuating the traditional curve of pursuit attack. Nor could they see through cloud, which reduced seeker range drastically. For this reason, they are not really an all-weather weapon.

The most successful of the breed was the AIM-9 Sidewinder, which was first test fired in 1953 and entered service three years later. The AIM-9B had a brochure speed of Mach 2.5 and a range of about 1.75nm (3.2km), making it very much a clear air weapon. In seeker sensitivity, speed and range, it was inferior to both the IR Falcon variants and the British Firestreak and Red Top, but it was much simpler and cheaper than these. Nor did it require any special handling. Later Sidewinder variants were evolved with much longer range, improved seekers, and all-aspect homing, but in the late 1950s that was still many years in the future.

The advances in aircraft performance taking place at this time were such that early warning and tracking were assuming an ever-increasing importance. Ground-based radars were too limited. What was needed was something to enable the defenders to see over the horizon. The obvious solution was Airborne Early Warning (AEW). By lifting a search radar to about 30,000ft (9,144m), its range was increased to something over 200nm (371km). Moreover, an AEW aircraft could patrol well forward, out over the sea, over jungle or desert, in places where a ground radar station was impracticable.

Experiments with AEW in World War 2 had proved promising, notably those of the USN in the Pacific. Then, in August 1945, American scientists began work on Project "Cadillac", the requirements of which were to detect individual aircraft in small formations at more than 150nm (278km) under all-weather conditions, with a height accuracy of plus or minus 1,000ft (305m) at 60nm (111km).

Project "Cadillac" proceeded in three easy stages. Cadillac 1 was a standard ASV radar with an antenna extension carried by an Avenger. It first flew on 13 November 1946. Cadillac 2 was a converted B-17 which carried a production S-band APS-20A search radar, with an 8ft (2.44m) rotating scanner in a ventral radome. With the USN designation of PB-1W, it was described as a limited combat information centre. Cadillac 3 was a Lockheed PO-1W Constellation fitted out as a command information centre. The APS-20A was supplemented by an APS-45 height finding radar, and a tall but narrow dorsal radome was added.

Cadillac 3, which was developed to become the EC-121 Warning Star, was to be able to stay in the air for 30 hours on internal fuel, have five stations for fighter controllers who could each conduct two interceptions simultaneously, and detect low flying aircraft over water at between 70 and 90nm (130-167km). In the event, this proved to be a trifle ambitious, although it showed promise during interception exercises off New York early in 1951. But overland operations were bedevilled by clutter for many years. The technology of AEW and AWACS was in its infancy, and it was a long time in reaching maturity.

With the high flying supersonic jet bomber apparently just around the corner, the next generation of fighters had to be even faster, and have greater ceilings. Moreover, interception would become even more a matter of split second timing, calling for an even more highly automated fire control system than that of the F-89 and F-94. The interceptor was increasingly becoming an integrated weapons system.

The first fighter designed to meet these requirements was the Convair F-102A Delta Dagger. Development of this aircraft was scheduled to take place in two stages. The first was to be an interim type, brought into service quickly, while the second was to be the ultimate automatic interceptor.

As the poet said, the best laid plans of mice and men gang oft agley. He might have added fighter designers to the list. First flown on 24 October 1953, higher than predicted drag made the pre-production YF-102 firmly subsonic, and a massive redesign was initiated. Nor was this all. The selected engine and the FCS failed to meet requirements and had to be changed. Roll coupling was encountered, and the fin made larger in consequence. Far from an in-service date of 1954, the first deliveries to Air Defense Command were not made until April 1956, with initial operational capability (IOC) later that year. This delay meant that the F-102A was no longer regarded as an interim type, and it was ordered into service in large numbers.

Powered by a single Pratt & Whitney J57-P-23 rated at 16,000lb (71kN) with full afterburner, the Delta Dagger could wind up to Mach 1.175, and had a combat ceiling of 51,800ft (15,788m) – both figures less than originally specified. Only in operational radius was it better, although its maximum of 566nm (1,050km) was only achieved by using drop tanks, with which of course it was firmly subsonic. Development of the Hughes MG-10 FCS had lagged and the significantly less capable MG-3 was initially installed.

The Deuce, as the F-102 was popularly called, was the first production fighter to use a tail-less delta configuration. It was large – almost as long as a World War 2 Lancaster bomber, and fully laden weighed around 14 tonnes. A 60-degree swept delta wing provided plenty of area and a light wing loading, together with volume for fuel tanks. This was as well, because the sleek fuselage was packed full of black boxes – roughly three-quarters of a tonne of them, plus an internal weapons bay. In fact, the only wasted volume was in two aerodynamic fairings on either side of the tailpipe, added as a fix for excessive drag and called Yellow Canary.

The windshield was a sharp V-section, excellent for clearing rain away. There was of course a penalty in optical distortion, and yet another in annoying reflections from cockpit instruments at night. This last was partially cured by using a thin matt black screen on the centreline, past which the pilot had to peer.

The radar display was located high on the dash. Like others of its era, it was not bright enough to be seen in daylight and was fitted with a deep viewing hood. In

127

the interception phase, it was necessary for the pilot to lean foward to peer into the hood, manoeuvring the fighter with the control column in his right hand while manipulating the radar with a control stick in his left. Side to side stick movement deflected the scanner, while a thumbwheel adjusted the scan from between 37.5 degrees up to 20 degrees down. Fore and aft movement swept the range gate and aligned the radar on the target. Automatic modes were still way in the future.

Guns had supposedly been made obsolete by the new magic missiles and the Deuce was not fitted with any. This was a new trend which was to have unhappy consequences for the future. Armament consisted of six AIM-4 Falcons, three SARH and three IR homing, carried in an internal bay. With the FCS locked on, one or more missiles selected and the system armed, the rest was automatic. When the clever electrons decided that they had the problem licked, the weapons bay doors flicked open, the chosen missile(s) extended on arms, its rocket motor ignited, and the Falcon went inexorably on its way. The weapons bay doors would then click shut. Trim changes during this procedure were automatically compensated by the flight control system.

Alternative weaponry for the Deuce consisted of two AIM-26B Nuclear Falcons, or one AIM-26B and three AIM-4s. As a belt and braces measure, the weapons bay doors were designed to hold a dozen Mighty Mouse FFARs, but once the main system was found to work as advertised, these were no longer carried.

In 1958 the Deuce was retrofitted with the MG-10 FCS and still later with an Infra-Red Search and Track (IRST) seeker in a dome just ahead of the windshield. The MG-10 was linked into the Semi-Automatic Ground Environment (SAGE) which was then being deployed across the North American continent. In essence this was an overlapping system of radar and GCI stations, forming a network into which the fighter could be hooked. But by this time, the Deuce had been overtaken by events in the form of the far more potent "ultimate interceptor", at first designated F-102B, but later as the F-106 Delta Dart.

The "Six", as it was known, was basically a refined Deuce. Externally it looked very similar. A broad chord flat-topped fin, the absence of the ugly Yellow Canary fairings at the base of the fuselage, and inlets set well back behind the cockpit were the only major external differences. Beneath the skin however it was a very different bird.

The Pratt & Whitney J75-P-17 turbojet gave nearly 50 per cent more power. Added to a less draggy fuselage and a wing with the significantly lower thickness/chord ratio of five per cent, the Six could comfortably exceed Mach 2. It climbed nearly twice as fast as the Deuce, and had a ceiling of 57,000ft (17,373m). A slightly longer fuselage allowed fuel tanks to be located there, giving an increase of nearly 50 per cent internal fuel, and with external tanks the Six had an operational radius of 633nm (1,173km).

The F-106A reached IOC in October 1960 and became the mainstay of Air Defense Command until well into the 1980s. The Hughes MA-1 FCS had finally reached maturity, which is to say that it worked perfectly for some of the time. A bonus here was that the tie-in to SAGE now included the automatic pilot, which could thus be controlled directly from the ground. This made the pilot more or less a system manager, responsible for take-off and landing, making tactical decisions, and monitoring fuel status, while the weapons system – one hesitates to say the aeroplane – flew a fully automatic interception.

One of the more advanced gismos was a tactical display indicator (TDI) which was a little round screen located low in the centre of the dash, to accommodate which the control column was moved over to the right. Working on film strips, the TDI showed terrain, landmarks, airfields and navaids for normal flight, while for air combat it displayed two little moving bugs, one of which was the Six and the other its opponent.

To fly, the Six was a delight, sensitive and responsive, and able to out-turn anything at high altitude. Like all deltas, it had no clearly defined point of stall, and if the speed got too low, would merely sink, without the slightest inclination to drop a wing and spin. Like the Deuce it carried four Falcons in an internal weapons bay; generally these were late models, AIM-4Fs and Gs, although AIR-2A Genie was sometimes carried. All the Six needed to be outstanding in the air superiority role was a gun, but apart from a podded version, this was never fitted, although one was projected in the late 1960s.

Traditionally, the night and all-weather interceptor had been inferior to the dedicated air superiority fighter in daylight, due to the need to carry a heavy and bulky load of electronics, and often a second crew member. By the end of the 1950s the technology explosion meant that the gap was closing fast. This notwithstanding, the reliance of the Six on SAGE and automation made it rather specialised. There was room for another type of all-weather fighter, one with autonomous interception capability to provide greater flexibility.

The first of these was McDonnell's F-101 Voodoo, which was initially ordered as a long range escort fighter by Strategic Air Command, then cancelled on 29 September 1954 – ironically the same day as its first flight – because its projected operational range was far short of that of the bombers it was supposed to escort.

It was then adopted as a tactical fighter-bomber, a role to which it was basically unsuited, and in which it served with only one fighter wing. There followed a reconnaissance variant with a rehashed camera nose. Finally it was discovered by Air Defense Command, which adopted it to supplement the Deuce, to be used in areas outside or on the periphery of SAGE coverage.

In appearance and concept the Voodoo could hardly have been more different from the Convair deltas. For a start it was a two-seater. The tiny swept wing had little more than half the area of the Deuce, while the maximum all-up weight approached 52,000lb (23,587kg), giving the incredibly high wing loading of 141lb/sq ft (687kg/sq m). Stalling speed was frighteningly high, 184kt (341kmh) at sea level, rising to 472kt (874kmh) at 50,000ft (15,239m), at which altitude and maximum speed it was limited to a sedate 1.2g turn.

Although rate of roll was quite adequate, the Voodoo was a complete turkey in any situation which required a moderate amount of manoeuvre, and this was not helped by the high set tailplane, which was blanketed by the wings at quite low angles of attack. When this happened, pitchup would result and the aeroplane would tumble end over end. A pitchup inhibitor was introduced at an early stage, but like so many systems of that era, it usually didn't work. Handling left much to be desired; flying the F-101B has been described as balancing the aircraft on top of a pencil point, wobbling back and forth without ever finding the right place. Another frequent problem was that a shorting electrical junction could cause the canopy to jettison, leaving the crew exposed to the elements in a high speed cabriolet.

This notwithstanding, the F-101B had its good points. Two Pratt & Whitney J57-P-55 afterburning turbojets, each rated at 14,782lb(65.7kN), gave an adequate thrust/weight ratio of 0.71 at combat weight. Combined with low drag, this resulted in a climb rate that few fighters of its era could match, and considerably better than that of the Six, plus sparkling acceleration. It was also fast for its day, as was demonstrated on 12 December 1957, when a single-seat Voodoo flown by Major Adrian Drew set a new absolute speed record of 1,207mph (1,942kmh).

The escort fighter origins of the Voodoo showed in its large internal fuel capacity of 13,345lb (6,053kg), more than one-third greater than that of the Six, which, with two external jugs, gave a combat radius of 720nm (1,334km) and endurance of 3.04 hours. Flight refuelling allowed transatlantic deployments to be made.

The FCS was the Hughes MG-13 which needed a specialist operator, and three AIM-4 Falcons were carried in an internal bay. It was later modified to carry two Genies on underwing pylons, and an IRST was fitted at much the same time.

Meanwhile McDonnell were designing a new carrier aircraft to follow on from their not very inspiring Demon. Not being very sure what the USN would want next, they produced a basic airframe layout which could have a variety of different cockpits and noses grafted on to fit it for various missions. Initial studies showed one or two seats, and one or two engines. If required, it could perform day fighter, photo-recce, electronic warfare, or attack missions. Essentially it was a design in search of a role.

Indecision came to an end when the USN decided they wanted a two-seat missile-armed fleet air defence interceptor with a three-hour endurance, able to loiter on station 250nm (463km) from its carrier. McDonnell configured it for this mission and the prototype took to the air on 27 May 1958. It was duly called the Phantom II, thus perpetuating McDonnell's line of spooks.

It was a strange looking beast. The two General Electric J79 turbojets were set in a mid-position like those of the Voodoo, with the tail surfaces carried on a boom above them, with the stabilators canted down at a steep angle to prevent them being blanketed by the wings during manoeuvring flight. The wing was nearly a delta, with the outer panels canted upwards to give added stability. A really innovative feature was the semi-submerged carriage of four AIM-7 Sparrow missiles under the fuselage, which gave a tremendous saving in drag over the more orthodox external carriage on pylons. It is an interesting point to note that drag is slightly less when missiles are carried than when the wells are empty.

Radar in the early models was the Westinghouse APQ-50, with a 24in (610mm) diameter scanner, but the quest for greater range soon saw it replaced by the same company's APQ-72. This had a 32in (813mm) scanner, to accommodate which the nose had to be enlarged, giving the Phantom its characteristic droopy look.

At the same time the cockpit was raised to improve forward view over the nose, an essential feature for carrier landings.

Despite its ungainly appearance, the Phantom was soon turning in better than predicted performances and between December 1959 and April 1962 set a hatful of world records, which included absolute speed at 1,606.3mph (2,585kmh); absolute altitude at 98,557ft (30,048m); sustained altitude at 66,443.8ft (20,252m); and the entire range of time to height records, during one of which it passed the 50,000ft (15,239m) mark in less than two minutes. This attracted the attention of the USAF and, although reluctant to buy a Navy fighter, Operation "Highspeed" showed that the Phantom with the APQ-72 radar was in many ways superior to the highly automated Six. Modified for land-based operations, it became the F-4C in USAF service, following the US Navy's F-4B. The Phantom, in many variants, dominated the fighter scene for the next 15 years and was bought by many overseas air forces. We shall meet it in combat in the next chapter.

There had been several attempts to push speeds up past Mach 3 and altitudes up to 80,000ft (24,383m), but with one notable exception, which was Russian (and which we will come to later), these came to naught. Fighter performance reached a plateau at just past Mach 2 and just over 50,000ft (15,239m). It was not intended, it was just the way things happened.

Of the three American Mach 3 plus projects, only one ever flew. The futuristic Republic XF-103, which was to use a turbojet and a ramjet coupled in tandem to reach Mach 3.7, and in which pilot forward vision was through a periscope, was cancelled in 1957 in favour of the North American F-108 Rapier. This aircraft, which was in effect a scaled down fighter version of the Valkyrie bomber and which used a special high energy fuel, itself fell victim to a combination of budget cuts and controversy current at that time as to whether surface-to-air missiles could do an equal job more cheaply. It was therefore left to Lockheed to carry the Mach 3 fighter banner in the West.

The YF-12A had its origins in a dedicated reconnaissance vehicle, the single-seat A-12, which first flew in April 1962. Not only was the A-12 intended to cruise at Mach 3 at ultra-high altitudes, but it was designed for minimal radar reflectivity. These features were retained in the experimental interceptor variant, which was modified to have a second crew position and three internal weapons bays, resulting in a slightly longer fuselage, ventral fins, and a revised nose to hold the radar, with the chines cut away from around it. Infra-red sensors were installed on the leading edges of the chines. The first of three YF-12As made its maiden flight from the top secret Groom Lake facility on 7 August 1963.

The FCS was the Hughes ASG-18, originally developed for the Rapier. This was the first coherent pulse-Doppler radar to fly, the technology having been made possible by replacing the magnetron with the newly developed travelling wave tube, allied to advances in digital computers. ASG-18 was excellent at detecting high speed closing targets at previously unattainable ranges, although it suffered from range ambiguity due to the fact that several pulses were emitted before the first echo returned. It had a certain amount of look-down capability, but for various technical reasons it was less effective against contacts with a low closure rate.

Also taken from the Rapier were the missiles. These were enormous AIM-47 Falcons, with a maximum speed of Mach 6 and a range of 100nm (185km). Guidance was SARH, switching to IR for the terminal homing stage. While we saw earlier that IR was not really suitable for an all-weather weapon, it was anticipated that the ultra-fast, ultra-high bomber would generally be up above the weather.

While the speed and range of the YF-12A were well suited to the long range interceptor mission, in other respects it was less than satisfactory. Acceleration at the slow end was very average as was rate of climb, while its powers of manoeuvre were severely restricted by structural limits of +3g/-1g. In addition, the exotic JP-7 fuel had to be warmed prior to take-off, making a rapid scramble difficult if not impossible. Its death knell was sounded when it became obvious that an orthodox fighter, carrying "snap-up" missiles, could do the job equally well.

Whereas the defence of North America offered opportunities for early warning and forward interception, no such luxury was available to Britain and France. Early warning times were likely to be short, and there was little margin for error. This placed the accent on exceptional rates of climb, even at the expense of endurance.

Britain managed to produce just one type of supersonic fighter. That this one happened to be exceptional is hardly relevant; scores of good schemes were simply thrown out. The Saunders Roe SR177 was a mixed power fighter, using a turbojet for normal flight conditions, and a liquid fuel rocket to augment rates of climb and manoeuvre at high altitudes. The SR53 proof of concept aircraft worked very well, but the project was junked in 1957 when the official mind decided that manned fighters were no longer needed.

There were others. The Gloster G50 was basically a scaled up Javelin with the high set tail removed, and a much thinner, supersonic wing. It promised a maximum speed of Mach 1.77 and carried four Red Dean AAMs with a range of 35nm (65km), which used SARH for midcourse guidance and active radar terminal homing. The Hawker P1092 was a slender delta with a lot of wing/body blending, which was to have carried two Red Top AAMs at Mach 1.5, while the Fairey F155T had a wing planform similar to that of Eurofighter 2000, and should have reached Mach 2.5 at 59,000ft (17,982m).

The sole success was the English Electric Lightning, which as the P1 research aircraft, first flew on 4 August 1954. In many ways its design was unique. Wing sweep was a startling 60 degrees, for which a considerable penalty in structural weight was incurred. At the time it was said that it was a delta wing with the areas of least lift cut out, but this was obviously a nonsense. The planform is best described as having a steeply swept trailing edge inboard, and a straight trailing edge outboard on which the ailerons were mounted. The tailplane was set low to obviate problems with pitchup, while to minimise drag the engines were mounted staggered one above the other, fed by a single pitot intake. This last design characteristic did nothing to ease engine changes or maintenance.

The use of a pitot intake meant that the only place for the Ferranti AI.23 radar was in the centrebody, which naturally restricted the size of its scanner. This apart, it was a particularly good system which used monopulse techniques, a type that is singularly hard to jam. Range was about 22nm (41km). Its main failing was that it had no look-down capability, but as it was expected to intercept over the North Sea, where ground clutter was minimal, this was less important than it might otherwise have been. Weaponry consisted of two 30mm Aden cannon, though not on all variants, and two Firestreak (replaced later by Red Top) missiles, the latter having all-aspect capability.

Ordered by the RAF in November 1956, the Lightning was sufficiently far advanced to escape the great fighter purge of the following year. Entering service in June 1960, it was a potential world beater in many respects. Two afterburning Rolls-Royce Avons, each rated at (in the Mk 6) 16,300lb (72.4kN) gave a thrust/weight ratio of better than 0.80, allowing it to pull into a near vertical climb straight off the runway, and giving an initial climb rate of 50,000ft/min (254m/sec). Maximum speed was Mach 2.1, and service ceiling 60,000ft (18,287m).

Handling was responsive, but at the same time pleasant and vice-free. On one occasion a Mk 1 ran away with a maintenance officer on board. Although his only flying experience was on Chipmunk trainers, he was able to gain control, circle, and bring it in for a successful landing. It is difficult to think of another Mach 2 aircraft with which this could have been done. The only real shortcoming was critically low internal fuel capacity on the early variants. While this was almost doubled on later aircraft, lack of endurance was always a potential problem which was only partially alleviated by flight refuelling.

On the other side of the English Channel, France was less hampered by the ramblings of the official mind. Avions Marcel Dassault had already established themselves as front runners in the postwar French aircraft industry. Their first venture into the all-weather fighter field had been the Mystere IVN, a single-engined two-seater of similar appearance to the American F-86D, which was passed over in favour of the Vautour. Dassault's next venture into the specifically all-weather fighter field was a long time in coming. This was the two-seat Mirage F2, the prototype of which was first flown in June 1966 but which also failed to enter production. In between they produced a very successful fighter fitted with AI radar which gave it a moderate degree of night and all-weather capability.

This was the Mirage IIIC, a single-seater of tail-less delta configuration which entered service in July 1961. At first rocket motors were fitted to enhance rates of climb and high altitude manoeuvre capability, but one of the fuels used was a dangerous and volatile substance called red fuming nitric acid. When in the mid-1960s the high altitude threat receded, the rocket motor fell into disuse.

A single SNECMA Atar 9B afterburning turbojet rated at 13,225lb (58.8kN) gave the modest thrust/weight ratio of 0.67. Like most tail-less deltas, wing loading was on the low side, and while a maximum speed of Mach 2.15 and a service ceiling of 54,136ft (16,500m) could be reached, rate of climb was on the low side. The Cyrano II radar was generally reckoned to be less capable than the British AI.23. Early armament consisted of two 30mm DEFA cannon and a single large and not very effective Matra 530 missile with either SARH or IR homing.

While all this was going on in the West, the Soviet Union was far from idle. Many of their standard fighters, notably the MiG-17, -19 and -21 were fitted with small radars which gave them a marginal all-weather capability, while others were designed specifically for the task. Of these there were five major types.

The Soviet tradition of screwing every ounce of capability from a proven format saw the Yak-25 "Flashlight" developed through many variants, culminating in 1960 with the supersonic Yak-28P "Firebar". Although it retained the same basic layout as its forebear, and with it some pretty horrible asymmetric handling problems with one engine out, "Firebar" differed considerably in detail. The wing, set much higher on the fuselage, was more sharply swept and its area increased by about one-fifth. Extended nacelles housed two afterburning Tumansky R-11AH2-300 turbojets each rated at 12,680lb (56.4kN), which could push "Firebar" up to Mach 1.8 and 53,000ft (16,154m), and give a rate of climb equalling that of the MiG-21. Radar was the "Orel-D", with a range believed to be of the order of 16nm (30km). Cannon armament was omitted and standard weaponry consisted of two R-30 (AA-3 "Anab") missiles with both IR and SARH homing, the latter ranged to match the radar. The later Yak-28PM carried two R-3 (AA-2 "Atoll") short range AAMs in addition to "Anabs".

In many ways the air defence of the USSR resembled that of Canada. Vast wastelands, few airfields and terrible weather all demanded a very long range interceptor capable of functioning with minimal assistance from the ground. This gave rise to the huge Tu-28P "Fiddler", the heaviest interceptor ever, weighing over 100,000lb (45,360kg) fully laden. First flown in 1960, little is known for certain about "Fiddler". It has an orthodox swept wing layout, with two afterburning turbojets, possibly Lyulka AL-21Fs, each rated at 26,500lb (117.8kN) located along the sides of the fuselage. This would give an unexceptional thrust/weight ratio, but its mission is to loiter in the air until needed, rather than to scramble and go tearing off in pursuit of an intruder. The two-man crew is seated in tandem and, like the F-102, the windshield is V-shaped.

"Fiddler's" radar is known in the West as "Big Nose". Scanner size is unknown, but very large, and emitting in I-band is reported to give a tracking range of 43nm (80km) against fighter sized targets. Weaponry is four huge AA-5 "Ash" missiles, which are about 12in (305mm) in diameter and over 17ft (5.18m) long. Of these two use SARH homing, with a range of about 30nm (55km), while the other two are heat seekers with the shorter range of 11nm (20km).

Despite its size, "Fiddler" is believed to be capable of Mach 1.5 and 60,000ft (18,287m), while its vast internal fuel capacity of over 30,000lb (13,608kg) gives an operational radius of about 809nm (1,500km) including a supersonic dash. However, there has been a tendency in the West to overestimate the capabilities of Soviet aircraft, and these figures may be yet another example.

Not all the area of the Soviet Union demanded long range fully autonomous interceptors. Strategically important regions were given a close ground control network. In these, as in the Western SAGE and NADGE, automatic interception was quite feasible and this allowed high performance single-seaters to be used, rather than lumbering two-seaters such as "Fiddler".

Traditionally, Soviet single-seaters had been the agile sports cars of the fighter world, potentially very effective in daylight, but much less so in adverse conditions. Their radars were of limited capability; they were behind the West in transistors and micro-miniaturisation. Furthermore, their missiles tended to be short ranged. To get any worthwhile reach, missiles had to be large, but hanging large missiles on a small fighter was like putting an anchor on it, increasing drag and reducing thrust/weight ratio, which penalised performance to an unacceptable degree.

The simple answer was a bigger fighter, which duly emerged as the Sukhoi Su-15, NATO reporting name "Flagon", the first really effective all-weather interceptor produced by the Soviet Union. In later models, two afterburning Tumansky R-13F-300 turbojets each rated at 15,875lb (70.5kN) gave an initial climb rate of 45,000ft/min (229m/sec) and a maximum speed in excess of Mach 2. "Flagon" was optimised for performance rather than manoeuvrability. Aerodynamically it was remarkably clean, but the delta wing, which had a cranked leading edge, was very small, giving the high wing loading of 108lb/sq ft (527kg/sq m). This notwithstanding, operational ceiling is generally quoted as 65,620ft (20,000m). Operational radius is 540nm (1,000km) carrying four AAMs externally, plus two drop tanks.

The adoption of side intakes left the nose free for a large radar. At first this was the Uragan 5B, codenamed "Skip Spin" by the West, but almost certainly with a larger scanner, but later variants carry "Twin Scan". This probably has a Cassegrain antenna with a track while scanning system which, although not a pulse-Doppler type, may well have a limited look-down shoot-down capability. Detection range is believed to be about 30nm (56km), which is quite adequate for automatic interception. Like the Delta Dart, "Flagon's" fire control system is linked to the GCI system via the autopilot.

Four AAMs are routinely carried: Advanced AA-3 "Anabs" as described for the Yak-28, but rather longer ranged, or possibly two R-23R "Apexes". "Flagon" has no integral gun, but has been seen with two twin-barrel GSh-23 cannon pods. Precisely why is uncertain, unless it is to fire the traditional warning shot across the bows of an interloper in peacetime.

In the late 1950s the Soviet Union spent many unhappy hours tracking American U-2s across the sky without ever being able to do a thing about them. When in May 1960 they finally managed to knock one down, the Lockheed A-12, with performance maxima of Mach 3.6 and 95,000ft (28,955m), was less than two years away from its first flight. It was this, rather than the threat posed by the bisonic B-58 Hustler, which entered service in August 1960, or the projected trisonic B-70 Valkyrie, that led to what was to become the world's fastest fighter.

The Soviet Union, lagging the West in all respects, be it propulsion, electronics, missiles or metallurgy, was faced with having to produce a counter with the resources available. They succeeded brilliantly and in doing so started a hare which misled their opponents for many years to come.

The Mikoyan MiG-25, NATO reporting name "Foxbat", is best described by comparing it with its American contemporary, the YF-12A. Whereas the latter had rather clever turbo-ramjets, "Foxbat" was powered by two large but crude low pressure Tumansky R-15 turbojets optimised for high and fast flight using afterburning, but with an incredibly high specific fuel consumption without it. Like the

YF-12A, special high density fuel was used, in this case T-6. Both aircraft were little more than flying fuel tanks, but whereas the American fighter could cover over 2,000nm (3,706nm) at Mach 3, the full afterburner interception radius of "Foxbat" was a mere 160nm (296km).

Whereas the US machine was built mainly of titanium to resist aerodynamic heating, the Russians used nickel steel where they had to, aluminium alloy where they could get away with it, and some titanium where it was unavoidable. This incurred a heavy weight penalty and, like its American counterpart, "Foxbat" was structurally very limited, to 2g with full internal fuel, rising to 5g at half fuel.

The A-12 and its successors were designed for low radar signature. This obviously posed problems to the Russians, to which their solution was extreme power as a cure for all ills. "Smertch-A", which in the absence of transistors used old fashioned thermionic valves, was reported to put out about 600kW, and was popularly supposed to kill rabbits at 200m. Be that as it may, it was as good a way of detecting low reflective targets and burning through jamming as more sophisticated measures. Radar range was about 50nm (93km) -half that of ASG-18 – and "Smertch-A", although far from being a coherent pulse-Doppler type, had a certain amount of look-down capability.

Normal weaponry was four R-40T and R-heat and SARH missiles respectively (AA-6 "Acrid"). Despite the latter being 19.33ft (5.90m) long, 15.7in (400mm) diameter, and weighing roughly 1,765lb (800kg) at launch, range was just 43nm (80km); no more than half that of the much smaller AIM-47 Eagle.

"Foxbat" could achieve Mach 2.8 with a full bag of missiles, and could operate at 78,000ft (23,773m). In extremis it could be wound up to Mach 3.2, although this meant wrecking the engines through overspeeding. Intended to fly a fully automatic interception, "Foxbat" was tied into ground control by a digital data link, which took it from shortly after take-off until shortly before landing, with the pilot acting as systems manager. In many ways a classic example of making the best of what was available, when launched against its primary target, the SR-71, it was unable to catch it, as recorded by Soviet defector Viktor Belenko.

11. Vietnam and its Aftermath

Up to 1965, the development of the all-weather fighter had been almost entirely theoretical. The next eight years saw a certain amount of practical proof in a series of limited wars. With one exception, these were of short duration, even though the air fighting was often intense. In the Middle East, air actions of the Six Day War of 1967, the War of Attrition in 1969-70 and the October War of 1973, were in the main fought in clear weather, in daylight. There was comparatively little night air activity, and so far as has been released, no night air combat, although a handful of actions took place around dusk.

Farther east, India and Pakistan fought two short wars in 1965 and 1971. As in the Middle East, most of the air fighting took place in daylight at fairly low level, with visibility often reduced by haze and dust, but a few night actions ensued. The first war between India and Pakistan began on 6 September 1965 and was of particular interest in that both countries operated jet bombers at night; India using Canberra B(I)58s, while Pakistan was equipped with the almost identical B-57. Both sides lacked a really capable night fighter, and were forced to make shift with what was available. The Pakistani Air Force (PAF) used the F-104A Starfighter which had a totally inadequate radar, and the F-86F with no search radar at all. India was in a similar plight with MiG-21s and Hunters.

On the first night of the war, at least 14 Indian Air Force (IAF) Canberras were detected approaching Rawalpindi and Peshawar at high altitude, using stream tactics to confuse the PAF GCI. Three PAF Starfighters were scrambled to intercept them. Time and again the Pakistani controllers attempted to vector the F-104s in behind the raiders but these, warned that they had company by GCI or by their Orange Putter tail warning radar, took evasive action. This was quite enough to prevent the PAF fighters from gaining contact with their very limited radar.

After a few days, the IAF adopted a hi-lo-hi profile, approaching Pakistan at high level, then descending beneath the radar coverage as they crossed the border, pulling up to medium altitude for the attack run, then descending again for the egress. This compounded the difficulties of interception considerably, and not until 13 September did a Starfighter even so much as make radar contact, and then an electrical failure prevented it from firing any ordnance. On the following night, a Starfighter actually managed to launch a Sidewinder in a blind stern attack. A flash was seen as the missile exploded, but whether it had struck home, or had detonated prematurely, could not be established. Further AI contacts were made by other aircraft, but could not be held due to evasive action by the IAF Canberras.

Ironically, the first night victim of the war fell to a Sabre. Flight Lieutenant Cecil Choudhry was vectored by GCI after a climbing Canberra. Even though it was a bright moonlit night, he was unable to get a visual, but at 30,000ft (9,144m) he managed to get a missile tone from one of his Sidewinders, indicating that it had detected a possible target.

The first AAM was launched blind and missed, and the IAF aircraft, by now aware that all was not well, commenced evasive action. GCI vectored Choudhry in pursuit and shortly after, still without visual contact, he got another good missile tone. Launching, he watched the missile begin tracking, then after about three seconds saw an explosion. GCI then reported that the target was descending fast over Indian territory.

The sole Starfighter night success came right at the end of the war, when Wing Commander Khan Jamal intercepted a Canberra at 33,000ft (10,058m) and shot it down with a Sidewinder, also without gaining visual contact. Luck had been on his side. At low level, the tail warning radar gave spurious warnings when the beam touched the ground, and so had been switched off. The Indian crew had forgotten to turn it on again for the climbout. This was confirmed by the pilot, who ejected successfully and was taken prisoner.

PAF B-57s were also busy, mainly on low level strikes at IAF airfields, although some close air support sorties were flown at night. Low level operations ensured that IAF night fighters had even greater difficulty in intercepting than their PAF counterparts, and while a few encounters were reported, no B-57s were lost to fighters at night.

The second war between India and Pakistan occurred in December 1971. In many ways it was a rerun of the previous clash, most of the air action taking place in daylight in support of the ground forces. At night, PAF B-57s and IAF Canberras attacked airfields and other targets; in the IAF case some assistance was rendered by Antonov An-12 transports fitted out as bombers, attacking from low level.

As in the 1965 conflict, night interceptions were few, even though the PAF now operated the Mirage IIIP. On the night of 8 December an IAF Canberra, taking violent evasive action to evade a Starfighter, was reported to have crashed into the sea without a shot being fired. Then in the later stages of the war, a Mirage nearly collided with an An-12 before losing contact. Finally, a Mirage IIIRP on a night photo mission was intercepted by two Indian MiG-21s, but escaped unharmed at high speed. PAF sources then state that one MiG-21 was shot down by the other. If this was the case, and no confirmation has been forthcoming from the IAF, it simply underlines the old rule that night fighters should operate singly.

To summarise, losses to interceptors at night in both conflicts were minimal. As in World War 2, operational losses due to night and bad weather were rather higher than losses to enemy action. While both IAF and PAF bombers were able to operate virtually unhindered by fighters, they were unable to cause much damage and thus had little effect on the air war as a whole. This being the case, it hardly mattered that both sets of night fighters were ineffective. This also meant that there was little incentive to improve the situation between the wars. In daylight there was little in the way of adverse weather to contend with, so this was not a significant factor either, although at least one PAF Sabre pilot crashed as a result of becoming disoriented in cloud at low level in the 1965 conflict.

It was in 1964 that US air power first became embroiled in Vietnam, in a conflict which lasted until January 1973. While the Indo/Pakistan fracas of one year later had been essentially low-tech and localised, the Vietnam air war saw the most modern technology of the time tested in the crucible of combat.

A feature of the South East Asia conflict was the appalling weather that existed for much of the year. From November to April the monsoon brought solid cloud cover, often with heavy rain and appalling visibility below it. Thunderclouds reached as high as 48,000ft (14,630m). A laden fighter could not fly over them; mission requirements or fuel considerations often made it impossible to go around them, so if the mission was to be accomplished it had to go through them. Inside the thunderheads were spectacular displays of lightning, icing, and extreme turbulence, with visibility reduced to a few tens of feet. From May to October things were better, but often visibility was restricted by haze.

Conditions notwithstanding, the war had to go on. Often a strike force, complete with its escorting fighters, would launch and fly to the target area, only to find it completely socked in. They would then drag their munitions back to base, ready and eager to go through the whole performance again next day.

Distance was another consideration. Many USAF fighter units were based in Thailand and had to fly a distance equivalent to that from London to Berlin in order to raid North Vietnam. This made refuelling essential for both the outbound and inbound legs. While flight refuelling is a more or less routine operation in peacetime, in South East Asia in the monsoon it was less so.

First the fighters had to struggle through the weather while maintaining formation integrity, which was far from easy. Then they had to find the tanker. Finally they had to formate on it to take on fuel, often in very turbulent conditions while carrying a heavy load of ordnance. On a bad day, this was close to the ultimate in all-weather flying.

The North Vietnamese Air Force (NVAF) operated MiG-17s and MiG-21s and in the final two years of the war, F-6s, which were Chinese-built MiG-19s. With all these aircraft, on-board radar capability was minimal, while blind flying instrumentation and navaids were basic. Consequently the NVAF rarely flew at night, or in really bad weather. To compensate for these shortcomings, they flew combat missions under close ground control. Frequent American raids, all too often using stereotyped attack profiles, gave them plenty of practice, and they quickly became proficient.

The USAF based a detachment of F-102 Delta Daggers in South Vietnam from 1962 to 1969, to guard against the possibility of raids by Ilyushin Il-28 jet bombers, of which the NVAF had a small number. In the event, this threat failed to materialise and this highly automated interceptor spent much of its time in search of mysterious low and slow radar contacts. At least one of these came from a flock of ducks! The only real contact came in 1968, when a Deuce was shot down by an NVAF fighter.

However, the lion's share of air combat over North Vietnam fell to the ubiquitous Phantom, by now in service with the USAF, USN and USMC. Theoretically this was a mismatch as the Phantom, with its sophisticated AI radar and Sparrow missiles, would kill the NVAF MiGs at far beyond visual range, without ever seeing them. For several reasons this failed to work out.

First, the Phantom's radar could only scan a relatively small sector of sky ahead, while early models had an analogue display which, when looking down, showed a great deal of clutter, making it difficult to detect a low flying target. The North Vietnamese controllers became adept at keeping their fighters out of the search area of the Phantoms and working them round astern at low level before commencing an interception. Area surveillance by AEW aircraft was the obvious American counter, but as these operated out over the Gulf of Tonkin they were often unable to detect the low flyers well inland.

The next problem was that the MiG-21 in particular was a small radar target, and the Phantom's radar was unable to lock on for missile guidance at more than about 12nm (22km). In a head-on engagement, closing speeds approached one nautical mile (1.85km) every four seconds, giving little time for a successful missile attack.

But the greatest factor of all was the need for positive identification. It is not widely known that very early in the war, beyond visual range missile attacks resulted in two own goals. In theory, IFF should have prevented this, but as in many other fields theory was not borne out in practice, because there was simply too much which could, and often did, go wrong. The result was that almost invariably, visual identification was demanded, thus negating the Phantom's radar/missile capability.

Young Lieutenant Bill Lafever, a Phantom back-seater with the 555th Tactical Fighter Squadron (TFS) in 1967, recalled:

"Sometimes we'd get low contacts out ahead, below the undercast where we couldn't see them to identify them. We were often pretty sure they were MiGs, but had to be absolutely certain. This was difficult, because if they were coming head on, we couldn't get down and round in time, and would lose radar contact as they passed beneath us.

"Once we knew MiGs were in the area, we had to fly with one eye on the radar and the other looking out of the window. The rear view from the Phantom was poor, and we were more concerned about what was coming up from behind where we had no radar cover.

"The MiGs would suddenly pop out of the clouds; one minute there was nothing, the next there would be a MiG. They had a trick of vectoring MiGs onto us from different directions. We'd see the first one and break into it, then the second would pop out of the clouds at our six o'clock. It called for very good timing, which they didn't always quite manage, but when it did it was difficult to counter. Our answer was teamwork, mutual cover and support at all times."

Neither did the theory of beyond visual range (BVR) combat meet expectations, nor did the magic missiles. Sparrow and Sidewinder had been designed to kill non-manoeuvring targets, but the MiGs were rarely so obliging. At launch, the Phantom was restricted to manoeuvres of not more than 2.5g; neither missile was very agile, although on rare occasions they surpassed expectations, while there was a short delay between trigger squeeze and the missile firing. Finally, the switchology between SARH and IR missiles took too long. These factors conspired to prevent split second chances being taken.

Another problem was that both missiles had rather long minimum ranges, and Phantoms often got too close, which rendered their weaponry ineffective. After many missed opportunities to this cause, F-4Ds were fitted with gun pods.

The AIM-4D Falcon saw limited use in South East Asia. Designed for fighter-versus-fighter combat, it had less restrictive launch limitations, greater manoeuvrability, and a more sensitive seeker than Sidewinder. In the event it proved rather less successful, due to the fact that the seeker had to be cooled before firing, and the supply of coolant was limited. Once readied, if it was not fired before the coolant was exhausted, it became unusable.

The final factor affecting all AAMs of the period was lack of reliability. The overall success rates for the war were about eight per cent for the Sparrow and 15 per cent for the Sidewinder. On many occasions a missile would fail to light up on launch and fall to earth, while on others it would fail to track the target. In part this was due to lack of maintenance. AAMs would be hung on an aircraft and left there through mission after mission. With this treatment it was small wonder that the sensitive electronics often failed to work properly.

American incursions over North Vietnam ceased in 1968 and did not resume until 1972. By this time, several advances had been made. New and improved Phantoms had entered service. The AWG-10 FCS of the F-4J was a first in many ways. It was the first multi-mode pulse-Doppler set to enter service; the first transistorised interceptor radar, and the first with a digital computer. Furthermore, all weapons launch data was displayed on the HUD.

The F-4J was a US Navy aircraft; its equivalent in the USAF was the F-4E, which had the APQ-120 radar, similar in many ways to that of AWG-10 but with a smaller scanner, adopted partly to allow the installation of a 20mm M61 cannon in the nose. The F-4E also had slatted wings, which gave it greater manoeuvrability.

Performance of *Red Crown*, the radar picket cruiser in the Gulf of Tonkin, and the AEW aircraft patrolling outside the borders of North Vietnam had been, in the early part of the war, something less than impressive. Operating at extreme ranges, and trying to survey small targets over often mountainous terrain, this was hardly their fault. Two improvements were now put in hand to allow greater use to be made of the Phantom's BVR missile capability.

The first of these was "Combat Tree", a codename concealing an IFF interrogator which was only fitted to aircraft of the 432nd Tactical Reconnaissance Wing (TRW), and which enabled Phantom crews to establish identity at far beyond visual range. The second was the increasing use of SIGINT (SIGnals INTelligence) aircraft to monitor NVAF radio traffic. This was concealed by an elaborate message relay system. To the best of the writer's knowledge this has never been officially admitted, but nothing else accounts for the fact that a ship stationed many miles offshore could consistently know that fighters on a base well inland were about to take off.

Although raids on North Vietnam ceased in 1968, the ground war in the south continued, with Viet Cong forces supplied down the Ho Chi Minh trail through Laos. B-52 bombers of the USAF flew missions to interdict the supply routes, and gradually NVAF fighters started operating in the area. USAF Phantoms started to fly combat air patrols to oppose them, and it was one of these that obtained the first night victory of the war.

The successful pilot was Major Robert Lodge, with Lieutenant Roger Locher in the back seat. On the night of 21 February 1972 they were flying an F-4D of the 432nd TRW over north-eastern Laos when *Red Crown* vectored them towards incoming MiGs. Descending to low level, beneath the NVAF radar coverage, they closed, and Locher gained a radar contact coming head-on. Locking on, they launched a Sparrow at 11nm (20km), followed by two more at intervals of approximately 12 seconds and eight seconds.

The first missile appeared to miss, but the detonation of the next was followed by a large secondary explosion. With no more Sparrows left (this was probably a "Combat Tree" aircraft, which carried specialised equipment in the fourth Sparrow well) Lodge and Locher turned and egressed the area at low level and high speed, pursued for 30nm (56km) by two MiG-21s.

Using "Combat Tree", the same tactics worked equally well by day as by night. In the initially successful "Oyster Flight" action of 10 May, a vector from "Disco", an EC-121 AEW aircraft, was supplemented by more information from *Red Crown*. A high speed low level charge followed, ending in a front-quarter Sparrow attack, which downed two out of four MiG-21s from beyond visual range. One fell to Lodge and Locher for their third victory of the war. As the two surviving MiGs swept past, the four Phantoms turned in behind them, and a third was shot down with a Sparrow by future aces Steve Ritchie and Charles DeBellevue. This action gave further credence to the involvement of SIGINT aircraft, as two F-6s, believed to have been piloted by Lieutenants Le Thanh Dao and Vu Van Hop, joined the party with no prior warning, shooting down Lodge and Locher with cannon fire. The lack of warning is significant. *Red Crown* could not possibly have detected them on its own radar; "Disco" obviously did not, while if the two young NVAF pilots had observed radio silence, SIGINT could not have detected them either.

Whatever the means of identification, this new capability of *Red Crown* proved invaluable, and never more than in the final months of the war. In December 1972, B-52s made a series of raids on Hanoi at night, with Phantoms flying barrier patrols between the bombers and the MiG bases. The heavy bombers could hardly be ignored, and the NVAF made several attempts to intercept. The protective Phantoms, cleared to fire by *Red Crown*, picked several of them off at quite long distance.

While the MiG-21 was a capable day fighter, once the US forces had acquired a reliable method of BVR identification, its limitations at night or in adverse weather were ruthlessly exposed.

Historically, dedicated night and all-weather fighters, penalised by a heavy and bulky load of electronic gear, and often by a second crew member, were supreme only in their chosen domain. In clear air they were vulnerable to light and agile fighters. Given sufficient power to provide a high level of performance despite the extra weight and bulk and a superior weapons system, they were at last the equal of the aerial sports cars, even in daylight. While many theoretically very capable aircraft preceded the Phantom into service, it was the big McDonnell Douglas fighter that first passed the test of combat, giving a practical demonstration that the all-weather fighter had at last come of age.

The Phantom was the great all-rounder of its era. It had shown that it could operate around the clock; in daylight it had demonstrated that it could, if handled correctly, outfight the MiG-21, not only in South East Asia but in the Middle East also; it was a great bomb truck; was one of the best tactical recce machines around, and could fly the demanding "Wild Weasel" defence suppression mission as well as, if not better than, anything else.

This notwithstanding, combat experience in the 1960s and early 1970s showed that it was not without faults. The avionics fit showed only what was in front, with inadequate indications of threats coming from behind. It was a poor performer in a turning combat and, if pushed too hard, would depart controlled flight. When this happened, it was not easy to recover. Finally, while the Phantom had done well against the MiG-21, the Soviet Union was developing new fighters with more advanced weapons systems and these would be far more formidable opponents.

As we saw in the preceding chapter, the MiG-25 was a single-mission aircraft, with very limited capabilities in other roles, but in the late 1960s US Intelligence had no way of knowing that. Working on disconnected snippets of information, they arrived at performance levels and abilities far beyond those "Foxbat" actually possessed, such as long range, an operational maximum speed of Mach 3.2, and full agility in close combat.

Closely contemporary with "Foxbat" was a Mikoyan tactical fighter, the MiG-23 "Flogger". A single-engined single-seater, "Flogger" was, like the Phantom, a multi-role design. A Tumansky R-29 afterburning turbojet rated at 25,350lb (112.7kN) gave it a respectable thrust/weight ratio, with what has been described as "jackrabbit acceleration", and a rate of climb of about 50,000ft/min (254m/sec). A multi-mode pulse-Doppler radar codenamed "High Lark" gave a search range of 43nm (80km) and a tracking range of 30nm (56km), these figures reducing significantly in the look-down mode. Armament was typically a 23mm GSh-23 cannon, two R-23 (AA-7 "Apex") medium range missiles and four R-60 (AA-8 "Aphid") short range missiles.

Like "Foxbat", "Flogger" was mistakenly credited with being a rather better fighter than it was. In part this was because its wings featured variable sweep, which it was thought could be optimised for the entire range of the flight envelope. In conjunction with high lift devices, this would have made it very agile at low to medium speeds. The truth was more prosaic. Swing wings had been adopted solely for good short field performance, and at minimum sweep were very g-limited. "Flogger" was never intended to be agile, and in combat it turned like a tram.

The new threat, real or imagined, was therefore the new generation of Soviet fighters, coupled with jet bombers armed with long range air-to-surface missiles. Once more the USN led the way. Defence against stand-off missiles called for a long range interceptor, but on its own this was not enough. A pure interceptor was too limited; it also needed to double in the air superiority and escort fighter roles.

The radar and weapons were already to hand. These were the Hughes AWG-9 FCS and AIM-54 Phoenix long range missile, developed from the ASG-18 and AIM-47 Eagle AAMs tested by the YF-12A and intended for the F-111B carrier interceptor. When it became evident that the latter would fall well short of specification, Grumman designed a new fighter around them. First flown in December 1970, this was the F-14 Tomcat. The Tomcat was large. To carry a load of six AIM-54s and a crew of two, it had to be. Learning from the South East Asia experience, it had an integral 20mm M61 cannon and alternative weapon loads were four or six Sparrows supplemented by four or two Sidewinders. It was also given a huge transparent canopy which allowed a really good all-round view, something sadly lacking in the Phantom and even more so in "Flogger".

Like the latter it had variable sweep wings, but computer controlled to give the optimum position under all flight conditions. Coupled with a battery of high lift devices, this provided excellent agility at subsonic speeds, while for the supersonic regime, glove vanes were used to offset excessive stability and improve manoeuvrability. Unlike the Phantom, the Tomcat had almost completely vice-free handling. Its only real weakness lay in the over-sensitive Pratt & Whitney TF30 turbofans, but it was never intended that these should be the definitive engines. Only when costs threatened to spiral out of sight was the decision taken to stay with the TF30.

At the heart of the Tomcat, AWG-9 was way ahead of any other fighter radar of its time. A 36in (914mm) diameter slotted planar array antenna and a power output of 10.2kW, combined with high prfs, allowed it to reach out to more than 115nm (213km) in search mode. Other modes included range while search, track while scan, single target track, and several air combat manoeuvring modes. But the most impressive thing of all was that whereas AWG-10 of the Phantom could handle only one target at a time, AWG-9 could guide all six AIM-54s at different targets simultaneously. This was done by "time-sharing" the target tracks and updating the course of the missiles in flight. Phoenix uses active radar homing for the final few miles of flight.

The AWG-9/AIM-54 combination provided a long range/multiple kill capability which has never been matched. In April 1973 it "destroyed" a target drone from a launch range of 110nm (204km), the Phoenix covering a total distance of 72.5nm (134km) – a figure that has never been bettered by an AAM – while the only six-target test carried out resulted in four direct hits and one "no-test" when the augmentation in one of the drones failed.

Apart from its outstanding long range detection/kill capability, AWG-9 also introduced a new era into traditional air combat. The Naval Flight Officer (NFO) in the back seat has two displays with which to monitor events. At the top is the Detail Data Display, which presents basic target information, while below it is the circular Tactical Information Display (TID). Both present information in a clutter-free alpha-numeric format which shows contacts with attitude and heading, and identified as friendly or hostile.

The TID picture can be presented in one of two ways. The first has the Tomcat at the bottom pointing upwards, which gives essentially the view in front. The second is north-oriented, with both the Tomcat and aircraft all around it shown. Contacts which are not within the radar scan are supplied from GCI, AEW, or from other aircraft, via a two-way data link. This provides all-round coverage, minimising the chance of the Tomcat being surprised from behind. In all, 24 contacts can be shown and the NFO acts as a battle manager, constantly advising the pilot of the current tactical situation.

The McDonnell Douglas F-15 Eagle first flew in July 1972, some 20 months later than the Tomcat. Like the Tomcat, its design had also been influenced by the largely mythical performance of the "Foxbat", but there were other considerations. In many projected scenarios, the F-15 would be heavily outnumbered by agile lightweights such as the latest MiG-21 variants. It therefore needed to combine the virtues of high performance interceptor and daylight air superiority fighter, while retaining full night and all-weather capability.

To meet these demands, armament consisted of a single 20mm M61 cannon and eight AAMs, a mix of Sparrows and Sidewinders, combined with a capable but one-man operable radar. The airframe had therefore to be large and two Pratt & Whitney F100 augmented turbofans, each rated at 23,830lb (105.9kN), were selected to give the new fighter a thrust/weight ratio exceeding unity. This conferred a tremendous rate of climb: the F-15 could be hauled into the vertical immediately on leaving the runway and continue to accelerate straight up. To give the required agility, a large wing area kept the loading moderate at 68lb/sq ft (333kg/sq m) at normal take-off weight.

Radar was the Hughes APG-63 pulse-Doppler multimode type, with a maximum detection range of 100nm (185km). Whereas AWG-9 in the Tomcat had difficulty in ranging accurately and in detecting targets with a low closure rate, these were now overcome by interleaving medium prf with high prf and using a digital signal processor, rather than the fixed circuit hardware filter banks of the earlier type.

Inevitably, the workload involved in flying the aircraft while operating an advanced multi-mode radar, navigating and using various communications systems, was enormous, and McDonnell Douglas evolved a new concept to reduce it. This was HOTAS – Hands On Throttle and Stick – in which all controls likely to be needed in combat were grouped under the pilot's hands. It needs remarkable manual dexterity to operate effectively, but as one F-15 pilot said to the writer: "It's like learning to play the piccolo; it gets easier with practice."

The F-14 and F-15 were very large, extremely capable, and incredibly expensive, to the point where the world's richest nation was unable to afford as many of them as were needed. The new buzzword became affordability, and this in turn led to the advent of the General Dynamics (now Lockheed) F-16 Fighting Falcon.

First flown in January 1974, the F-16 was a classic example of the smallest possible fighter wrapped around the largest possible engine, in this case the Pratt & Whitney F100. Armed with a 20mm M61 cannon and just two Sidewinders, and originally intended to be fitted with a simple search radar, it was designed for maximum agility, a totally unstable aeroplane which used computers to keep it under control. The F-16 was the first of the fly-by-wire fighters.

What happened next was inevitable. It was criticised for lack of all-weather capability, which led to the adoption of the Westinghouse APG-66 multi-mode radar with a range of 39nm (72km) against fighter-sized targets. Later models were given the even more capable APG-68 and a Sparrow missile capability was added. In the West at least, there was no longer a place for a fighter without a medium range missile and all-weather capability.

Further advances in radar and cockpit systems management came in the McDonnell Douglas F/A-18 Hornet, the prototype of which first flew on 18 November 1978. Its origins however lay much further back.

The Northrop YF-17 had been a contender for the lightweight fighter contest won by the F-16 in 1974. In the normal way of things, it should have sunk into obscurity, but the USN was at that time looking for an aircraft to fill both the fighter and the attack roles. The twin-engined (GE F404s) YF-17 was deemed more suitable than the F-16 for carrier missions and McDonnell Douglas was tasked with producing a navalised version.

The F/A-18 Hornet, as it became, was rather larger and considerably heavier than the YF-17. Basic armament consisted of a 20mm M61 cannon, two Sparrows carried semi-conformally, and two Sidewinders on wingtip rails. To allow it to perform both fighter and attack missions with equal facility, it was given what was the most versatile multimode radar of its day, the Hughes APG-65.

Air combat radars need variable waveform flexibility for all-aspect, all-altitude target detection, with extremely fast rates of data processing, while air-to-surface systems require a large amount of data storage, with processing facilities for ground mapping. Greater flexibility than had previously been available was needed, and this was provided by a programmable signal processor. The digital signal processor of APG-63 in the F-15, constrained by hard-wired logic, gave a fixed repertoire of modes. With APG-65, existing modes could be modified; Doppler filter and range gates could be altered, while new Electronic Counter Counter-Measures (ECCM) features could be introduced to match a changing threat simply by changing the software. The new buzzword was "programmable".

In addition to several air-to-ground modes, APG-65 featured no less than nine air-to-air modes. Velocity Search provided maximum detection range against closing targets; Range While Search for use against all-aspect targets out to about 80nm (148km); and Track While Scan could maintain 10 track files while displaying eight at ranges below 40nm (74km). Single Target Track used two-channel monopulse angle tracking and track extrapolation logic to follow a contact through the 180-degree angle off zone where the radar echo appeared to move in conformity with ground returns, where Doppler filtering tended to throw out the baby with the bathwater. Gun Director mode used pulse to pulse frequency agility to reduce glint. Raid Assessment mode allowed the pilot to expand the region around a single echo, allowing radar resolution of targets in close formation at distances below 30nm (56km). Finally there were three Air Combat Manoeuvre modes for ranges less than 5nm (9km), each with its own scan pattern and all giving automatic target acquisition.

With APG-65, the Hornet pilot was seated in the middle of an information explosion. The problem became how best to handle it. HOTAS, as used in the same company's F-15, was only a partial answer. All the information needed in flight and in combat had to be readily available in an easily assimilable form.

The solution adopted by McDonnell Douglas was to abandon the plethora of dials and switches and channel everything into three multi-function CRT displays, which were also made interchangeable at need. A press of a button would call up the information needed at any specific moment, while critical information could also be displayed on the HUD. This was the forerunner of the "glass cockpit" now found in every modern fighter and in many airliners.

Vietnam and Middle East wars had convincingly demonstrated that Mach 2 was never reached in tactical air combat. To the best of the writer's knowledge, the highest speed ever attained in Vietnam was Mach 1.6 and the Hornet, like the F-16, was never intended to be Mach 2-capable. However, it did have a very respectable level of performance, and handling was pleasant and vice-free, with first class high alpha capability. If the Hornet was in some ways inferior to the F-16 in close combat, it had an altogether better radar and weapons system. Meanwhile the Europeans had not been idle.

France seems always to have regarded the high speed, high altitude intruder as the primary air threat, and taken the attitude that anything that can deal with this would be able to handle all other interception and air combat tasks. The tail-less delta configuration of the Mirage III, while ideal for high speed, high altitude flight, had shortcomings in other regimes. It bled off energy at an alarming rate in hard turns, while long runways were needed to cope with high speed take-offs and landings. To overcome these problems, Dassault reverted to an orthodox swept-wing layout for their next fighter. This was to have been the Mirage F2, a two-seater powered by a single Pratt & Whitney TF306 turbofan. This proved too expensive and the Mirage F1, a scaled down single-seater powered by a SNECMA Atar 50K, was produced in its stead.

Relaxed stability and fly by wire (FBW) then allowed Dassault to overcome the inherent problems of the tail-less delta, which was adopted for their new fighter, the Mirage 2000. First flown in March 1978, the Mirage 2000 proved to be very agile, with quadruplex digital FBW conferring carefree handling. The new SNECMA M53 augmented turbofan provided a thrust/weight ratio approaching unity, and gave a maximum speed of Mach 2.35, an initial climb rate of 49,212ft/min (250m/sec), and a ceiling of 60,042ft (12,300m).

A detection range of about 54nm (100km) using high prf was given by the Thomson-CSF RDI pulse-Doppler multi-mode radar. Matched to this was the main air-to-air weapon, Matra's Super 530D SARH missile, which has in-built Doppler filters to allow snapdown attacks against low flying targets. With a reported speed of Mach 4.6 and a range of 22nm (40km), the Super 530D can also snap up to home on targets at 80,384ft (24,400m). Two are routinely carried for the interception mission, plus two R550 Magic 2 heat seekers, which have a better off-boresight capability than Sidewinder. For close range work, two 30mm DEFA 554 cannon are fitted.

For the RAF, the situation was different. Forward defence, far out over the North Sea, involving long patrol times over extended ranges, often in terrible weather, in the face of intensive ECM, was the priority. The threat to be countered was the supersonic Tu-22M "Backfire" bomber or Su-24 "Fencer" long range attack aircraft, at high or low level, operating unescorted.

The project started as the Multi-Role Combat Aircraft, built by Britain, Germany and Italy. This was to be a tactical strike and interdiction aircraft, optimised for long range and low level penetration of defended airspace, with short field performance that allowed it to operate from austere or damaged runways. To meet these demands, it had economical RB199 augmented turbofans and variable sweep wings with a whole bag of high lift devices to offset the very high wing loading. It was a far cry from a dedicated interceptor.

Development started in March 1976, nearly two years after the first flight of the Tornado IDS, as the strike variant was called, and considerable revision was needed. First, the fuselage had to be lengthened in order to carry four Skyflash SARH missiles semi-submerged. This had the advantage of increasing internal fuel capacity by 11 per cent, which was a promising start. The engines, although very economical, were far from ideal for the interception mission, mainly due to the high bypass ratio of 1:1, which was ideal for subsonic cruise but became a hindrance in the supersonic regime. All that could be done about this was to increase afterburning thrust by a small percentage, but the thrust/weight ratio remained on the light side. Other changes involved fully variable automatic wing sweep, which was introduced on the Tornado F3, and the Spin and Incidence Limiting System, (SPILS), which gave carefree handling.

The main changes concerned the avionics fit. The original terrain-following radar was replaced by the Marconi AI.24 Foxhunter, an I-band multi-mode radar with a detection range exceeding 100nm (185km) even in the look-down mode. Unusually, a Cassegrain antenna was used rather than the more fashionable planar array. This gave more consistent performance over a wide range of frequencies, while minimising sidelobes. The receiver was designed for low signal levels amid high clutter returns.

Long range search used Frequency Modulated Interrupted Continuous Wave techniques, which can be most easily described as the next step on from pulse-Doppler. While this gave good results against rapidly closing targets, the problem remained, as with AWG-9 and other high prf radars, detecting tail-on targets with low closure rates. This was overcome by using low prfs and pulse-compression modulation.

As with the F-14, the Tornado back-seater acts as a battle manager, collating the information from all the sensors – radar, data link, radar warning receiver etc. In the back is a Plan Position Indicator similar in concept to that in the F-14. The RAF has always been rather coy about exactly what AI.24 can do, but it is believed that it can track at least 20 contacts simultaneously and receive yet others from AWACS or GCI.

The Tornado F3 can reach Mach 2.27 at altitude, or Mach 1.2 at low level, which is good by any standards. Initial climb rate is 40,000ft/min (203m/sec) which is modest for the era, and service ceiling is 50,000ft (15,239m). What it does best is to patrol far out over the sea and stay on station for two hours at a distance of between 300 and 400nm (556–741km).

Air-to-air armament consists of a 27mm Mauser cannon, two or four Sidewinders, and four Skyflash SARH missiles. Skyflash is essentially a Sparrow with British designed monopulse seeker which gives far greater accuracy than its American counterpart. Another advantage is in warm-up time. In Vietnam, the obligatory count of "four potatoes" often allowed a potential victim to escape. With Skyflash, warm-up is reduced to two seconds.

To summarise, the Tornado F3 has few equals in medium range combat, but at close quarters would be disadvantaged by its high wing loading and lack of thrust.

12. Further Wars, Developments and Conclusions

he term "all-weather" was initially used to describe an aircraft which could operate in conditions too bad for an orthodox day fighter. In the early days, this generally meant during the hours of darkness, but as capabilities gradually increased, the night fighter was increasingly used in daylight in weather conditions where the fighter reliant solely on the unaided vision of its pilot was ineffective. It was not a truly all-weather machine inasmuch as it was too vulnerable in clear skies when enemy fighters were abroad. This gradually changed as the performance of radar-equipped fighters began to equal that of the visual-only aircraft. Then as radar and other avionics systems improved, they were used to expand the situational awareness "bubble" of the pilot to far beyond that of his unaided eyesight, even on the clearest day. This was made even more effective by the widespread use of medium range homing missiles. All-weather finally came to mean just that: a fighter effective around the clock, in fair weather or foul.

The Beka'a Valley action in 1982 clearly demonstrated the art of what had become possible, when the Israeli Air Force trounced the Syrians. Their first move was to take out the Syrian detection systems. This was coupled with intensive ECM, which forced the Syrian fighters to fly electronically blind. The Israeli fighters, mainly F-15s and 16s, set ambushes by lurking in the radar "shadows" cast by mountains, then aided by E-2C Hawkeye AEW aircraft, climbed rapidly to attack.

Whereas the Israeli fighters at all times had a broad picture of events, the Syrians, operating mainly MiG-21s and 23s were only aware of what they could see "out of the window". The consequences of this were clearly shown by an 84 to nil score in the Israelis' favour.

In that same year, the Falklands War between Britain and Argentina showed a similarly lopsided scoreline, primarily because the Argentinians were forced to fight on British terms. There was however an interesting sidelight on adverse weather operations in this conflict. Aircraft could be launched from the giant American carriers in quite appalling weather, but landing them back was quite another matter. Automatic Carrier Landing Systems were first produced in the early days of the Phantom, but for various technical reasons they were never entirely successful. Getting a fast-moving aircraft back onto a carrier deck in conditions of almost nil visibility remained beyond the capabilities of contemporary technology. In the appalling weather of a South Atlantic winter, it was found that Sea Harriers, with their slow flying and vertical landing capability, could be safely recovered in weather too bad for conventional fast jets to operate. This notwithstanding, two Sea Harriers flying a combat air patrol in appalling visibility were lost on 6 May, probably due to a mid-air collision.

While the Sea Harrier emerged from the war in the South Atlantic with the desirable tag "combat proven", various shortcomings had been evident. The first of these was lack of a BVR weapon; the second was a lack of on-board kills – two Sidewinders were simply not enough; and the third was that a pulse-Doppler radar was needed to replace the pulse-only Blue Fox. This resulted in the Sea Harrier FRS2 with a rejigged nose holding the Ferranti Blue Vixen multi-mode radar, and the adoption of four AIM-120 Amraam missiles as main armament, trials with which were commenced in April 1993.

The superb range of fighters produced in the USA from 1970 onwards totally outclassed those of the Soviet Union, which took immediate steps to close the qualitative gap. As a result, three new Russian fighters entered service during the next decade. These were the Mikoyan MiG-29 "Fulcrum" and MiG-31 "Foxhound", and the Sukhoi Su-27 "Flanker".

"Fulcrum" was a small and agile twin-engined single-seater, in size somewhere between the F-16 and F/A-18 and with comparable air-to-air performance, though lacking the endurance of the US types and, in its early version, without a FBW flight control system. What really surprised Western observers was the fire control system. This consisted of the Phasotron NO-93 "Zhuk" pulse-Doppler multi-mode radar, with a maximum search range of 54nm (100km), and capabilities closely comparable to those of the APG-68 of the F-16C. The radar is interlinked through the fire control computer with an Infra-Red Search and Track (IRST) system, a laser ranger, and a helmet-mounted sight. IRSTs had been in service in the West for many years, but were widely regarded as supplementary equipment. In the "Fulcrum" they are an integral part of the FCS and allow interceptions to be made in radar silence. On the other hand, if a target vanishes into cloud, thereby losing the IRST, the radar automatically switches on and takes over. Guns attacks are mainly made with IRST coupled with the laser ranger, a combination said to give exceptional shooting accuracy, while the helmet-mounted sight allows missiles to be fired at large off-boresight angles. Later MiG-29s have so-called "glass cockpits", with CRT displays replacing conventional instrumentation.

"Fulcrum's" stablemate, the MiG-31 "Foxhound", is by contrast a pure interceptor. Mikoyan, using the "Foxbat" as the baseline, installed two new Perm D-30F6 two-spool turbofans each rated at 41,843lb (186kN) maximum, with considerably better fuel economy than the R-31s of the "Foxbat", to give a supersonic interception range of 389nm (720km), and a maximum speed of Mach 2.35. Leading edge slats were used to offset the very high wing loading, and a few structural tucks and gussets were added to strengthen the airframe. Internal fuel capacity is 36,045lb (16,350kg), giving a maximum endurance of 3.6 hours.

Whereas "Foxbat" and other Soviet air defence interceptors relied heavily on GCI and automatic interception, "Foxhound" was a major departure, designed to operate semi-autonomously. At the heart of the fire control system was the enormous SBI-16 "Zaslon" radar, which has a maximum search range of 162nm (300km), can track up to 10 targets, and guide four long range AA-9 "Amos" missiles simultaneously. Like the "Foxbat" before it, "Foxhound's" radar is enormously powerful to burn through jamming.

A major advance was the use of a phased array antenna with electronic steering, the first time this had ever been done in a fighter. The scan pattern for tracking and firing is plus/minus 70 degrees on either side of the boresight, and 70 degrees up/60 degrees down. It is of course much wider than this for a pure search mode. A retractable IRST is located on the underside of the nose and this interacts with the radar as described for "Fulcrum". To increase autonomous operation a second crew member handles the systems, while a secure data link connects the MiG-31 with the ground and up to three other aircraft, and the standard patrol pattern shows four "Foxhounds" in line abreast at 108nm (200km) spacings.

Standard weaponry consists of four AA-9 "Amos" long range AAMs, two AA-6 "Acrid" medium range AAMs or four AA-8 "Aphid" dogfight missiles, plus a 23mm GSh-23 cannon.

The third of the Russian trio was Sukhoi's Su-27 "Flanker", a huge twin-engined single-seater which was very much an F-15 equivalent, but with FBW to allow it take take advantage of relaxed stability. Wing loading is moderate, thrust/weight ratio is very high, and the big fighter is in consequence very agile. It has been described by Western pilots as a delightful aircraft to fly.

Standard procedure on Western fighters has for many years been to increase range by using external tanks. This increases drag, degrades performance, increases radar signature, and sterilises pylons which could otherwise be used for munitions. "Flanker" was a bold attempt to overcome this trend by providing a simply enormous internal tankage of 11 tonnes, a considerable portion of this only being used in the overload case, but which gives the impressive operational radius of 809nm (1,500km).

Whereas Western fighters can drop their external tanks when combat is joined, no such option is open to "Flanker", although presumably a fuel jettison capability is provided. On the other hand, the Russian heavyweight can carry no less than 10 AAMs in a combination of AA-8 "Aphids", AA-10 "Alamos", and AA-11 "Archers". Like "Fulcrum", "Flanker" carries a 30mm cannon.

"Flanker's" large radome houses a multi-mode pulse-Doppler radar with a scanner only slightly smaller than that of "Foxhound". Estimated search range was 130nm (240km) and tracking range 100nm (185km). Troubles with the radar delayed service entry, and it has been reported to have a high false alarm rate and a short mean time between failures. Only one target could be engaged at a time, although the recent emergence of the Vympel RVV-AE "Amraamski", the latest Russian medium range fire-and-forget missile, will have altered this. Like "Fulcrum", an IRST is an integral part of the fire control system, with the seeker mounted just in front of the windshield where surprisingly, it does not obstruct forward view.

Later "Flankers" have "glass" cockpits, while the Su-35 variant first revealed at the 1992 SBAC Farnborough Air Show has added canards for greater manoeuvrability, carries up to 14 AAMs, and its radar has a claimed maximum detection range of 216nm (400km).

The Gulf War of 1991 clearly demonstrated the value of round the clock operations and, inadvertently, due to the worst weather conditions in the region for 20 years, all-weather operations also. The overwhelmingly powerful Coalition air forces had far greater capabilities in this field than their Iraqi opponents, and for this reason the all-important initial assault was made at night.

As we have seen, air defence systems have become integrated, with ground-based detection, control and command playing an ever-increasing part in the whole. With this in mind, a goodly proportion of the initial strike was aimed at air defence radars, command and communication centres. As the old Russian saying goes: "Destroy one third, jam one third, and the rest will just collapse!" And so it proved, with central control lost, great holes in the ground radar coverage, and the remainder subjected to a barrage of jamming.

Bereft of effective GCI, few Iraqi fighter sorties were flown on that first night, but those that did encountered a new ploy. Tactical Air Launched Decoys (TALD) and BMQ-74 drones with enhanced radar signatures to make them look like tactical aircraft on Iraqi screens, preceded the incoming strikes. While their primary functions were to bring ground radars on line so that they could be attacked, and to soak up the surface-to-air missiles, several were intercepted by the Iraqi fighters. Thus distracted, the Iraqis became more vulnerable to the Coalition fighters that followed.

The first kill of the war went to Captain Steve Tate, flying an F-15C of the 1st TFW on 17 January. The son of a former USMC fighter pilot, he described it thus:

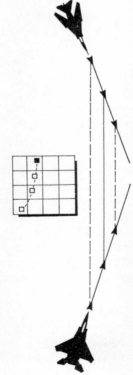

"A few minutes after the beginning of operations, around 3am, my radar showed a plane climbing and coming rapidly towards us. Soon he came up to the tail of one of my squadron's F-15s. I don't know if the bogey was chasing him, but I locked him up at 12nm (22km) range, confirmed he was hostile, and closing to 4nm (7.4km), fired a Sparrow. When it hit the whole sky lit up. It (a Mirage F1) continued to burn all the way to the ground and then just blew up into a thousand pieces."

Also airborne were F-15 pilots Captains Richard Tollini and Larry Pitts of the 33rd TFW. Tasked to provide cover for incoming strike aircraft, they were refuelling when an AWACS alerted them that the strike was under attack from Iraqi fighters. Breaking off from the tanker, they headed north. Larry Pitts recalled:

The B-Scope of the F-15 needs careful interpretation. The radar scans a segmental area, but the information is presented on a square screen. Although the target is always at the same angle, it appears to drift wider as the range closes.

"Our radar scopes were filled with friendlies, 60–80 of them. Night conditions combined with bad weather made it difficult to fire missiles even if we acquired targets. There were just too many friendlies out there!"

Although Pitts made several contacts, all were lost in the multi-bogey confusion before he could fire. However, all was not lost. Two days later he and Tollini accounted for a MiG-25 "Foxbat" each with Sparrows.

Other 33rd TFW formations had better luck on this first night. Captain Jon Kelk downed a MiG-29 with a Sparrow at 0315, then five minutes later Captain Robert Grater picked off two Mirage F1s, also with Sparrows.

The destruction of the Iraqi GCI system badly disadvantaged the defending fighters, which failed to score, the much vaunted MiG-29s losing five of their number in air combat, while on the Coalition side, the F-15C accounted for almost all the air-to-air victories. The Gulf War showed up the weakness of a centralised GCI system and pointed up the need for fighters able to operate autonomously in the face of heavy ECM. In addition there were other lessons to be learned.

The conflict saw the first intensive use of low observables technology, in the angular shape of the Lockheed F-117A. Designed to give exceptionally low radar and IR signatures, and to operate using no emitting systems, the F-117A flew deep into Iraq with impunity. Even had the Iraqi early warning system been intact, it seems improbable that they could have been detected except by sheer chance, using catseye fighters. At least one tale has emerged of an F-15C on combat air patrol, getting a fleeting glimpse of a black jet as it flashed past, without the faintest trace of it on his radar.

According to an official USAF document, a strike force of 32 F-16s needed 16 F-15s as escorts; four EF-111s for ECM cover; and eight F-4G Wild Weasels for defence suppression, the whole being supplied with fuel by 15 KC-135 tankers. By contrast, just eight F-117As, their pilots undistracted by the defences, could achieve a level of accuracy sufficient to do the same job, with no support needed other than two KC-10 tankers. Quite apart from the stealth implications, this gave the Iraqi defenders a target-poor environment in which to operate.

It should of course be remembered that air combat does not exist in isolation, but is a means to an end – that of attaining air superiority to allow the attack aircraft a free run against their surface targets. The Gulf War demonstrated that this is an area in which weather is still a major player. Many attack aircraft were forced to return with ordnance unexpended when their briefed targets could neither be seen nor identified. This was a fairly frequent occurrence with the F-117A, which lacked target-finding emitters such as synthetic aperture radar. This was of course the penalty of using precision attacks. Area attacks can still be made in almost any weather, therefore the requirement for an all-weather fighter remains paramount.

It would be only too easy to think that modern radar has reached a pitch of sophistication and reliability wherein the fighter with the most capable equipment wins. This is far from the case. Radars, nor yet the computers behind them, are not yet 10 feet tall, and even though capabilities may have increased by many orders of magnitude since the early days, reliability has not kept pace.

Let us take for example the Vietnam War. Even as just a few fighter pilots claim the lion's share of victories, so a few Phantoms did significantly better than others simply because, for whatever reason, their fire control systems were more reliable. In this connection, on the sortie when USAF ace Steve Ritchie scored his double-kill, it is not widely known that his radar went down barely 15 minutes later. Such is the knife edge between success and failure.

Nor have radars been made totally idiot-proof; a great deal of skill is required to get the best out of them. As an example, let us take the Westinghouse APG-68 as fitted to the F-16C. For the early stages of an engagement, two main modes are available: Range While Search (RWS) and Track While Scan (TWS). Search areas are variable. RWS has longer range than TWS, and scan areas are

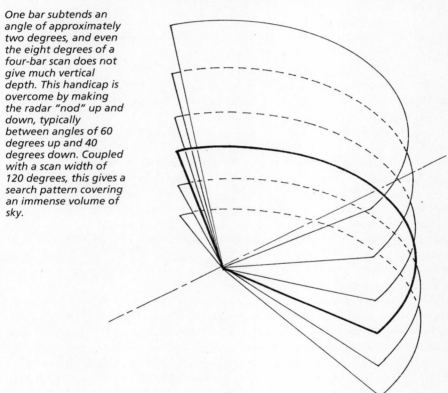

One bar subtends an angle of approximately two degrees, and even the eight degrees of a four-bar scan does not give much vertical depth. This handicap is overcome by making the radar "nod" up and down, typically between angles of 60 degrees up and 40 degrees down. Coupled with a scan width of 120 degrees, this gives a search pattern covering an immense volume of sky.

+/-60 degrees; +/-30 degrees, and +/-10 degrees in azimuth, with 1, 2 or 4-bar in elevation, bar spacing being 2.2 degrees in elevation, which gives roughly a 50 per cent overlap between bars.

By contrast, TWS has a scan area of +/-25 degrees with 3-bar, or +/-10 degrees with 4-bar, which gives a considerably reduced area of search in azimuth. Another difference is that bar spacing in TWS is 3.3 degrees which, while it gives greater coverage in elevation, reduces the probability of detection for a target mid-way between the bars compared to the narrower bar spacing of RWS.

In RWS, to lock on, the pilot slews the cursor over the target and designates and, when conditions are right, the radar automatically goes to Single Target Track (STT) until the attack is complete or broken off.

TWS operates rather differently. It has both manual and automatic modes. In TWS manual, a steady contact is turned into a radar file, and the on-screen presentation changes. Designation turns this into a full Fire Control Computer (FCC) file, the priority of which is determined by the order of designation.

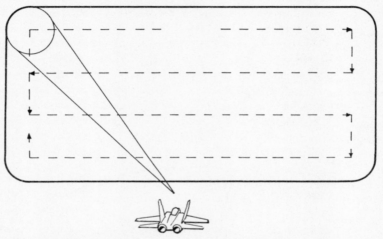

Fighter radar scan is usually in bars, as seen here. Four bars is fairly typical, but on modern radars the number can be selected. A smaller number of bars reduces the total scan time and increases the ability of the radar to track a contact. The scan width can also be selected.

In TWS auto mode, steady contacts automatically become FCC files and closer contacts are given priority. This means less work for the pilot. Both TWS modes have Multi-Target Track, which updates files as each contact is renewed, but neither will allow the radar to be slewed off the priority target, which is indicated with a bug.

If the radar fails to pick up an established contact in about eight seconds, the target indication begins to flash. This is a warning and if the target is not recontacted within a further five seconds, the indication will be lost. The main difference between RWS and TWS is that the former is real time, whereas TWS is historical, and will extrapolate to fill the gaps, thus sometimes giving a picture which is not strictly accurate.

To get a better picture of what is out there, scope expansion is available in 10, 20 and 40nm (18, 37 and 74km) sectors. This is not however able to show anything below the resolution limit of the radar; it just makes it easier to see. Expansion should be used briefly, as staying in it may cause overall situational awareness to be lost.

In a multi-bogey situation, the sweep restrictions of TWS may require a reversion to RWS, in order to cover a larger area. There could also be a situation where a hostile aircraft makes a violent manoeuvre which takes it outside the scan. What happens here is that the computer continues to extrapolate the track for about 13 seconds before it vanishes from the screen. And in 13 seconds, much can happen.

What can be done to avoid this? Track loss can sometimes be avoided by anticipation; changes in velocity vector direction and closing velocity are clues that this may be about to happen. Reversion to RWS from TWS may be one answer, as this increases the search area, but doing this in TWS auto will result in all files dumping, leaving a clean scope. This is a strong argument for using TWS manual rather than auto.

For the terminal portion of the intercept, the pilot may well wish to go STT in order to gain greater tracking capability against a hard manoeuvring contact, even though this will probably alert the target via his Radar Warning Receiver. There are three ways to go from MTT to STT. At close range Air Combat Mode is probably the best option; otherwise the bugged target can be designated on TWS, or simply go RWS and let the radar automatically go STT when it is ready. But whatever the option, be ready to react if the transfer to STT from another mode fails. Just one final point here. In TWS, the FCC will hold track files for up to 13 seconds, so if the transfer to STT fails, a quick switch back to TWS should re-establish contact.

Easy, isn't it. And all the pilot has to do in addition is to fly the aeroplane into an attacking position while maintaining formation integrity, selecting appropriate weaponry, maintaining communications where necessary, and planning ahead, while keeping a sharp visual lookout in all areas, especially six o'clock low and into the sun.

The answer to this horrendous workload is of course training and practice; sticking rigidly to the correct procedures until they become second nature. There is however a variation on Murphy's Law which states that as the wheels leave the ground, the IQ halves, and this was never better demonstrated than in an incident which took place in 1990.

The mission consisted of practice night interceptions on an oversea range. On completion, the leader called for a rejoin and commenced a gentle turn. His wingman had lost sight and almost immediately experienced a double generator failure. Recovering on emergency instruments, he turned towards land, then spotted a red flashing light in the direction where he assumed the leader to be. Lighting afterburner, he turned towards it to rejoin.

Fifteen minutes later the wingman joined up with the flashing light, which turned out to be an airliner. Extended use of afterburner had depleted his fuel, and by now too far out over the sea to return to land, he took a Martin Baker departure. Loss of situational awareness, failure to adopt radio out procedures, and failure to turn towards land, all contributed to the loss of an aircraft. The moral of the story is that when training fails, all else goes pear-shaped!

And what of the future. One thing seems obvious. The successful projection of air power will depend to a very great degree on detectability. If an aircraft can be detected, it can be shot down. If it can remain undetected, it can carry out its mission without hindrance. The F-117A clearly demonstrated this in the skies over Iraq in 1991.

The art of low observables has been with us since 1917, although it did not make any appreciable strides until the advent of the Lockheed A-12 in the 1960s, followed by the SR-71. The next step was the accent on reducing signatures in the design of the Rockwell B-1B, which reportedly reduced the radar cross section of this aircraft by an order of magnitude. Next came the angular and unaerodynamic shape of the F-117A which was only made possible by advances in computer technology which allowed it to be flown safely. As Lockheed has said, we have now reached the stage where the Statue of Liberty could be made to fly. Given the shape of the F-117A, this is quite believable. The most recent advance was the Northrop B-2 which combined a pleasing aerodynamic shape with minimal radar and heat signatures. The stage then seemed set for a stealth fighter which would yet be agile enough to fly the air superiority mission.

Only four truly new fighter types are set to enter service in the coming years, three European and one American. The Europeans have paid lip service to low observability, but far greater accent has been placed on manoeuvrability, with the result that all three are unstable canard deltas.

Sweden has produced the Saab JAS 39 Gripen, a truly tiny single-engined single-seater. A Volvo RM12 afterburning turbofan (actually General Electric's F404) gives it a thrust/weight ratio approaching unity, while wing loading is moderate. Saab are coy about performance details and it seems likely that the Gripen will have figures closely matching those of the F-16. Radar is an Ericsson PS-05/A pulse-Doppler multi-mode set. The slim contours of the Gripen's nose indicate that the scanner must be of small diameter and while Ericsson will give no details, a capability close to that of the Westinghouse APG-68 can be expected. Like all modern fighters, the Gripen features a wide angle HUD and cockpit MFDs. A maximum of six AAMs can be carried, supplemented by a 27mm Mauser cannon. There are few apparent concessions to low observability, apart from very small size.

Back in the days when small NATO air forces faced their Warsaw Pact opponents in Central Europe, it seemed obvious that a fighter was required which was capable of operating successfully in a heavily outnumbered, multi-bogey scenario. Five nations got together to define their requirements for a joint project, but failure to agree ended in the development of two rather similar but separate aircraft.

The French offering was Dassault's Rafale. Powered by two SNECMA M88-2 afterburning turbofans, when configured for the air-to-air mission it has a thrust/weight ratio in excess of unity coupled with a moderate wing loading, giving exceptional manoeuvrability. Radar is the RBE 2 pulse-Doppler set developed jointly by Thomson-CSF and Electronique Serge Dassault, which uses an active array scanner. This is stated to have a detection range of 54nm (100km) against fighter-sized targets in the look-down mode and presumably rather better than this in look-up. Like the latest Russian fighters, IRST is part of the detection suite.

With the relaxation of international tensions in Europe, the Rafale's mission increasingly became air-to-surface rather than air-to-air, and the majority of production aircraft will now be two-seaters. For the interception mission, up to eight

Mica medium range missiles can be carried, with the heat seeking Magic 2 as an alternative, supplemented with a 30mm DEFA 554 cannon.

Far slower in development was the Eurofighter 2000, produced by a consortium from Britain, Germany, Italy and Spain. Rather larger than Rafale, air-to-air performance was primary in the concept although air-to-ground capability was also built in. Like the Rafale, the Eurofighter 2000 is a super-agile canard delta with a rather long moment arm on the canards which may at some future date allow it to enter the post-stall manoeuvrability regime. Two Eurojet EJ200 afterburning turbofans each rated at 20,000lb (89kN) give a thrust/weight ratio of 1.06 even at maximum take-off weight. Combined with a wing loading of only 69lb/sq ft (340kg/sq m), this should give a sparkling performance to go with unmatched agility.

Radar is the GEC/Ferranti ECR.90 which, like the Rafale, will be coupled with an IRST. Few details of ECR.90 are available, but it is known to have 31 different modes, including air-to-surface and navigation. It has been claimed that it has superior target detection, with range against fighter-sized targets in excess of 100nm (185km), and will include adaptive scanning and fine range resolution, as well as superior automated functions. Basic air-to-air weaponry will be four AIM-120 Amraams and four Sidewinders or Asraams, plus a 27mm Mauser cannon.

Low observables feature in both the Eurofighter 2000 and the Rafale, notably the intake of the former, but these appear to be merely compromise measures, apparently intended to reduce the RCS to between one-quarter and one-fifth of that of an orthodox fighter. In both, agility has been stressed at the expense of stealth, while cost is also a factor in the equation.

Meanwhile, across the Atlantic the USAF had been planning their next generation fighter. They concluded that what was needed to take them to the year 2025 was a stealthy aircraft that was agile enough to look after itself in close combat, and yet very fast. A combination of stealth and speed looked unbeatable.

Many years earlier, radar had been used to expand the situational awareness of the fighter pilot. Now stealth was to be used to shrink that of his opponent, while high speed would reduce the opponent's reaction time, even if he did manage to detect the fighter before getting a faceful of missile. High speed is also an excellent panacea for negating attacks from astern, by drastically reducing the range at which a missile could be launched, always assuming that the signatures were enough to allow it to home. Mach 1.4 was the magic speed to clear the vulnerable six o'clock area.

There was no difficulty in attaining Mach 1.4. The clever bit was in sustaining it for a useful length of time without either running out of fuel, or building a flying fuel tank like the SR-71. Afterburning was not on, as it greatly increased the IR signature. What was needed was a fighter that could cruise at Mach 1.4 or above in military power. Not only were new stealth technology and new avionics needed, but a new propulsion system.

In 1990 two contenders finally emerged for evaluation: the Northrop YF-23 and the Lockheed YF-22. Many details remain classified and it is difficult to comment authoritatively, but it seems to the writer that the former concentrated more on stealth, while the latter was more, for the want of a better word, "operational".

Both aircraft were twin-engined single-seaters, and both carried their AAMs in internal bays, a feature that caused a certain amount of comment by those who had forgotten the F-102 and F-106. The YF-23 was very sleek and very unorthodox, while the YF-22 was vaguely reminiscent of a customised F-15 with stealth features.

Details of detection systems are not known, but neither has a bulbous radome and it seems probable that a radar with a small electronically scanned phased array antenna will be used; failing that a conformal array. Both aircraft are believed to have met the specification, but the Lockheed contender was selected to become the next fighter for the USAF, perhaps because it showed greater agility (described by Lockheed as "unprecedented") at subsonic speeds.

The F-22 will not enter service until the next century. When it does, it will stand at the peak of all-weather fighter development for many years, if only because the demise of the Soviet Union has ended the hi-tech fighter race.

Appendixes

These cover aircraft specifically designed or adapted for night and all-weather air combat and which, for the most part, have seen significant service in this role. There are, however, one or two exceptions where a particular type is of outstanding interest. In order to compare like with like, the figure quoted for range is generally that obtainable on internal fuel while carrying a full air-to-air weapons load. The use of external tanks and/or flight refuelling where applicable, makes this figure extremely variable, while combat radius also varies widely according to the mission profile flown.

APPENDIX 1. WORLD WAR 1 NIGHT FIGHTERS

Type	Avro 504K	Morane Saulnier L	BE2C
Span (ft/m)	36.00/10.97	33.79/10.30	37.00/11.28
Length (ft/m)	29.50/8.99	20.75/6.32	27.25/8.31
Height (ft/m)	10.50/3.20	10.33/3.15	11.12/3.39
Weight (lb/kg) (Normal T/O)	1,829/830	1,499/680	2,142/972
Engine	Le Rhone	Gnome/Le Rhone	RAF 1a
Rating	110hp	110hp	90hp
Max Speed (kt/kmh)	83/153	89/164	63/116
Rate of Climb	16min to 10,000ft/3,048m	12min to 10,000ft/3,048m	20min to 6,500ft/1,981m
Ceiling (ft/m)	16,400/5,998	13,100/3,883	12,000/3,657
Endurance	3hrs	1.75hrs	3.25hrs
Crew	1	1	1
Armament	1xLewis mg Anti-Zep bombs	1xLewis mg Anti-Zep bombs	1xLewis mg Anti-Zep bombs

Type	Sopwith F.1 Camel	Bristol F2B
Span (ft/m)	28.00/8.53	39.25/11.89
Length (ft/m)	18.75/5.71	25.83/7.87
Height (ft/m)	8.50/2.59	9.75/2.97
Weight (lb/kg) (Normal T/O)	1,422/645	2,779/1,261
Engine	Le Rhone	R-R Falcon III
Rating	110hp	275hp
Max Speed (kt/kmh)	103/191	109/201
Rate of Climb	6min to 6,500ft/	6.5min to 6,500ft/
Ceiling (ft/m)	1,981m	1,981m
Endurance	19,000/5,791	20,000/6,096
Crew	2.5hrs	3hrs
Armament	1	2
	2xLewis mg 1xLewis free mg	1xVickers mg

APPENDIX 2. WORLD WAR 2 NIGHT FIGHTERS

BRITISH

Type	Bristol Blenheim IF	Bristol Beaufighter VIF	Boulton Paul Defiant II
Span (ft/m)	56.33/17.17	57.83/17.63	39.33/11.99
Length (ft/m)	39.75/12.12	41.67/12.70	35.33/10.77
Height (ft/m)	9.83/ 2.99	15.83/ 4.82	12.16/ 3.71
Weight (lb/kg) (Normal T/O)	11,800/5,352	21,600/9,798	8,600/3,901
Engines	2xBristol Mercury VIII	2xBristol Hercules VI	Rolls-Royce Merlin XX
Rating	840hp	1,670hp	1,260hp
Max Speed (kt/kmh)	226/418	289/536	274/507
Initial Climb (ft/min-m/sec)	1,540/7.82	2,350/11.94	1,900/9.65
Ceiling (ft/m)	27,280/8,315	26,500/8,077	30,350/9,250
Range (nm/km)	977/1,810	1,277/2,366	404/748
Crew	2/3	2	2
Armament	5x.303in mg, 1xVickers K in turret	4x20mm cannon 6x.303in mg	4x.303in mg in turret

Type	Douglas Havoc I	De Havilland Mosquito NFXIX
Span (ft/m)	61.33/18.69	54.16/16.51
Length (ft/m)	46.98/14.32	42.16/12.85
Height (ft/m)	5.83/ 4.82	15.25/ 4.65
Weight (lb/kg) (Normal T/O)	19,040/8,636	20,600/9,344
Engines	2xPratt & Whitney Twin Wasps	2xRolls-Royce Merlin 25
Rating	1,200hp	1,620hp
Max Speed (kt/kmh)	256/475	328/608
Initial Climb (ft/min-m/sec)	1,850/ 9.40 26,000/7,924	2,700/13.72 36,000/10,972
Range (nm/km)	868/1,609	1,216/ 2,253
Crew	2	2
Armament	8x.303in mg	4x20mm cannon

GERMAN

Type	Messerschmitt Bf 110G-4	Dornier Do 217J	Junkers Ju 88G-7
Span (ft/m)	53.41/16.28	62.34/19.00	65.62/18.00
Length (ft/m)	41.56/12.67	59.06/18.00	51.12/15.58
Height (ft/m)	13.12/4.00	16.31/4.97	15.91/4.85
Weight (lb/kg) (Normal T/O)	20,723/9,400	29,057/13,180	28,880/13,100
Engines	2xDaimler Benz DB 605B	2xBMW 801ML	2xJunkers Jumo 213E
Rating	1,475hp	1,580hp	1,880hp
Max Speed (kt/kmh)	297/550	264/489	338/626
Initial Climb (ft/min-m/sec)	2,165/11.00	c1,350/6.86	1,640/8.33
Ceiling (ft/m)	26,248/8,000	29,530/9,000	32,810/10,000
Range (nm/km)	491/910	1,133/2,100	1,214/2,250

Type	Messerschmitt Bf 110G-4	Dornier Do 217J	Junkers Ju 88G-7
Crew	2/3	3	3
Armament	2x30mm and 2x20mm cannon 2x7.98mm mg in rear cockpit	4x20mm cannon 1x13mm turret 1x13mm ventral	4x20mm cannon 2x20mm Schräge Musik, 1x13mm rearward

Type	Heinkel He 219A-7	Messerschmitt Me 262B-1a
Span (ft/m)	60.70/18.50	41.05/12.51
Length (ft/m)	50.99/15.54	38.55/11.75
Height (ft/m)	13.45/ 4.10	12.57/ 3.83
Weight (lb/kg) (Normal T/O)	33,730/15,300	15,653/7,100
Engines	2xDaimler Benz DB 603L	2xJunkers Jumo 004
Rating	2,100hp	1,980lb/8.8kN
Max Speed (kt/kmh)	362/670	437/810
Initial Climb (ft/min-m/sec)	1,810/9.19	3,937/20.00
Ceiling (ft/m)	c36,091/11,000	c36,091/11,000
Range (nm/km)	834/1,545	410/ 760
Crew	2	2
Armament	2x20mm, 2x30mm forward cannon, 2x30mm Schräge Musik	4x30mm cannon

UNITED STATES OF AMERICA (INCLUDING KOREAN WAR PROP TYPES)

Type	Lockheed PV-1 Ventura	Northrop P-61B Black Widow	Vought F4U-5N Corsair
Span (ft/m)	65.50/19.96	66.06/20.13	41.00/12.50
Length (ft/m)	51.75/15.77	49.58/15.11	33.50/10.21
Height (ft/m)	11.92/3.63	14.67/4.47	14.75/4.50
Weight (lb/kg) (Normal T/O)	31,077/14,096	29,700/13,472	14,106/6,398
Engines	Pratt & Whitney 2xR-2800-31 2,000hp	Pratt & Whitney 2xR-2800-65 2,250hp	Pratt & Whitney 1xR-2800-32 2,100hp
Max Speed (kt/kmh)	271/502	314/583	408/756
Initial Climb (ft/min-m/sec)	2,230/11.33	2,550/12.95	3,780/19.20
Ceiling (ft/m)	26,300/8,016	30,500/9,296	41,400/12,618
Range (nm/km)	1,442/2,671	816/1,512	973/1,802
Crew	3	3	1
Armament	2x.50in hmg 2x.30in ventral 2x.50in turret	4x20mm cannon 4x.50in hmg in dorsal barbette	4x.50in hmg

Type	Grumman F6F-3N Hellcat	Grumman F7F-3N Tigercat	North American F-82G Twin Mustang
Span (ft/m)	42.83/13.05	51.50/15.70	51.58/15.72
Length (ft/m)	33.33/10.16	46.70/14.23	42.21/12.86
Height (ft/m)	14.42/4.40	16.58/5.05	13.83/4.22

Type	Grumman F6F-3N Hellcat	Grumman F7F-3N Tigercat	North American F-82G Twin Mustang
Weight (lb/kg) (Normal T/O)	12,186/5,528	25,720/11,667	21,819/9,897
Engines	Pratt & Whitney 1xR-2800-10 2,000hp	Pratt & Whitney 2xR-2800-34 2,100hp	2xAllison V-1710 1,930hp
Max Speed (kt/kmh)	327/605	378/692	399/740
Initial Climb (ft/min-m/sec)	3,650/18.54	4,530/23.01	3,770/19.15
Ceiling (ft/m)	37,500/11,429	40,700/12,405	38,900/11,856
Range (nm/km)	942/1,746	1,042/1,931	1,945/3,604
Crew	1	2	2
Armament	6x.50in hmg	4x20mm cannon	6x.50in hmg

JAPANESE

Type	Nakajima J1N1-S Gekko	Kawasaki Ki-45 Kai-D Toryu
Span (ft/m)	55.71/16.98	49.27/15.02
Length (ft/m)	41.90/12.77	36.08/11.00
Height (ft/m)	14.97/4.56	12.15/3.70
Weight (lb/kg) (Normal T/O)	18,042/8,184	12,125/5,500
Engines	2xNakajima NK1F Sakae	2xMitsubishi Ha-102
Rating	1,130hp	1,080hp
Max Speed (kt/kmh)	274/507	295/547
Initial Climb (ft/min-m/sec)	1,850/9.40	2,350/11.94
Ceiling (ft/m)	c28,000/8,534	30,479/9,290
Range (nm/km)	2,039/3,779	1,079/2,000
Crew	2	2
Armament	3x20mm cannon firing upwards	1x37mm cannon 2x20mm cannon firing upwards

APPENDIX 3. EARLY JET NIGHT AND ALL-WEATHER FIGHTERS
BRITISH

Type	De Havilland Vampire NF10	Armstrong Whitworth Meteor NF11	De Havilland Venom NF3
Span (ft/m)	38.00/11.58	43.00/13.11	41.67/12.70
Length (ft/m)	34.58/10.54	48.50/14.78	36.67/11.18
Height (ft/m)	6.58/ 2.01	13.83/ 4.22	6.50/ 1.98
Weight (lb/kg) (Normal T/O)	11,350/5,148	22,000/9,979	12,417/5,632
Powerplant	de Havilland 1xGoblin 3	2xRolls Royce Derwent 3	de Havilland 1xGhost 104
Thrust (lb/kN)	3,350/14.9	3,600/16	4,950/22
Max Speed (kt/kmh)	478/885	503/932	547/1,014
Initial Climb (ft/min-m/sec)	4,500/23	5,797/29	8,762/45
Ceiling (ft/m)	42,000/12,801	43,000/13,106	49,200/14,995

Type	De Havilland Vampire NF10	Armstrong Whitworth Meteor NF11	De Havilland Venom NF3
Range (nm/km)	634/1,175	800/1,481	868/1,609
Crew	2	2	2
Armament	4x20mm cannon	4x20mm cannon	4x20mm cannon

Type	Gloster Javelin FAW9	De Havilland Sea Vixen FAW1
Span (ft/m)	52.00/15.85	51.00/15.54
Length (ft/m)	56.75/17.30	55.58/16.94
Height (ft/m)	16.25/ 4.95	10.75/ 3.28
Weight (lb/kg) (Normal T/O)	42,930/19,473	35,000/15,876
Powerplant	Bristol Siddeley 2xASSa.7R Mk 209	Rolls-Royce 2xAvon 208
Thrust (lb/kN)	13,390/59.5	11,230/49.9
Max Speed (kt/kmh)	538/998	613/1,136
Initial Climb (ft/min-m/sec)	c10,000/51	c10,000/51
Ceiling(ft/m)	49,500/15,087	50,000/15,239
Range (nm/km)	808/1,497	741/1,373
Crew	2	2
Armament	2x30mm cannon 4xFirestreak AAMs or 148 2in rockets	4xFirestreak AAMs or 148 2in rockets

AMERICAN

Type	McDonnell F2H-2N Banshee	North American F-86D Sabre	Douglas F3D-2 Skyknight
Span (ft/m)	44.83/13.66	37.12/11.31	50.00/15.24
Length (ft/m)	40.16/12.24	40.77/12.43	45.42/13.84
Height (ft/m)	14.50/4.42	15.00/4.57	16.08/4.90
Weight (lb/kg) (Normal T/O)	17,200/7,802	17,100/7,757	23,575/10,694
Powerplant	Westinghouse 2xJ34-WE-34	General Electric 1xJ47-GE-17B	Westinghouse 2xJ34-WE-36
Thrust (lb/kN)	3,250/14.4	7,500/33.3	3,400/15.1
Max Speed (kt/kmh)	499/925	621/1,151	425/789
Initial Climb (ft/min-m/sec)	3,910/20	17,800/90	2,970/15
Ceiling (ft/m)	44,800/13,654	54,600/16,641	33,000/10,058 Range
(nm/km)	1,042/1,931	726/1,345	995/1,844
Crew	1	1	2
Armament	4x20mm cannon	24 FFARs 4xSparrow I	4x20mm cannon

Type	Northrop F-89D Scorpion	Lockheed F-94C Starfire	McDonnell F3H-2N Demon
Span (ft/m)	59.71/18.20	37.33/11.38	35.33/10.77
Length (ft/m)	53.79/16.39	44.50/13.56	58.92/17.96
Height (ft/m)	17.50/ 5.33	14.92/ 4.55	14.58/ 4.44
Weight (lb/kg) (Normal T/O)	37,190/16,869	18,300/8,301	39,000/17,690

Type	Northrop F-89D Scorpion	Lockheed F-94C Starfire	McDonnell F3H-2N Demon
Powerplant	2xAllison J35-A-35	Pratt & Whitney 1xJ48-P-5	1xAllison J71-A-2E
Thrust (lb/kN)	7,200/32.0	8,750/38.9	14,250/63.3
Max Speed (kt/km-hr)	552/1,023	556/1,030	559/1,036
Initial Climb (ft/min-m/sec)	7,440/38	7,975/41	14,350/73
Ceiling (ft/m)	49,200/14,995	51,400/15,666	42,650/12,999
Range (nm/km)	1,187/2,200	700/1,297	1,025/1,899
Crew	2	2	1
Armament	104 FFARs	48 FFARs	4x20mm cannon FFARs or 4xSparrow III or 4xSidewinder I

CANADIAN   **FRENCH**

Type	Avro Canada CF-100 Mk 4B	SNCASO 4050 Vautour IIN
Span (ft/m)	53.58/16.33	49.54/15.10
Length (ft/m)	54.08/16.48	56.75/17.30
Height (ft/m)	15.54/4.74	16.42/5.00
Weight (lb/kg) (Normal T/O)	40,000/18,144	45,635/20,700
Powerplant	Avro Canada Orenda 11	2xSNECMA Atar 101E-5
Thrust (lb/kN)	7,275/32.3	8,160/36.3
Max Speed (kt/kmh)	573/1,062	626/1,160
Initial Climb (ft/min-m/sec)	9,200/47	11,811/60
Ceiling (ft/m)	47,000/14,325	49,215/15,000
Range (nm/km)	2,200/4,077	1,813/3,360
Crew	2	2
Armament	108 FFARs	4x30mm cannon 1xNord 5103 or Matra R511 AAM

RUSSIAN

Type	Yakovlev Yak-25P	Yakovlev Yak-28P	Tupolev Tu-28P
Span (ft/m)	36.08/11.00	38.37/11.69	59.00/17.98
Length (ft/m)	51.37/15.66	71.04/21.65	89.25/27.20
Height (ft/m)	12.48/3.80	14.10/4.30	23.00/7.01
Weight (lb/kg)	22,149/10,047	35,273/16,000	100,000/45,360
Powerplant	2xMikulin AM-5A	2xTumansky R-11AH2-300	2xLy'ulka AL-21F
Thrust (lb/kg)	7,275/32.3	12,680/56.4	26,500/117.8
Max Speed (kt/kmh)	615/1,140	Mach 1.8	Mach 1.5
Rate of Climb (ft/min-m/sec)	9,843/50	c19,686/100	24,936/127
Ceiling (ft/m)	45,600/13,900	53,000/16,154	60,000/18,287
Range (nm/km)	1,620/3,000	1,052/1,950	2,698/5,000
Crew	2	2	2
Armament	2x37mm cannon	2xR30 "Anabs"	4xAA-5 "Ash"

4. SECOND GENERATION ALL-WEATHER FIGHTERS

EUROPEAN

Type	British Aerospace Lightning F6	Dassault Mirage IIIC	Dassault Mirage F1C
Span (ft/m)	34.83/10.62	27.00/8.23	27.58/8.41
Length (ft/m)	53.25/16.23	48.46/14.77	50.00/15.24
Height (ft/m)	19.58/5.97	13.96/4.26	14.75/4.50
Weight (lb/kg) (Normal T/O)	39,940/18,117	19,004/8,620	25,353/11,500
Powerplant	Rolls-Royce 2xAvon 301	SNECMA 1xAtar 9B	SNECMA 1xAtar 9K50
Thrust (lb/kN)	16,300/72.4	13,250/59.2	15,870/70.5
Max Speed	Mach 2.14	Mach 2.15	Mach 2.2
Initial Climb (ft/min-m/sec)	50,000/254	16,400/93	41,930/213
Ceiling (ft/m)	57,000/17,373	54,103/16,490	65,620/20,000 Range
(nm/km)	696/1,290	c809/1,500	c890/1,650
Crew	1	1	1
Armament	2x30mm cannon 2xRed Top AAMs	2x30mm cannon 2xR550 Magic or 2xSidewinders	2x30mm cannon, 2x Super 530F, 2xR550 Magic

AMERICAN

Type	McDonnell F-101B Voodoo	Convair F-102A	Convair F-106A
Span (ft/m)	39.67/12.09	38.08/11.61	38.29/11.67
Length (ft/m)	67.42/20.55	68.25/20.80	70.73/21.56
Height (ft/m)	18.00/5.49	21.16/6.45	20.28/6.18
Weight (lb/kg) (Normal T/O)	51,724/23,462	28,150/12,770	39,195/17,779
Powerplant	Pratt & Whitney J57-P-55	Pratt & Whitney J57-P-23A	Pratt & Whitney J75-P-17
Thrust (lb/kN)	16,900/75.1	16,000/71.1	24,500/108.9
Max Speed	Mach 1.63	Mach 1.175	Mach 2.0
Initial Climb (ft/min-m/sec)	39,250/199	17,400/88	42,800/217
Ceiling (ft/m)	52,100/15,879	54,000/16,458	57,000/17,373
Range (nm/km)	1,320/2,446	1,172/2,172	1,570/2,910
Crew	2	1	1
Armament	4xFalcons 2xGenies	12xFFARs 4xFalcons or 2xAIM-26	1xGenie & 4xFalcons

Type	Lockheed YF-12A	McDonnell Douglas F-4E Phantom
Span (ft/m)	55.58/16.94	38.41/11.71
Length (ft/m)	101.67/30.99	63.00/19.20
Height (ft/m)	18.25/ 5.56	16.25/ 4.95
Weight (lb/kg) (Normal T/O)	c127,000/57,607	45,750/20,752
Powerplant	Pratt & Whitney	General Electric

Type	Lockheed YF-12A 2xJ58	McDonnell Douglas F-4E Phantom 2xJ79-GE-17
Thrust (lb/kN)	32,500/144.4	17,900/79.6
Max Speed	Mach 3.5	Mach 2.2
Initial Climb	n/a	28,000/142
Ceiling (ft/m)	85,000/25,907	55,000/16,763
Range (nm/km)	2,171/4,023	1,400/2,596
Crew	2	2
Armament	3xAIM-47A	1x20mm M61 4xSparrow 4xSidewinder

RUSSIAN

Type	Mikoyan MiG-23MF	Mikoyan MiG-25P	Sukhoi Su-15
Span (ft/m)	46.75/14.25	46.25/14.10	30.00/ 9.14
Length (ft/m)	55.50/16.92	74.83/22.81	68.00/20.73
Height (ft/m)	14.33/ 4.37	20.00/ 6.10	16.50/ 5.03
Weight (lb/kg) (Normal T/O)	34,171/15,500	81,570/37,000	c40,000/18,144
Powerplant 1xR-29B	Tumansky 2xR-31	Tumansky 2xR-13F-300	Tumansky
Thrust (lb/kN)	25,350/112.7	27,120/130.5	14,500/64.4
Max Speed	Mach 2.35	Mach 2.83	Mach 2.00
Initial Climb (ft/min-m/sec)	50,000/254	40,947/208	35,000/178
Ceiling (ft/m)	54,957/16,750	78,088/23,800	c55,777/17,000
Range (nm/km)	1,511/2,800	696/1,290	c1,403/2,600
Crew	1	1	1
Armament	1x23mm cannon 2xAA-7 "Apex" 4xAA-8 "Aphid"	4xAA-6 "Acrid" or AA-7 "Aphid"	2x23mm in pods, 4xAA-3 "Anab" 2xAA-8 Aphid

APPENDIX 5. PRESENT AND FUTURE FIGHTERS

EUROPEAN

Type	Panavia Tornado F3	Dassault Mirage 2000C	Dassault Rafale M
Span (ft/m)	45.58/13.89	29.96/9.13	35.76/10.90
Length (ft/m)	61.00/18.59	48.07/14.65	50.20/15.30
Height (ft/m)	19.67/6.00	17.06/5.20	17.52/ 5.34
Weight (lb/kg) (Normal T/O)	55,200/25,039	20,944/9,500	c32,849/14,900
Powerplant	Turbo-Union 2xRB199Mk104	SNECMA 1xM53-P2	SNECMA 2xM88-2
Thrust (lb/kN)	16,520/73.4	21,385/95.0	16,400/72.9 Max
Speed	Mach 2.27	Mach 2.2	Mach 2
Initial Climb (ft/min-m/sec)	40,000/208	60,000/305	c60,000/305
Ceiling (ft/m)	70,000/21,335	59,058/18,000	59,058/18,000
Range (nm/km)	2,100/3,892	799/1,480	c1,349/2,500
Crew	2	1	1

Type	Panavia Tornado F3	Dassault Mirage 2000C	Dassault Rafale M
Armament	1x27mm cannon 4xSkyflash and 4xSidewinder or 6xAmraam	2x30mm cannon 4xSuper 530D or Mica 2xR550 Magic	2x30mm cannon 8xMica

Type	Saab JAS 39 Gripen	Eurofighter EFA 2000
Span (ft/m)	27.56/8.40	34.46/10.50
Length (ft/m)	46.26/14.10	47.58/14.50
Height (ft/m)	14.76/4.50	n/a
Weight (lb/kg) (Normal T/O)	17,637/8,000	c37,500/17,001
Powerplant	Volvo/GE RM12(F404)	Eurojet EJ200
Thrust (lb/kN)	18,000/80.0	20,250/90.0
Speed	"supersonic"	Mach 2+
Initial Climb	n/a	c60,000/305
Ceiling (ft/m)	n/a	c60,000/18,287
Range (nm/km)	n/a	n/a
Crew	1	1
Armament	1x27mm cannon 4xSkyflash 2xSidewinder	1x27mm cannon 4 or 6xAmraam 4xSidewinder

AMERICAN

Type	Grumman F-14A Tomcat	McDonnell Douglas F-15C Eagle	Lockheed(GD) F-16C F/Falcon
Span (ft/m)	64.13/19.55	42.81/13.05	31.00/9.45
Length (ft/m)	62.88/19.17	63.75/19.43	49.25/15.01
Height (ft/m)	16.00/4.88	18.46/5.63	16.58/5.05
Weight (lb/kg) (Normal T/O)	58,571/26,570	44,500/20,185	26,536/12,037
Powerplant	Pratt & Whitney 2xTF30-P-414A	Pratt & Whitney 2xF100-P-220	General Electric 1xF110-GE-100
Thrust (lb/kN)	20,900/92.9	23,450/104.2	28,982/128.8
Max Speed	Mach 1.88	Mach 2.5	Mach 2
Initial Climb (ft/min-m/sec)	30,000/152	50,000/254	50,000/254
Ceiling (ft/m)	56,000/17,068	65,000/19,811	50,000/15,293
Range (nm/km)	c1,200/2,224	c1,200/2,224	1,300/2,409
Crew	2	1	1
Armament	1x20mm M61 6xPhoenix or 4xSparrow & 4xSidewinder	1x20mm M61 4xSparrow or 4xAmraam 4xSidewinder	1x20mm M61 2xSparrow or Amraam 2xSidewinder

Type	McDonnell Douglas F/A-18C Hornet	Lockheed F-22A
Span (ft/m)	37.50/11.43	43.00/13.11
Length (ft/m)	56.00/17.07	64.16/19.56
Height (ft/m)	15.29/ 4.66	17.74/ 5.41

Type	McDonnell Douglas F/A-18C Hornet	Lockheed F-22A
Weight (lb/kg) (Normal T/O)	36,970/16,769	62,000/28,123
Powerplant	General Electric 2xF404-GE-400	Pratt & Whitney 2xF119-P-100
Thrust (lb/kN)	16,000/71.2	35,000/155.6
Max Speed	Mach 1.7	cMach 2 plus
Initial Climb (ft/min-m/sec)	50,000/254	n/a
Ceiling(ft/m)	50,000/15,239	n/a
Range (nm/km)	2,000/3,706	c3,000/5,559
Crew	1	1
Armament	1x20mm M61 4xSparrow or Amraam, and 2xSidewinders	1x20mm M61 6xAmraam?

RUSSIAN

Type	Mikoyan MiG-29 "Fulcrum"	Mikoyan MiG-31 "Foxhound"	Sukhoi Su-27 "Flanker"
Span (ft/m)	37.27/11.36	44.18/13.46	48.23/14.70
Length (ft/m)	54.18/16.51	74.44/22.69	71.97/21.94
Height (ft/m)	15.52/4.73	20.18/6.15	19.46/5.93
Weight (lb/kg) (Normal T/O)	33,069/15,000	90,389/40,000	48,501/22,000
Powerplant	Tumansky 2xRD-33	Perm 2xD30F6	Ly'ulka 2xAL-31F
Thrust (lb/kN)	18,300/81.3	41,843/184	27,558/122.5
Max Speed	Mach 2.3	Mach 2.45	Mach 2.35
Initial Climb (ft/min-m/sec)	65,000/330	c41,000/208	c60,000/305
Ceiling (ft/m)	55,777/17,000	68,901/21,000	59,058/18,000
Range (nm/km)	1,133/2,100	1,619/3,000	2,159/4,000
Crew	1	2	1
Armament	1x30mm cannon 6xAA-10 "Alamo" 6xAA-11 "Archer"	1x23mm cannon 4xAA-9 "Amos" 4xAA-8 "Aphid"	1x30mm cannon 10 AAMs inc AA-8, AA-10, AA-11 and Amraamski

Index